Cybernetics, Artificial Intelligence, and Ecology

Cybernetics, Artificial Intelligence, and Ecology

Proceedings of the
Fourth Annual Symposium
of the
American Society for Cybernetics

Edited by
Herbert W. Robinson
and
Douglas E. Knight

SPARTAN BOOKS

NEW YORK · WASHINGTON

Library of Congress Catalog Card Number 79-157733
International Standard Book Number 0-87671-167-0

Sole distributor in Great Britain, the British Commonwealth, and
the Continent of Europe.

THE MACMILLAN PRESS LTD.
4 Little Essex Street
London, WC2R 3LF

Printed in the United States of America

Contents

The Participants

DR. CARL F. ALBRECHT
Oak Ridge National Laboratory
Oak Ridge, Tennessee

DR. JAMES S. ALBUS
Data Techniques Branch
Goddard Space Flight Center
Greenbelt, Maryland

DR. W. ROSS ASHBY
Borden Neurological Institute
Bristol, England

DR. STAFFORD BEER
Science in General Management, Ltd.
Surrey, England

DR. SIDNEY GALLER
Science and Technology for
Environmental Affairs
Department of Commerce
Washington, D.C.

DR. WILLIAM D. GENNARO
Youngstown Hospital Association
Youngstown, Ohio

DR. FREDERICK F. GORSCHBOTH
International Business Machines Corporation
Federal Systems Division
Gaithersburg, Maryland

DR. JAMES R. HILL
Youngstown Hospital Association
Youngstown, Ohio

DR. WALTER JACOBS
American University
Washington, D.C.

DR. WILLIAM L. KILMER
Division of Engineering Research
Michigan State University
East Lansing, Michigan

DR. TURNER McLARDY
Myerson Research Laboratory
Boston State Hospital
Boston, Massachusetts

DR. EDWARD MATALKA
Worcester Foundation for
Experimental Biology
Shrewsbury, Massachusetts

DR. ANTHONY N. MUCCIARDI
Adaptronics, Incorporated
McLean, Virginia

DR. TUNCER I. OREN
Computer Science Department
University of Ottawa
Ottawa, Canada

DR. GORDON PASK
Brunel University
Uxbridge, Middlesex, England

DR. ARTHUR E. RAPPOPORT
Youngstown Hospital Association
Youngstown, Ohio

DR. W. R. SPILLERS
Department of Civil Engineering
and Engineering Mechanics
Columbia University
New York, New York

DR. DAVID STONE
Worcester Foundation for
Experimental Biology
Shrewsbury, Massachusetts

DR. LOUIS L. SUTRO
Charles Stark Draper Laboratory
Massachusetts Institute of Technology
Cambridge, Massachusetts

DR. M. W. THRING
Queen Mary College
University of London
London, England

Cybernetics, Artificial
Intelligence, and Ecology

Introduction

These are the fourth proceedings of the annual symposia of the American Society for Cybernetics. Each of the three preceeding symposia was a forum for presentation of work generally in the field of cybernetics, but it included some topical theme of major significance—purposive systems; management of large systems; conflict resolution. This symposium, held October 8–9, 1970, followed the same pattern. It had as a featured topic "management of ecological systems." Parallel sessions covered "artificial intelligence and robotics," "cybernetics and public policy," and "behavioral cybernetics and societal interactions," as well as "ecological cybernetics." Of thirty-five papers presented at the symposium, sixteen are included in this volume under the headings "General Cybernetics," "Artificial Intelligence and Robotics," and "Ecological Cybernetics." Some of the others will be published in the Society's journal.

Perhaps the most impressive aspect of these annual symposia is that well-qualified experts from a wide variety of disciplines—philosophy, natural science, life science, and social science—come together with the conviction that they have a common interest in a new discipline which transcends, but amplifies, their own specialty—cybernetics. The growth in the size of these annual volumes—from 192 pages in 1967 to 352 pages today—demonstrates the rapidly rising interest, and the serious work being done, in this young field of scientific endeavor. Even more impressive is the fact that the relatively small group of practitioners in this new science feel no compunction in tackling the most challenging and vital problems of the day as they arise (or even before they arise), believing sincerely that they have, in cybernetics, a powerful inter-disciplinary weapon for solving the most baffling social, economic, and political problems of civilization.

In light of this excitement and enthusiasm for a relatively new field on the part of many of the intellectual *elite* of diverse disciplines, it might be worthwhile to try to elaborate what cybernetics is all about. Many scientists profess extreme doubt whether cybernetics is not really a "charlatan" science. They fail to find anything really interesting or useful in the concept of cybernetics to aid them in applying their own expertise to problems, either in their own domain or in the world at large. In truth, it cannot be denied that these critics gain support from the fact that much written under the general heading of "cybernetics" is hardly distinguishable from work done generally in some particular discipline, especially in operations research, management science, statistics, computer technology, or neurology. On the other hand, many feel that cybernetics gives them a more comprehensive, thorough, systematic, and penetrating approach to the work they do in their own discipline. I believe that much of the conflict between these two viewpoints stems from a failure to define cybernetics or the cybernetic approach.

Cybernetics ("steersmanship") was defined by Norbert Wiener in 1947 as "the science of control and communication in the animal and the machine." It is hard to see how control can be exercised without communicating, so that this definition could be condensed to "the science of control in the animal and the machine." [This would leave communication as a component science which must deal in terms of message *content*, *language*, physical *communication*, and *optimizing* of communication systems (cost/effectiveness)]. As Sutro explains in his contribution to this symposium, this latter definition has, through much discussion, been expanded to "the science of command and control in the animal and the machine."

But what is "command and control?" The existence of a

"*will*" is obviously implicit, since only a "will" can exercise command and control over something. And what is meant exactly by "control?" Clearly, it is the imposition of the achievement of the goals and objectives of the "will" on that which is being controlled (x_1, x_2, x_3, etc.) in place of either the independent goals and objectives of x_1, x_2, x_3, etc. or of complete randomness, or both. And the end being sought by the will is to use the properties and behavior of x_1, x_2, x_3, etc. and their interactions with each other optimally to achieve maximum satisfaction of its goals and objectives. Thus, the definition might be condensed to "the science of achieving the maximum satisfaction of goals and objectives (of a will) through optimal use of all possible interactions of all available resources."

Once this basic concept is accepted, it is clear that the science of cybernetics cannot be applied except to some *cybernetic system* which presents the problem of achieving maximum satisfaction of goals and objectives through the command and control of a number of interacting variables. It is obvious that there are several requirements, all of which must be satisfied before such a cybernetic system can exist. These are:

1. a sustaining and constraining environment, external to the whole system, in which the system must operate, which has its own set of "laws" and initial conditions (e.g., an economy, the ocean). This environment also may contain, of course, other similar or dissimilar systems;[*]

2. a "will" *of* the system (e.g., of a fish in the ocean) or which a higher authority imposes *on* the system (e.g., the orders given to an admiral embarking on a mission);

3. a set of "goals and objectives" of the will (e.g., maximizing profit, survival of the species);

4. a set of basic "resource elements" of the system which are needed for the various activities of the system (e.g., an existing organ, a steel mill, etc.);

---

[*]Obviously, the more complete the system, the less remaining in the "environment," and the more determinate the behavior of the system. The ultimate cybernetic system is thus the entire universe.

5. the set of all possible activities which can be carried on by the system; the precise requirements of resource elements, material, and energy needed for each activity; and the precise output and other results of each activity (the building of new and additional resource elements are possible activities);

6. the initial internal inventory of useable material, energy, resource elements, etc. (e.g., blood, electrical energy, and organs);

7. a "brain" which is capable of performing the logical processes needed to determine the sequence of activities which will maximize achievement of the goals and objectives of the will—i.e., optimum use of available internal resources and technological relationships within the constraints and sustaining capability of the environment—and capable of commanding the execution of this sequence. Optimization is obviously a highly complex and laborious process, involving millions of bits of information. Such a "brain" must, therefore, have a substantial memory, data-processing capability, and data-receiving and data-sending capability. It may, of course, be a computer; and, finally

8. a nervous system through which information and control are transmitted to the individual resource elements in the system (e.g., nerves, computer terminal networks).

Without any one of these requirements, we are not dealing with a *complete* cybernetic system. We can, it is true, abstract from the total system and consider only a part or some combination of parts as a cybernetic *subsystem* by assuming specific states of the missing parts, thereby eliminating the feedbacks to and from those parts which, in practice, should really be taken into account. Results of such partial analyses will not, in general, be the same, or as effective, as those derived from complete analysis.

Perhaps the most important characteristic of the cybernetic approach is that it considers the *total system*, with all its interacting elements, as one inseparable organism. In this respect, in most cases, it denies the validity—for a complete solution—of optimizing a component part separately. The approach insists that the analysis be *comprehensive* and *simultaneous*. Thus, it considers the total organism—brain, nervous system, energy system, muscular system, organs, etc.—maximizing achievement of its goals and objectives in its total environment. And in this respect it might be noted that the *communication and control* of Wiener become component parts, or facets, of the system, rather than the system itself. While there are, of course, problems of tremendous complexity and fundamental importance in the domain of communication and control problems in a cybernetic system, especially when huge masses of data are implicitly involved, the central problem remains optimization of the organization and operations of the organism itself to maximize achievement of its goals and objectives.

Any lack of understanding of the nature of this total systems approach results in focus on individual parts of the whole, inability to find much new in cybernetics, and skepticism that cybernetics can add anything worthwhile to an individual discipline. But once the true nature of the cybernetic approach is appreciated, a common framework for the communication of ideas and for collaboration and cross-fertilization between disciplines is revealed, and the role of any one discipline itself becomes less distinct. Participation of many disciplines is obviously essential if all aspects of a real world total system of any complexity are to be dealt with adequately. These facts, and the ambition implicit in taking such a comprehensive approach, account for the enthusiasm of those who have fallen under the spell of cybernetics.

The following diagram summarizes a total cybernetic system:

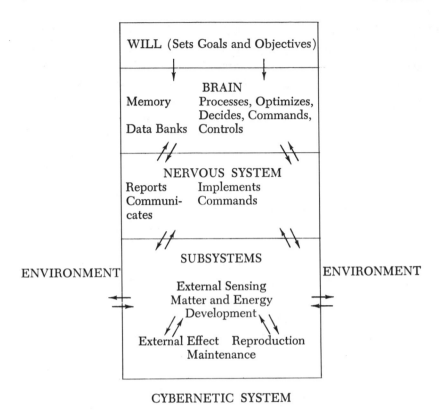

CYBERNETIC SYSTEM

The attraction of the cybernetic approach is that it optimizes comprehensively, taking account simultaneously of all goals and objectives, all available resources, all interrelationships, and all constraints. Because it is comprehensive, it is multidisciplinary; because the disciplines must cooperate, it is interdisciplinary and promotes common language; and because even the most elementary cybernetic system requires elaborate communication between the brain and resource elements through a nervous system, it recognizes the vital importance of *flows of information, communication and control,* and *feedback* to the efficiency of the system. Many practitioners in a single discipline have failed to appreciate cybernetics because they have not fully understood these fundamental features of the cybernetic approach.

Cybernetic systems of all types, by their very nature, display the attributes of *living* systems. Much of the work done in the fields of neurophysiology, biology, and medicine is, in fact, cybernetic. For example, an excellent series of articles on living systems by Dr. James G. Miller, Provost of Cleveland State University,[1] covering basic concepts, structure and process, and cross-level hypotheses, attempts to identify in great detail the essential elements and functions of a generalized living system and its matter-energy and information-processing subsystems. One senses that, in the years ahead, a more systematic *general theory of cybernetic systems* will evolve, complete with a precise terminology, and this will facilitate the further communication of ideas and interdisciplinary applications of the science to complex problems in many diverse fields, including physiology, medicine, politics, economics, sociology, and ecology.

These proceedings include papers on many aspects of cybernetic systems. Beer, in his keynote address "The Liberty Machine," brings out the urgent need for governments to consider man and his enviroment as a complete cybernetic system and, especially, for them to build the capability of simulating the future of the system by high-speed processing of huge quantities of detailed information, thereby anticipating political, economic, social, and ecological problems and solving them in advance. Perhaps the only examples of complete cybernetic systems are Jacobs' "How a Bug's Mind Works" and Gorschboth's "Environmation." Ashby, in "Setting Goals in Cybernetic Systems," focuses on the problem of defining goals and objectives. He points out not only the fantastic, completely unmanageable, size of the data-processing problem under complete mathematical generality, but also how real-world natural constraints reduce the problem by many orders of magnitude to manageable proportions. It is gratifying to note that eight of the sixteen papers describe actual applications of cybernetics, as distinct from purely theoretical work. Three of these, by Rappoport *et al.*, Stone and Matalka, and Sutro, describe actual live applications to important real-world problems, namely a cybernetic clinical laboratory, chain-effects of pollution on animals, and a robot for exploring Mars. And the invited paper by Thring describes actual laboratory models of prototype robots which, if perfected, could eliminate huge areas of human drudgery. Papers by Kilmer and Mc-Lardy, Mucciardi, and Oren show the growing importance of the computer and simulation techniques in cybernetics, providing the cyberneticist, in effect, with a remarkably cheap, but comprehensive, laboratory. The philosophical and theoretical papers by Pask, Albus, Spillers, Albrecht, and Galler are examples of the stimulating intellectual activity which characterizes these symposia. The papers on ecological cybernetics show clearly the need to approach the ecological problems that will face mankind—as population exceeds 7 trillion (7,000 million) and the economy multiplies to over four times its present size by the year 2000—by considering them as problems of a complex *cybernetic* system.

I am deeply indebted to my coeditor, Mr. Douglas E. Knight, International Business Machines Corporation, who edited Part III, "Ecological Cybernetics"; to my wife, Mrs. Elsie Robinson, who graciously performed the tedious chores associated with the preparation of the manuscript; and, of course, to Spartan Books for their unstinting cooperation in preparing the text and for the outstanding quality of their final product.

HERBERT W. ROBINSON

International Management Systems Corporation, Washington, D.C.

REFERENCE

1. Miller, James G. "Living Systems: Basic Concepts." Vol. 10, no. 3 (July 1965); "Structure and Process." Vol. 10, no. 4 (October 1965); and "Cross Level Hypotheses." Vol. 11, no. 1 (January 1966). *Behavioral Science*.

Keynote Address

The Liberty Machine

STAFFORD BEER

Science in General Management, Ltd.
England

Of Optimism and Pessimism

It is characteristic of man's way of thinking for him to contemplate entities rather than systems; to disconnect systems rather than relate their parts; to record inputs and outputs to systems rather than measure systemic behavior itself. When it comes to managing affairs, we characteristically try to deal with that dismantled system—piece by piece—rather than redesign the totality so that it actually works.

Thus, the current awareness of ecological crisis is based upon a catalog of stark and unbearable facts. They sound like this.

In the United States during 1966, man-made pollution by carbon monoxide amounted to eighty-five million tons.

Last year, 8.1 million automobiles were written off; 57,742 of these were abandoned in New York City.

The population of the earth is growing at the rate of one hundred persons a minute.

9

One does not know what any of this really means, but it certainly sounds bad. And the catalog of cataclysm goes on and on and on. Each item usually is accompanied by an extrapolation of the existing trend into the future.

For example, the loudest noises to which man is exposed have increased by one decibel a year for the last forty years. *If this goes on,* in about ten years we shall have passed a noise level already proven lethal for cockroaches and rats. This is one of the less terrifying examples, because we tend to think that man may be somehow superior to the cockroach—and besides, the postulated rate of increase is merely linear.

People really begin to blow their minds when confronted by exponential rates of growth—extrapolated, of course, to a point of singularity. Many years ago, Heinz von Foerster demonstrated that the population explosion would not starve us but crush us to death—by achieving an infinite population some sixty years from now.

But surely, people respond, this cannot be. Nature is widely known for its ability to maintain ecological homeostasis. Explosive tendencies on the part of threatening variables in our situation will be held in check by counterbalancing forces. Thus, we shall escape not only Armageddon, but, far more importantly, the intellectual agony of trying to contemplate these frightful things.

With this statement we have reached the limits of cybernetic sophistication for the average educated man. As far as the argument goes, it is correct; not even the worst mismanagement of affairs can have the effect of repealing the cybernetic laws of nature.

"Are you optimistic or pessimistic about all this?" asks the man. "I am optimistic," replies the perennial optimist in us all. "Then why are you scowling?" "Because my optimism is not justified. . . ."

We cyberneticians know very well that homeostasis will be achieved in the face of all threats because Nature inexorably moves from one equilibrial condition to another. However, this national symposium must speak out plainly (using as many noise-polluting decibels as it can muster) about the likely consequences. What should we say?

The laws of ecosystem are not answerable to a criterion of success which necessarily includes the survival of man. The most likely systemic outcome of the things we are up to is a sudden, catastrophic population decline. This is a sufficiently familiar experience for many species, observable today (in corals, for example) as it is in the geological record. That record suggests that sometimes there may be a little too much positive feedback in the control system. So, whereas the catastrophic population collapse typically cuts back the species to about a third of its peak strength, homeostasis sometimes overdoes it. Thus, whole species become extinct.

What we have to say to our educated cybernetician-in-the-street is that if this fate overtakes our species, Nature betrays no cybernetic law. She can afford to shrug off the incident, having been up evolutionary blind alleys before. Man seeks to impose his own objective function on the natural homeostat. His failure is his own failure; his extinction is his own affair.

The Metathreat Exposed

Let us try to make a constructive cybernetic approach to the crisis. I ask you first to contemplate the societary system by which ecological threats are currently recognized and handled. There seems to be a typical course of events.

First, a specific threat becomes known to a small group of experts endowed with acute perception. These people draw public attention to the threat, using the only machinery available to them: publication through the mass media, which handles such topics meretriciously. It is, of course, open to the experts privily to address government, which they have often tried to do. But frequently government will take no notice—until stimulated to do so by a public outcry that has been artifically engendered by publicity. I note here and now what an intolerable system this is, whereby we must sacrifice both dignity and scientific nicety and be turned into cathode-ray buffoons simply to alert our fellow human beings to danger.

This stage of the circuit is quite simply an amplifier, since although the facts may be rightly disseminated, people do not really believe them until we have bared our breasts and cut ourselves with knives. But given this high gain, the clamor may be sufficient to provoke action. What is to count as action? Because the threat is specific and has been made artificially more specific by the use of these communication circuits, only specific action is likely to count.

Studies will be financed to investigate this precise threat, experts who know about particular aspects of this threat will indulge in combat for their piece of the loot, and so society will be embarked on a familiar reductionist route. This machinery is guaranteed not to increase our knowledge of anything systemic.

The second thing that government will do is lay the precise threat squarely at the door of some explicit body or individual. Now there can be no accusations that the matter is being overlooked. For example, a recommendation has just been made to the mayor of Los Angeles to appoint an officer responsible for dealing with the problem of noise. The appointee is to have the unbelievably infelicitous title of "Noise Administrator." His terms of reference provide that he should know where the noise is coming from, create acceptable standards for the level of noise, and suggest methods of controlling noise in accordance with those standards.

Imagine yourself in this post. What would you do? Would you still expect your salary if you responded to this assignment by saying *everyone* is making a noise, the acceptable standard is *silence*, and the action required is to *shut up?* Again, I fear, we have machinery for talking about the problem but have no access to it—because the problem is just part of the pathology of a complex system, and the supposed solution has to do with peering and poking at a single symptom.

These measures will count as a solution because they will satisfy the clamor. Citizens with no comprehension of systems theory will think that everything possible is being done. This in itself defuses the societary bomb planted by the experts. The bomb is still there, but it does not look very dangerous. And now we encounter another subroutine of this total program. The researchers who got the money continue to discuss the problem in public to prove they deserved the funds. Those on whom responsibility has been laid continue to make pronouncements intended to show that they are ameliorating the situation or, at any rate, slowing down the appalling development of the threat which people had been led to expect. The result of all this is, very naturally, that the public becomes sick and tired of the whole thing.

We are confronted here with a phenomenon of social habituation. You, too, can live with the hydrogen bomb—even though the risks associated with this weapon steadily grow as more nations acquire nuclear capability. We have now completed a circuit, for we are back at the stage where there is a wide public knowledge of a threat in which no one really believes. With new knowledge, it is possible to reactivate this circuit, but this time the response will be less alarmed. Indeed, we may expect an exponential decay in the response we get each time round. We have laid bare a machine called "Cry Wolf."

Meanwhile, however, a new specific threat has been exposed and is ready to take over from the first threat in the public esteem. After the trauma of Hiroshima comes the Silent Spring. If we are now satisfied that we will not be blown up, pesticides will kill us. The societary machine goes into action again, and again the meretricious handling of the problem begins. Europe is alerted to the dangers of poisons building up in the human body with the bizarre cry: Americans are now unfit for human consumption. And when the rituals are complete, and society has become habituated to this threat, too, along comes Threat the Third. . . .

I have sought illumination about what happens next in Ross Ashby's model of general habituation, which he published in 1958. He explains that a new stimulus tends to free the original response from its habituation, so that if the original stimulus is again presented, the response will be restored to its initial value prior to habituation. But he goes on to show that if two stimuli have much in common, then the dehabituation may not work or at any rate will be less effective.

Clearly societary threats *do* have much in common, and Ashby's predicition seems to be coming true. The dehabituation mechanics are not working any longer. Scientists are now being cataloged by the public as prophets of doom, which is precisely to emphasize the commonality of the specific threats to which we draw attention. We are now likely to be discarded, like any good messenger bearing bad news who has his head cut off.

I think that Professor Ashby would expect me to record that his model was not intended to handle habituation in cases where special mechanisms of survival are involved, as they surely are here. We are not dealing simply with a stimulus representing *any* kind of disturbance likely to upset the system from an equilibrial state; we are dealing explicity with threats. A threat is a very special and particular kind of stimulus for any animal; it churns about in the recticular formation of the brain stem, promptly committing the whole organism to some special mode of action. If the threat turns out to be a wolf-crying false alarm, we may yet habituate. Even so, the experience is different from habituating to a neutral stimulus. If someone now cries "bear," another but different false alarm, and another "lion," and so on, what shall we make of that?

I want to suggest that this is the core of our problem. We might well become convinced that there really are no wolves, nor bears, nor lions, and so on, and yet we should soon begin to wonder why we found ourselves in this imaginary menagerie. Something else must be going on, something we do not understand, which keeps coming at us in the form of urgent alarm signals which turn out to be false. Then, although we shall not be eaten by wolves, crushed by bears, or mauled by lions, we are at least likely to have a nervous breakdown.

I believe that this stressful situation is the metathreat to our society. We cannot cope with it. It is the threat that society itself will collapse and with it all our over-sanguine mechanisms for dealing with specific threats. *There* is a dehabituating device if ever there was one. For, as we saw, habituation to threat depends on the confidence that there are institutional ways of handling the threat. Now the institution itself is threatened.

If the mechanisms I have criticized for dealing with explicit threats are not particularly satisfactory, it is perfectly clear that the aggregate of these solutions will not touch the metathreat at all. They are not even addressed to it. There is worse still: if we are dealing with a metathreat generated in a metasystem which we do not understand, our well-meaning attempts to cope with explicit systemic threats (that we now perceive to be no more than local manifestations of the metathreat) may, through our ignorance, do more harm than good.

Let me at once tie this theoretical construct to ecological realities. Endless stories are recorded about the disasters which often follow attempts at local biological control because of a lack of understanding of the ramifications of these actions in the ecosystem at large. I will not rehearse them here; you are all convinced. Should anyone wish to ponder the factual basis of this complex situation, however, I recommend to him a new book just published in England by Gordon Rattray Taylor. Significantly, in view of my recent remarks, it is called *The Doomsday Book.*

The burden of the argument so far is that threats derive from an unrecognized metathreat, and that this is why government and the public are so confused about the nature of ecological and societary crises today. Once this point is taken, so that we see apparently specific threats as being indeed manifestations of the metathreat, we are ready to recognize two truths.

The first is that we shall not be able to handle problems of threat by direct methods. Take the city. Noise, carbon monoxide, water failure, electricity failure, transportation failure, ghetto violence, street muggings, schoolgirl pregnancies, student revolt—all these and many more problems are generated metasystemically. That is to say, they are not problems about decibels, gases, logistics, color, greed, lust, and drugs, but problems about having cities. The city is a settlement grown beyond viable limits, technologically souped-up beyond the threshold of physiological endurance, and perhaps ten percent efficient in terms of its group purposes. It is a machine for generating problems of noise, carbon monoxide, logistics, ghettos, and so forth.

The second truth follows from this. We must redesign the machine that is the city and for that matter the machine that is the state. That is to say that the metaproblem of the metasystem that engenders the metathreat is a problem of organization.

Stereotypes of Organization, Time, and Planning

To put this point in less technical language, we may use the familiar metaphor with which I began. If we are not to attack symptoms, but rather the disease, we shall have to look at the body politic rather than the malfunctioning organs.

This seems an obvious thing to do. The difficulty is that it is almost impossible, because we have invented and perfected an unalterable organization for society that does not permit it. Federal organization everywhere in the world is delineated by function. Thus it is easy to talk about the health of the people, about the education of the people, and about the social security of the people. But there are no convenient means for discussing the integral state of a citizen, who ought after all to be healthy *and* educated *and* secure, especially since each one of these desiderata probably depends upon the other two.

Well, it is true that you cannot look at everything at once. I define organization as a structural device for reducing proliferating variety. By this I mean that when a large and complex system has been segregated into subsystems, it loses the appropriate combinatorial power to become more complicated still. Sensible attempts to institute horizontal cross-linkages in a vertically compartmentalized system of this kind are, and in a sense very properly resisted, because they would restore the variety-generating capability that the organization as such is meant to destroy. But it is a necessary corollary of this that everything we do is constrained in its effectiveness by the appropriateness of the divisions we made in the first place. Since our circumstances and above all our technology are so rapidly changing, the likelihood is very low indeed that particular organizational divisions that were once effective will remain so.

Great businesses have come to recognize this fact and to undertake evolutionary experiments in novel and adaptive modes of organization. Witness for example the president's office in a large corporation. Changes occur here so quickly that the staff lower down becomes disoriented. When it comes to public affairs, however, we are locked into an organizational stereotype. This is not ascribable merely to the immense inertia of so elaborate and ponderous a machine as we have come to know and hate, though that is a considerable factor. It is more importantly ascribable to the suspicion that any interference with this machinery is likely to be nefarious.

It is a relatively simple matter to reorganize the responsibilities of a firm's vice-presidents, and it is not all that difficult to move from a commercial system of geographic divisions to a commercial system of product divisions. But in affairs of state, this is hard indeed to accomplish without first destroying the machinery of state and going through a phase of anarchy. This is why I suggest the ever increasing and ever more apparent incompetence of a particular regime of state has been allowed, throughout human history, to continue its inoperable course to the point of collapse or revolution. Those who funk a phase of controlled anarchy in the interests of adaptation have bloody anarchy thrust upon them.

Here I pause to consider a philosophical foundation of this incorrigible resistance to change, since I regard it as a matter of profound professional interest to this audience. The point I want to make concerns the nature of time and the inherited view we have of processes that unfold with time. Our philosophic heritage has misled us seriously here, and the problem derives from the mysterious irreversibility of time—which irreversibility is not shared by any other dimension of our existence. This, of course, means that we cannot undertake the symmetric experiments in the temporal evolution of systems, involving the science of time and entropy, with which we are most at home, in the science of space and energy.

According to the inherited view, which we might dub Bergsonian, world systems are delineated by a complex pattern of trajectories which have been traced until *now*. With this *now*, the trajectories are annihilated, and the future is a void. The philosophers who first understood this view to be mistaken (and I mention particularly J. W. Dunne) pictured the temporal universe as a set of trajectories in which *now* was the name of a cursor, moving across the scene. As a result, philosophy became bogged down in a variety of problems that were fundamentally bogus.

If you could get ahead of the cursor—by moving outside the reference-frame where the trajectories interplay—then you could have precognition and telekinesis. Then what becomes of free will? In the 1930s and 40s we had fun and games galore with such spurious problems. It was only with the discovery of cybernetics that we began to see a new and more useful insight. The trajectories are generated by systems under perturbation. Then there is a component of the future that is inexorable, and a component that is adaptive.

I mention all this, however briefly, because it seems that there is a powerful contemporary school of thought in planning technology that has not grasped this point. It is the philosophic legatee of Bergson and Dunne and is responsible for those peculiar extrapolations of current specific trends which I began today by questioning. It sits in a philosophical halfway house between the views of the future as void and the future as predestined. Are world trajectories shot from the point *now* like arrows into the air, or are they launched on tramlines molded to the curve $e^{\lambda t}$?

Neither, I say to you emphatically. The trajectories are outputs of the systems which we have built and which we continue to underwrite even when we see that the trajectory is hellbent to disaster. It is no good blaming that on human impotence in the face of either the void or the tramlines. We are not impotent, because it is open to us to redesign the systems that generate the trajectories—maintaining predictive control of the inexorable component of outcome and adaptive control of the rest. No, we are not impotent—just stupid.

I return from this discursion to the theme that our accepted control systems for handling environmental threats are functions of the organization that we use. A threat being recognized, it must belong somewhere; someone must be responsible. Or, even if we are sufficiently sophisticated to say that the spread of this threat cuts across the organizational structure and to try and distribute responsibility under a metastructure, we shall still be caught out. The reason is that the practical processes which must be gone through in order to handle the problem at all are processes of *planning*, and these must be undertaken by staffs who belong—and see themselves as belonging—to the established structure.

The result is inevitable, not surprising, yet very curious, and I have not seen it commented on anywhere:

PLANNING IS HOMOLOGOUS WITH ORGANIZATION

It sounds trivial; it is certainly obvious. How can you have plans that are not couched in terms of the organization which must implement them? But just think carefully about the converse proposition. If the organization is no longer well adapted to the environment, how then can the plans be relevant to existing threats? It is just not possible. We have totally failed to grasp this point, despite overwhelming evidence that our plans do not work very well, and that the threats are not being competently met.

Nonetheless, there is indeed an abiding sense of unease. So what do we do? We throw into the situation all the resources we have, resources of money, time, and skill. This is done in the cause of efficiency: do it better, do it faster, do it cheaper. *That* will stave off the threat. The point is: do *what?* Obviously, implement the plans. But we have already shown as a lemma that the plans cannot possibly be rightly structured. Thus it is that we expend our resources in the ever more efficient implementation of irrelevant plans.

There is a second massive difficulty which is illuminated by these considerations. If planning is homologous with organization, then plans—which of their very nature ought to be syntheses of parts into a greater whole—become instead ever more detailed and localized sets of unrelated minor decisions. That is because, in deference to one of the major discoveries of the social sciences, we are trying to hold the level of decision at the lowest possible echelon as a matter of policy. I have no quarrel with participative management; in fact, I urge it forward. But this ought to mean that small decisions, made in the appropriate locale, are sucked upward and reformulated into a master plan expressed metalinguistically. Instead, it means that the making of decisions is a task pushed down and implicitly condemned to a stereotyped outcome.

If you wish proof of this assertion, consider the potent development of the decision tree as a technique of operations research. Now planning is a continuous process of decision. If it is homologous with organization, then the decision tree splits according to the organizational split; it cannot do otherwise. If it did otherwise, there would be no competent body to take the decision. So the continuous process of planning and decision rattles down the stereotyped organizational structure like a steel ball on a pin table and is awarded some score at the end of the line.

Using that model, you will notice that all is well as long as the pin table retains its structure, and that the metasystem of reward is maintained. If you had a pin table whose structure was constantly altering, and whose payoff function was constantly being changed by a higher-order system, there would be no point in playing the game. By the same token, there is not much point in playing the game of governing the environment in chunks.

The Metasystem and Human Liberty

We have reached the point of saying that plans to deal with environmental and societary threats do not work because the plans are homologous with organization, and the organization is not appropriate but cannot be radically changed.

There seem to be only two alternative courses ahead. The first is to do nothing, to carry on as we are. Then the component of future trajectories that is in principle adaptive will, I predict, fail to adapt, because it is frustrated by an organizational straitjacket. And the component that is inexorable will, I predict, take society on to structural collapse or to overthrow by revolution. The second available alternative is to create a metasystem to handle the metathreat.

Once again, this proposal is based on something more than a theoretical construct; there are many precedents for handling situations in this way. The trouble with the precedents is that they are mostly misleading. In the world of real organizations, characterized as it is by the tenacity of power and the lust for prestige, metasystems are found to masquerade as supra-authorities.

Subsidiary companies of a large corporation cannot be allowed to operate with wholesale autonomy in defiance of each other; therefore we think of them as subservient to the metasystem called the corporation. The same is true for departments of state, which are therefore subservient to their metasystem, the state itself. The father may intervene in a dispute between his subservient children. Using the higher centers of my brain, I may make an act of conation which overrides my subservient autonomic system—by holding my breath, for example.

These precedents are misleading, because they appear to achieve metacontrol by virtue of superior authority rather than by logical necessity. That is to say, we do not see them as metasystems in the proper sense, where they are supposed to employ a higher-order language in order to resolve systemic problems posed in local languages. Instead, we map them onto our hierarchic models of authority, so that it is always possible to erect a higher body, having more authority than any operational system, which is seen not as facing a dilemma but as causing trouble.

In fact, the corporation and the state, like the father, should be cybernetically regarded as servants of the subsidiary companies, the departments and the children. The realities of life are found at the operational level. If my brain sets out to kill my body by holding its breath for good, the autonomic nervous system will soon thwart that design. Finally the children and the subsidiary organizations will thwart authoritarian behavior at exactly the point when the metasystem is apparently acting *from authority* rather than from superior information and higher-order logic. This revolt is easily brought about, because the metasystem does not deploy sufficient variety to hold the lower systems down. If it wishes to turn itself into a genuine supra-authority *rather* than a metasystem, that is easily done as well—by destroying variety in the subservient system. In this way, my brain can kill my body by throwing it over a cliff, fathers and company presidents may become despotic, and the state may become totalitarian.

By confusing metasystems with supra-authorities, we have almost lost the chance of understanding what to do. Think of the limiting case, the United Nations. We wanted, and desperately needed, a world-level metasystem. Frightened of the risk to national sovereignty, we built in the famous Veto. This at once turned the required metasystem into a power system —one which automatically, and for very good reasons, cannot possibly work. The result is deadlock.

When it comes to the mastery of environmental problems, we observe such deadlocks everywhere. A government agency handling funds for research on pollution is in practice forced to recognize the sovereign rights of every responsible academic who has research to do in this area. A Secretary of State for the Environment, if there were such a person, would have to acknowledge the sovereign rights of every industry to continue polluting, while the industry concerned (if it had any sense) would disarm the higher authority and public opinion alike by supporting anti-pollution research with its own funds. In short, the failure of metasystems in society is due to their conception as higher authorities which cannot conceivably exert that authority in a free society. We have invented a self-defeating machine, a machine conceived to be unworkable. We have called it Liberty.

I stand here on very thin ice indeed. It could be made to seem that I am ready to forgo liberty in the interests of efficiency. That is a classical trap. In fact, I am not ready to forgo liberty at all. Nor do I want to talk politics, but societary cybernetics. If the Liberty Machine does not work, the answer is not to design an illiberal version. Indeed, there is plenty of evidence to suggest that to use a metasystem as a supra-authority whereby to ride roughshod over the interests of minorities is also inoperable. Such a machine is self-defeating too, in the long run, and, moreover, the cybernetician would not expect it to work in the short run for one simple reason.

The reason: informational overload. We may invest all power in a super-supra-authority, but it cannot exercise that power effectively in the very nature of cybernetic law. When we are talking about these large problems, there are not enough channels in the world to convey information within the limits of Shannon's Tenth Theorem. There are not enough computers in the world to constitute a cerebrum able to supply requisite variety within the contraints of Ashby's Law. Then I cannot, nor do I in good sense advocate a form of metacontrol which *means* supra-authority. And I seek your protection from any who may say that I have used this occasion for so illiberal an advocacy.

I must continue to advocate the fresh design of a metasystem, exerting metacontrols, as being the *only* solution to our problems, at whatever risk of being misunderstood. The problem is for cybernetics to discover, and to make abundantly clear to the world, what metasystems truly are, and why they should not be equated with the supra-authorities to which our organizational paradigms direct them. It is an appallingly difficult job, because it is so very easy to condemn the whole idea as totalitarian. Hence my use of the term the Liberty Machine. We want one that actually works.

The first test of the viability of this thinking is that I should be able to convince my cybernetic peers. In order to do that, perhaps I may be allowed a technical statement which would certainly not avail me outside this conference. The whole point about a metasystem is that it uses a metalanguage, and the whole point of a metalanguage is to be competent to decide propositions which are undecidable in the lower-order languages of the systems concerned. In short, I am making a straight appeal to the logical transcendence at the metasystemic level of limitations imposed on the lower logics by Gödel's Theorem.

For this contention my critics usually fire at me with both barrels. The message of the first bullet is that undecidability is an arcane property of abstract number systems, and that it is absurd to try to import the findings of metamathematics into sociopolitical thinking. The second bullet is inscribed "trivial." Since I always allow my critics to have it both ways, on the grounds that the two sides usually cancel each other out, I shall continue. The hypothesis that we are dealing with undecidable systems has at least the attraction that it explains why we do not seem able to decide them. Second, we are now entitled to suspect that a metasystem or Liberty Machine that has to be designed to provide a decidable metalanguage, rather than to exert despotic power in the paradigmatic sense earlier rejected.

The Liberty Machine

Once over this hurdle, which is in truth an emotional barrier (to the daunting fear of which we scientists are just as susceptible as anyone else), we can proceed quickly to specify some of the characteristics that the metasystem is bound to display.

If it breaks with the organizational stereotype of the pyramidal hierarchy, it is a disseminated network.

If it breaks with the stereotype whereby action is the product of authority, then action derives from the only available alternative, namely information.

If it cannot depend on protocol, which is the stereotype of orderly hierarchical and time-consuming procedures for implementation, then it is a fast-acting real-time regulator.

We see such metacontrols operating in all natural systems. They seem to me to operate through the rapid, discriminatory selection of information, followed by its amplification so as to promote an immediate and colossal shift in negentropy.

Think of a crystal seeding a supersaturated solution. Think of any piece of electronic control gear that you have ever seen work by error-actuated negative feedback. Think of the cataclysmic population changes, mentioned earlier, by which homeostasis is restored in the ecosystem. Think of the march of the lemmings. Think above all, as thanks to Warren McCulloch and Bill Kilmer we are able to do, of the recticular formation of the brain stem.

None of these arrangements is authoritarian in the power-hungry sense. Each constitutes a constraint on the liberty of the subsystems involved. But, insofar as survival is concerned for any of these systems, it is not liberty that stands to be lost— merely license. We humans of Western civilization are ready to pay a high price for liberty. Is it not a degradation of that ideal unthinkingly to pay bankruptcy price for a license that entails denaturing the very system in which we have some faith?

I am suggesting that in the doomsday trap in which humanity is locked today, liberty is not best preserved at the expense of all synergy and even coherence. But coherence and synergy are possible given metacontrol, and metacontrol is not incompatible with liberty once we see that it is *information* and not *legislation* that changes us.

I will go so far as to suggest a redefinition of liberty for our current technological era. It would say that *competent information is free to act,* and that this is the principle on which the new Liberty Machine should be designed. If we test this principle against our present difficulties, must we not agree that it is indeed the frustration of competent information, its inhibition from action, that forestalls progress?

That is all very well, people will say, but how can a disembodied information act? Where does the information reside?—for presumably wherever it is becomes the seat of power. I invoke your protection for the third and last time, before it is supposed that I am seeking to enthrone the modern technocratic equivalent of the philosopher-king. Scientists who suggest that it would be a good idea to have information from which to act are often assumed to be seeking power for themselves. That is because the organizational stereotype does not work on competent information, but on the equilibria of moral suasions. Its incumbents feel a sense of guilt when faced with people they suspect know more than they do. We must try to assure others that this is not at all the point we are making. If science is to offer society yet another tool, let us learn from dire experience and build *right into the package* adequate warnings against its ignorant abuse.

The tool I am proposing would be very powerful indeed. It is a tool directed toward instant decision. The pace of events will not brook delay. Then by whom should the tool be used? There is ineluctably only one answer. It should be used by those elected by the people to govern and by the agencies to which these governors delegate that responsibility. There are features of this situation that I think I understand and features which puzzle me profoundly.

As to the understanding, we surely have a shrewd idea as to what the Liberty Machine would actually look like. It is not too difficult to envisage, given the specification and the technology available. There ought to be a set of operations rooms, strategically placed in relation to the spread of the system concerned. These rooms would receive real-time data from the systems which they monitor, and they would distill the information content. (Note I do not say process the data.) Using this input to drive models, the people inside the rooms—who, I must repeat, would be responsible officials answerable to constitutional masters—would formulate hypotheses, undertake simulations, and make predictions about world trajectories. The metacontrol is of course constituted by the linkage of these rooms across the subsystems—using color television and a network of fast-acting real-time computer terminals.

Does not this begin to sound rather familiar? Do we not already have systems looking very much like this that were built in the cause of defense? Do we not have hot lines, installed on the premise that the organizational stereotype called diplomacy will not work in the face of the fast-acting thermonuclear threat, and that knowledge must constitute action?

But compare this outcome with the outcomes I discussed earlier for other kinds of threats—whereby committees are formed, officers are appointed, and research grants made. A Martian observer would be forgiven for inferring that we earthlings regard the thermonuclear threat as many orders of magnitude *more* threatening than the other environmental and societary threats which confront us. Then, if our Martian friend looked at the objective facts, he would classify us *Homo insapiens.*

As to the features of the situation which puzzle me, I refer first to the disrepute in which fast-acting metasystemic controls are currently held. As an Englishman, I should know: an election has recently been won in my country on the platform that instant decision is a shocking and improper thing. Time for reflection is required. The thesis well suits the scholarly tradition of European gentlemen. The rather obvious fact that you can be shot dead while debating the correct dress for a fight seems to have escaped attention for the moment, as have the pressure of technological advance and the manifest impatience for reform of that mass of the world's people who had nothing but their patience left to lose.

The second cause of my puzzlement is the total unawareness of governments that the tool of which I speak, a tool of this potency, could be forged by anyone commanding adequate resources. He might then, because of his infinitely superior decision-taking capability in complex, ramified international situations, take virtual control of affairs. If that sounds far-fetched, just contemplate an electronic Mafia. Information is what changes us; information constitutes control. But to put it to work requires a science of effective organization, called cybernetics, which neither racketeers nor governments understand.

Forgive me for the thought that, unfortunately, the future of mankind secondarily depends on the race between crooks and honest men for this insight, as it depends primarily on the race between nature and any men at all.

Responsibility and Finesse

I have already invited you to join me in sending out a call to anyone who will listen, urgently demanding that the Liberty Machine be redesigned. Experiments must be put in train, pioneering efforts made, and experimental systems tested. All this is easily done: we have the knowledge to do it, and the cost in all conscience, though high compared with ordinary research contracts, would be trivial compared with equivalently important programs on which we are embarked. The difficulties do not lie here. They lie in the trapped state of men's minds.

Who are *we* to say that we know best and everyone else is wrong? I have thought deeply about this question, not from a sudden access of unaccustomed humility, but because I honestly do find the sounding of clarions distasteful and acknowledge that I am fairly quick to condemn it in others. Here is the answer with which I emerge.

It is that we are *responsible*. We are not responsible because we have been elected to govern affairs; we are responsible because cybernetics, that science of effective organization, is our profession. Such understanding of this subject as there exists, is ours. Therefore we must speak out.

If my son brought home an innocuous-looking drug, I should not call the physician who warned me of this a megalomaniac; I should not draw attention to my authority in my own house; I should not beg him to refrain from interference in my son's freedom. On the contrary, were he to say nothing, on the grounds that he might be wrong, I should hold him culpable.

We do not know as much as we would like to know before making such a stand as I propose. But we have waited a hundred years in vain for the sociopolitical sciences to provide solutions. Instead, they have forfeited their claim to respect by inventing or embracing ideological frameworks for discussion and research which are antipathetic to scientific advance. As a result, man does not at all understand, and cannot therefore control, the complex forces which have pushed him to the edge of the evolutionary cliff.

We must use such tools as we have, and use them now. Just as we are responsible for displaying the problem, so we are responsible for the tools themselves. Cybernetics made and forged them. Some who are here, and some great men and wonderful friends now dead, guessed that the tool-kit would not be finished in time. Today we know that the moment has come for us to start work, and we must do the best we can.

I end in a minor key, not with that loud cry to the world for which I earlier asked, but with a thoughtful, personal word for my friends. Let us not be seduced by the sheer fun of redesigning the tools and honing their edges, when we ought to be using them to save our lives. Here in a different metaphor are the sad and evocative lines of the Bengali poet Rabindranath Tagore, which have haunted me for twenty-five years:

> The song that I came to sing remains unsung to this day.
> I have spent my days in stringing and in unstringing my instrument.
> The time has not come true, the words have not been rightly set;
> only there is the agony of wishing in my heart. . . .

Let us not come to this, for God's sake—and man's.

I
General Cybernetics

Setting Goals
in
Cybernetic Systems

W. ROSS ASHBY

Borden Neurological Institute
England

Getting clear the matter of goals is of the first importance in cybernetics, for most applications of cybernetics start with someone saying "I want . . . ". Here I am thinking of cybernetics not as a way of explaining things, but as a new science and technical method enabling us to tackle practical problems that would otherwise defeat us by their complexity. Coordinating the traffic around an airport, stabilizing the flows of money between international banks, normalizing the composition of the blood in a patient without kidneys—all these must start with the question "What do you want?" The process itself will end at the goal; the cybernetician's thoughts must start there.

What is a goal? We all know something about it, and a child of three frequently says "I want . . . ," so we all start with a personal awareness of intention, purpose, need, desire. But when we ask how a machine can have a desire, we find ourselves in difficulties. The difficulty becomes even greater if the system that is to have the goal is not even one machine but a mixture of machines and men, with the goal involving only the whole, not the parts. How can such a system have a purpose or desire?

The solution of this first difficulty, I suggest, is to do what the psychologists have done for a century: drop the introspectional aspect and turn to the aspect of *behavior*. Stop asking "Does this system feel a want?" and ask instead "How does it behave?"

Those whose knowledge of these matters is mainly introspectional may well hesitate to abandon their main source of information. But a century's work in psychology has shown that the introspectional approach, though vivid and apparently unquestionable, is in fact grossly unreliable. Look, for instance, at a piece of uncolored (white) paper: if anything is obvious and trustworthy, it is that there is no red present. Yet the physicists have convinced us that what we see is not the paper but a message from the retina saying that the three primary colors "balance." The introspective viewer sees only his own retina, not beyond it.

A report based on introspection is in fact simply the output of the brain's final, verbalizing stage. Such report can give only a coded version of what is happening earlier in the processes; to take a coding literally is an evident mistake. Psychoanalytic studies have shown in innumerable cases how mistaken a person can be when he describes his own motives or goals. Briefly, the introspectional approach, in science, has so far proved to be either just useless or positively misleading.

But if a goal is not a want, what is it? Ever since McDougall,[1] psychologists have understood that it can be treated equivalently as *a way of behaving*. "Take a timid animal," he wrote, "such as a guinea-pig, from its hole or nest, and put it upon the grass plot. Instead of remaining at rest, it runs back to its hole; push it in any other direction, and, as soon as you withdraw your hand, it turns back towards its hole." Just the same behavior is characteristic of the missile that persists in going toward a source of infrared rays, that reasserts its direction if diverted, and that will change direction if the source moves.

The experiences of a century in psychology and of thirty years in automatic control systems have shown that, for *practical* purposes, we can achieve clarity by replacing the idea of a felt need with the idea of a *focus* in a stable dynamic system.

When the system is as simple, essentially, as a missile that "seeks" infrared rays, the thesis will probably not be disputed. But what of the more complex? What of natural evolution, for instance, with organisms apparently developing their own goals? What of man? Can he not choose his own goals? Cannot the cybernetician make a machine that can choose its own goal?

To get our ideas untangled, let us first take the case of natural evolution, since here the facts are, today, beyond dispute. This case is that of a planet, subject both to unchanging laws (such as those of gravity, optics, hydrodynamics) and, over all of 10^{10} years, to a constant energy input. Through all this time, photons of the visible wavelengths have poured in and have left at infrared lengths to the night sky, in a steady flux of about 10^{29} ergs per day. This unceasing flow of free energy has kept the molecules on the planet in a mild but unceasing turmoil, during which the less stable combinations have incessantly been superseded by the more stable. Today, after 10^{10} years, what remains is mostly of extremely high stability, ranging from such minerals as granite to such dynamically stable forms as the mammal, a form older than the Alps and the survivor of several ice ages.

Looked at in this way, natural evolution and the emergence of forms such as the guinea pig, with its well-developed goal, are in no way unusual: they merely exemplify the fact that almost all state-determined systems tend to preferred regions. It is the exceptional system that does not show such preferred regions. Thus, the continuous state-determined system with equations

$$x_i = \phi_i(x_1, \ldots, x_n) \qquad (i = 1, \ldots, n)$$

shows *non*convergence only where div ϕ has the special value

$0.^2$ Take $\emptyset$'s at random, and the system resulting is almost certain to show stability at preferred regions, within which it will behave in the goal-seeking way.

"Making a system that seeks a goal" is thus trivially easy: one forms a state-determined dynamic system at random (e.g., let it be specified by the spins of a coin). One is then almost certain to have a system that, like a guinea pig, will show that it is actively goal-seeking for some preferred state. It is true that the preferred state may well be meaningless or useless to the designer, but we should notice at this point that getting a machine to have *some* goal is no problem at all.

Achieving an Assigned Goal

Having disposed of this pseudoproblem, we can now consider the real, and difficult, problem. This arises when the designer not only wants the system to be goal-seeking but also wants it to seek some goal already specified. Air-traffic control systems are required to make collisions minimal, not maximal, and a physiological stabilizer of blood composition must have as its goal just those values that the human finds normal. Here the majority of stable states that might occur on random assembly are not acceptable.

When the system is small (designing a room thermostat, say), the designer needs no further general theory; he goes straight to the particular details. But when the system is of "cybernetic" size, he may still be uncertain of the next steps. I want to suggest in this paper that the general nature of the situation can be made much clearer if we apply what is already known in information theory.

The situation is most evident when a designer faces a heap of components from which he is going to construct his machine (but it is equally so when he faces a sheet of paper on which he will write a program). The point is that by his *selection* of the assembly or program he wants, from the set that includes both what he wants and what he does not, he *transmits a message* to the end product, and all the laws of communication are applicable. To design a thermostat that will hold 72°F is to transmit the value "72" to the machine. Consider the less trivial example of the designer who wants to allot values −2, −1, 0, +1, or +2 to the four coefficients a, b, c, d in

$$\dot{x} = ax + by$$
$$\dot{y} = cx + dy$$

so that the system will be stable. In this case the quantity of information that must be transmitted from designer to system is calculable. 5^4 types are possible, of which 114 have the real parts of their latent roots both negative. In the worst case (if all values are equiprobable), the selection implies a transmission of $\log_2 (625/114)$ bits, i.e., just under 2½ bits. Thus, in this example, the channel represented by Fig. 1 *must* be able to transmit at least 2½ bits (per act of design).

Fig. 1.

The example is trivial: what matters is whether the principle is sound. If so, it will give us a deeper insight into problems that are anything but trivial.

Before we go further, however, we must notice a matter that might easily confuse us. Suppose some complex regulator accepts m inputs X_i (i = 1, . . . , m), data about aircraft at an airport perhaps, and emits orders, values on n variables Y_j (j = 1, . . . , n), to the aircraft. The designer is then asked to design it so as to be a "good" traffic controller. The basic situation may be represented as in Fig. 2. How the outputs

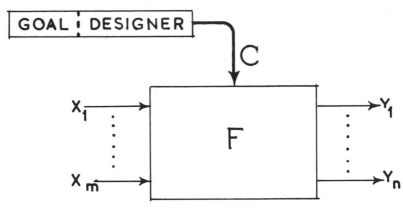

Fig. 2.

depend on the inputs is a relation F, the "transfer function" (in a general sense) of the system. The designer's task is to act so that the desired goal, selected from *all* the events (good and bad) that can occur at an airport, is transmitted to, and acts effectively as, a "good" F. This good F, it should be noted, comes from the set of all possible F's (not from the set of Y-values), so the transmission implied by the selection, along the channel C, is essentially independent of the transmission from X to Y. In this paper our attention will be focused on the quantities transmitted through such a channel as C.

The situation perhaps can be made intuitively more vivid if the designer's task be formulated as that of conveying to the heap of components what he means by the phrase "a successful airport," in the operational mode of getting the heap, when assembled, to separate the "good" set from its complement. Similarly, the problem of designing a pattern-recognizer (for genuine dollar bills, say) may be regarded generally as one of trying to tell the machine, in its *un*developed state, what is meant by "genuine, dollar, and bill." Again, this flow of design-information is essentially distinct from the flow that occurs later when the finalized machine scans an actual piece of paper and emits a verdict. Similarly, in information retrieval (getting from a library, say, the documents relevant to "social feedbacks in universities"), the difficulty can be regarded as essentially one of getting across to the machine what is meant by "society, feedback, and university." In general, thinking of the design process as one of telling the machine what you want helps to make more evident the flow of information that is intrinsic to the act of designing.

Sponsor and Designer

If this thesis is granted, we are led inescapably to the deduction that exactly the same situation exists at the prior stage, represented in Fig. 3.

Fig. 3.

Whence came the particular goal that the designer transmitted to F? Rarely is the designer himself the originator; more commonly, as in the example of the air-traffic control system, the goal comes from what I will call generically the *sponsor*. Again I argue, as before, that effects must have causes. Selection among the F's can be attributed to prior selection among the designer's possible goals. And this selection must be attributed to prior selection among the *sponsor's* possible goals. Further, it is axiomatic through information theory (though seldom stated explicitly) that complex effects, as "messages received," require at least as much complex causation as "messages sent." By as much we mean either the number of bits or, more simply, the number of possible messages. So with this axiom we can assert that there must be sufficient transmission, from sponsor to designer, for the selection made by the sponsor (among *his* possible goals) to reach the designer.

Often this requirement is so obvious that these remarks would appear to be unnecessary. But it also often happens that the requirement is not, in fact, adequately met. It is more than likely that at this meeting there are some designers who have been given nothing like sufficient information (channel B) about the sponsor's goal, yet who are expected to achieve high and appropriate selection in the system F. Sponsors must learn enough elementary cybernetics to appreciate when they are asking the impossible. The sponsor must learn, in fact, that he is as subject to Conant's First Theorem[3] as every other would-be regulator. He is a regulator insofar as, with some goal in mind, he is trying to bring the designer, who might design all sorts of things, to accept his particular goal (for transmission to the system F). If the designer misunderstands and designs for G' instead of G, the sponsor must correct him and keep acting until the designer has the sponsor's G as his guide. This is an act of regulation and so is wholly subject to Conant's Theorem, which asserts that transmission of the corresponding quantity of information (through B) is absolutely unavoidable. Armed with this theorem, the designer can *demand* that the sponsor transmit sufficiently.

The only worker in this field who seems to have clearly understood and stated these requirements was the elder von Moltke, who, in 1858, founded and organized the German General Staff. The key principle he gave it was that of the "directive." In this method the senior (corresponding to the sponsor here) gives no orders to the junior. Orders were replaced by the rule: the senior shall take all necessary time to explain to the junior what the senior wants *from the senior's point of view;* then he shall leave the junior free to use all personal initiative and local knowledge to achieve the goal. Von Moltke evidently had the clearest intuitive understanding of these quantitative flows.

Sometimes, however, the sponsor need not transmit everything. What is necessary is that *to* the designer shall come sufficient information (as determining factors) to enable him to select *his* goal adequately. But the determination need not all come from the sponsor. A sponsor may well specify so much and then say "I delegate the rest to ——————." He may delegate it to a junior, who must then supply the rest. He may delegate it to the designer himself. The designer may himself delegate further, to the spins of a coin, perhaps. But in all cases *the total of determination coming to the designer must be not less than the quantity required for the selection of his goal.*

Such supplementation may take various forms. One well-known form occurs when the genes set the goal for the living organism. But, in the higher organisms, the goal is too complex to be transmitted through the genetic channel, so a part of the determination is delegated to the environment. Says the gene-structure to the kitten, "I have told you something about mice—now go out and get the finer details from the mice themselves." We call such supplementation "learning." And a learning machine is simply any machine that is specified only partly by its designer, who delegates the remainder of the specification to some "teaching" environment.

Quantities of Information

Once these general principles governing goals are clear, the rest is a matter of special techniques in special cases. But there is one aspect that I would like to mention, as I believe it to be of central importance. It concerns the case in which the goal is of very high complexity, as in artificial intelligence, high-order pattern recognition, and high-order regulation.

Without stopping to examine closely the idea of "complexity," I shall assume that a complex goal is one which has many parts and in which the required relations between the parts show high *conditionality* of part on part; when, that is, the whole goal is a nonreducible function of many variables. I want to stress that the difference in information content between the simple (reducible) and the complex (nonreducible) goal is enormous. The basic argument can be given clearly by using set theory. Thus: If each of n variables can take k distinct values, then the number of reducible (i.e., rectangular) relations between them is the number of rectangular subsets. In the space of k^n points, it is 2^{kn}. But the number of relations in general, not restricted to the reducible, is $2^{(k^n)}$. Thus, specifying one of these relations (the subject of events acceptable as goal-achieving) requires, in the reducible case, kn bits, and in the nonreducible case, k^n bits.

The difference may be triflng to the printer, but numerically it is out of this world. Suppose, for instance, that the traffic at an airport involves only 100 variables (probably an underestimate) and that each variable need be distinguished in only 5 degrees (again, a very moderate demand). If the goal is reducible, specifying it may demand up to 500 bits; if it is *not* reducible, the quantity rises to 10^{70} bits, one bit for every atom in the universe! This fantastic leap is in no way exceptional; on the contrary, all that I have done in the last few years has shown that it is entirely typical. Allowing interaction commonly makes the informational content increase by vast orders of magnitude.

In these huge quantities we have a useful fixed point, and can keep some sense of proportion, by remembering Bremermann's limit.[4] Because of the quantal coarseness of matter, nothing made of it, machine or brain, can process information faster than about 10^{47} bits/p/sec. Take tons of computer and decades of time, and no feasible computation can handle more than about 10^{60} to 10^{70} bits. Thus, a generally complex goal, in the very moderate airport example just given, is already making demands quite beyond the achievable. I suggest that many of our troubles today, in our struggles with complex systems—especially in those researches that try to push into the really large and new—are basically ascribable to the fact that we are often attempting to handle quantities of information that are, by Bremermann's limit, actually unmanageable.

There are at least two ways in which the ideas and methods of information theory may help. First, even a rough approximation may suffice to warn us that we are attempting the impossible. Second, it may throw a quite unexpected light on the various *strategic approaches* to a problem. Here is an example that I encountered recently.

Suppose, as in Fig. 2, that the designer has to select the right function F in this system with the m inputs $X_1, \ldots, X_m$. Now this system has an obvious transmission from the X's to the Y's, but transmission in information theory means more than the driving of electrons along a wire. Essentially, *information theory is the science concerned with deviations from statistical independence.* If the values of the Y's are not independent of those of the X's, then the ordinary "transmission through" occurs, but other deviations are possible. Thus the X_i's may show deviations from independence (correlations, say) among themselves; then a transmission may be defined and measured between the X_i's. In Ref. 5, $T(X_1: \ldots : X_m)$ will not be zero. What effect will such correlation have on the quantity of information that must be handled by the designer?

Suppose $T(X_1 : \ldots : X_m) = 20$ bits. Another way of writing this fact follows.

$$2^{H(X_1, \ldots, X_m)} \;=\; 2^{\Sigma_i H(X_i)} \;\times\; 2^{-20}$$

Now "2 to an exponent entropy" is effectively the number of *independent* values, equivalent to the correlated. So the expression says that the transmission of twenty bits cuts the effective number of states at the input to the fraction 2^{-20}. Next, take the fact that the number of mappings of p input states into q output states (i.e., the number of F's from which the designer must select) is q^p. To select one F may demand up to $p \log_2 q$ bits. If q is fixed, the number of bits is proportional to p. But p has been cut by 2^{-20}, i.e., to one-millionth. Thus, the transmission, among the X_i's, of twenty bits does not just, for instance, subtract twenty bits from the designer's work: it cuts his work to a millionth part.

Having in mind this example and my other experiences of the last five years, I think it may reasonably be asserted that our most urgent need in artificial intelligence (and similar researches in highly complex systems) is that we be aware at every moment of whether the information content is dependent upon a multiplier or upon an exponent. Crude and elementary as this distinction is, without it a worker may struggle to achieve a ten percent saving in efficiency, unaware that, because of a wrong basic strategy, he is working at a level a million times too high.

REFERENCES

1. W. McDougall. *Psychology.* New York: Holt, 1912.
2. W. R. Ashby. "The Set Theory of Mechanism and Homeostasis." In *Automaton Theory and Learning Systems,* ed. by D. J. Stewart. London: Academic Press, 1967, pp. 23-51.
3. R. C. Conant. "The Information Transfer Required in Regulatory Processes." *IEEE Transactions* SSC-5 (L969): 334-338.
4. H. J. Bremermann. "Quantal Noise and Information." *5th Berkeley Symposium on Mathematical Statistics and Probability* 4 (1967): 15-20.
5. W. R. Ashby. "Two Tables of Identities Governing Information Flows within Large Systems." *Communications of American Society for Cybernetics* 1 (1969): 3-8.

Learning Strategies, Memories, and Individuals

GORDON PASK

Institute of Cybernetics, Brunel University
*England**

This paper introduces a number of theoretical ideas about human cognition: that memory is a reproductive process (in the abstract sense of "reproductive automata"), that learning is a sort of evolution, and that an individual may be profitably conceived as a self-reproducing system. More specific categories of learning and cognition (holist, serialist) also are specified and operationally defined.

As a preliminary, certain orientations, or attitudes, will be clarified, in order to minimize the chance of misunderstanding.

a. The theoretical ideas are concerned with computation. As stated, they refer to classes of computing systems rather than specific procedures. While there is no attempt to exemplify these classes by citing, for example, holist and serialist routines, or routines that are reproductive or not, there is no

*Dr. Gordon Pask is also Professor at the Institute of Educational Technology and the Department of Education, Open University; Director of Research, System Research Ltd.; and Director, Consumer Dynamics Ltd.

The research reported in this paper is supported by the Social Science Research Council of Great Britain under Research Grant No. HR 983/1, "Learning Strategies and Individual Competence," and, in its theoretical aspects, by United States Air Force Contract No. F61052-70-C-0011, "Cybernetic Learning Theory." The work was carried out at System Research Ltd.

difficulty in doing so, and the interested reader is referred to additional works.

b. As used in this paper, *learning* means a sort of problem solving. In particular, learning solves the "problem" engendered by the command "Solve P!" when the recipient has no adequate P-solving procedure in his repertoire. The solution to a learning problem is either the missing procedure or an attempt to create it. Clearly, this usage of learning has only a peripheral bearing upon the conditioning, behavior shaping, and adaptation with which many learning theorists are preoccupied.

c. A further postulate is that a human being's world is made up from relations that are learned and satisfied when problems are solved. Though fairly uncontentious, the point is important, since it provides the baseline from which the entire argument is started.

d. It is possible to build a human psychology on the basis of a language commonly understood by the subject and the experimenter (phenomenological psychology) or upon a quasiphysical model (behavioristic psychology). In the former case, statements of introspection and intention are primary data, and the constraints of an experiment are imposed upon the subject by normative restrictions contained in a contract that the subject accepts by mutual agreement with the experimenter.

e. Insofar as this paper is concerned with mindlike organizations and processes, a phenomenological point of view is adopted throughout the discussion. This orientation is intuitively proper to the subject matter and is taken for granted. The paper contains no attempt to defend it.

Empirical Data

The argument is supported by empirical data, most of which is gleaned from a recent series of experiments on human learning.[11, 15-18] These experiments are fully reported elsewhere,[16] and the following comments do not more than indicate their scope. The experiments were all concerned with modes, or styles, of learning and were designed to determine the free-learning strategies adopted by individual subjects and to assess the efficiency for individuals with differing mental makeup of different teaching strategies. In order to externalize the free-learning process (in which a student is at liberty to ask questions of his choice and direct his attention to different sub-problems), the design embodied a conversational technique. For some of the experiments, the dialogue took place in a formalized language, via an interface, with a partly mechanized tutorial system. In others, the subject conversed directly with the experimenter, who was, however, preprogrammed by fairly rigid rules.

All of the experiments can be conceived as experiments in relation learning; the relations in question, however, are complex and redundantly specified. For example, one task in the series involved the relations inherent in a taxonomy; another concerned the relations describing a cyclic system. Embedded in each redundantly specified set of relations there is a kernel of essential relations which a subject has to learn and re-capitulate. Though the subjects were aware of the essential relations, they generally learned and used redundant relations in order to access and manipulate essential relations while performing the test task which succeeded each experiment.

These are clearly experiments in learning and teaching, combined. The design was partly engendered by the educational objectives, but I also believe that theories of learning and theories of teaching do not exist as separate entities. There are theories of learning and teaching; that is all. The main foundations for that belief follow from the theoretical concepts developed in this paper.

Main Argument

If a relation, R, is described in the context of its domain, then it has an apparent *dimension,* n, equal to the number of properties *in* (descriptors *of*) its domain and an *order* of adicity, m, equal to the number of properties that R necessarily unites. The terms *apparent dimension* and *order* are easily interpretable (in case R is stated extensionally) as a subset of the product of variables (U_i) indexing the related properties, i.e., as $R \subseteq U_1x$ . . $U_n = U^*$ when an n-tuple* $[u_1, . . u_n]$ Σ $R \subseteq U^*$ satisfies R. Ashby provides an algorithm for determining the order, m, of an arbitrary subset of U^* (his "cylindrance"), and, in general, m is less than n. In particular, following Ashby's line of argument:

a. if n > m (as usual), then R is the intersection of sub-relations (cylinder subsets) of generally lower order and dimension;

b. there will often be several families of "cylinder subsets" that intersect on R; any one family specifies R; the set of families provides a redundant specification of R.

Relations may also be specified in a language where they are named by words or described by phrases, for example "Father of" or ">" or "the T.C.A. cycle" or "A allows B to do C" or "happiness" or "antelope" (a class of animals defined by relations between behavioral or physical properties). Sometimes, the order of the relation and the dimension of its domain are explicit; for instance, ">" has order 2 and is irredundantly specified (for numerical domains of dimension 2; similarly, "A allows B to do C" has order 3, though the dimension is not explicit). But, linguistically stated relations can be quite respectably underspecified. It is possible to list situations that engender happiness or relations supporting the antelope character ad infinitum.

I do not mean anything very mysterious by the idea of an underspecified relation. On the other hand, I do mean something interesting and important. An individual who understands the language in which the relation is stated can extensionally specify the relation, at a given instant, by ostending the n-tuples which belong to R and separating them from n-tuples that do not. But this specification is tied to the individual and to the instant; if R is underspecified, then n (and possibly also m) is a variable in any general statement that is independent of instants and individuals. Hence it may be deemed prudent, and it is certainly quite harmless, to regard underspecified relations as the open union of fully specified but redundant subrelations of possibly variable dimension.*

A goal is a relation that is entertained by a system which aims for it, satisfies it, or brings it about. A subgoal is a subrelation of a goal. If a goal relation is redundantly specified, and if n > m, then it may be satisfied by the achievement of several collections of subgoals, those corresponding to the families of subrelations intersecting on R.

Goal-directed systems (hereafter, G.D.S.) are conceived, for the present purpose, as problem solvers. A problem is posed, in the context of a goal, R, by inserting the values of an incomplete set of the variables indexing its domain; a solution is an n-tuple belonging to R. In general (as in the following section) a G.D.S. is built up from more elementary G.D.S. aiming for subgoals of R.

Strictly, a TOTE unit[1] is a G.D.S. The crucial feature, however, is that the operation of a G.D.S. is under the control of the problem itself, and probably the least organization to be seriously countenanced as a G.D.S. is a routine of the type that Manna[5] refers to as a nondeterministic program. A deterministic program represented as a collection of IF, THEN, ELSE loops is a special and limiting case of a G.D.S. obtained by requiring strictly serial operation.

It is profitable to distinguish between two major kinds of problem-solving computation. At one extreme, problems are solved by the serial application of basic routines; at the other extreme, they are solved by mustering these routines concurrently (an effectively parallel computation which may be mimicked, at the cost of much tagging, labeling, and housekeeping, by a complicated serial search). Amarel,[13] taking the position of a formalist, conceives the first type of problem

---

*Banerji[32] distinguishes between input properties (in a fine structure family) and noninput properties. Phrased in these terms an individual need not *specify* all noninput properties at the *outset*. But, if his goal is underspecified, he will *use* them and *could* specify them at some later stage.

solver as a macro-assembler, the second as a director and compiler combined. Making the same distinction in terms of artificial intelligence and psychology, we can say that the first sort of problem solving resembles the operation of a "TOTE hierarchy"[*] (Ref. 1), or a program such as Newell and Simon's "Logic Theorist,"[2] whereas the second sort of problem solving resembles the operation of an associative network like Quillian's "TLC"[3] or Reitman's "Argus."[4]

If R is redundantly specified (as it generally is), then the second sort of problem solver aims for several subgoals at once and is likely to achieve R as the intersection of various families of subrelations.

The choice of "problem solving" as an illustrative activity is a matter of convention; the pertinent distinction is familiar in this field. But the processes being distinguished are ubiquitous; they appear as part of all skilled and intellectual cognition. If, as is currently generally agreed, a *concept* is equated with a *procedure*, then the distinction demarcates two conceptual types, namely a *serialist* type and a *holist* type.

Consider a task involving a redundantly specified goal relation. (Nearly all tasks of practical concern are of this type, as are all educational tasks. The tasks used in the experiments were designed to be of this type, though the form and amount of redundancy were carefully controlled.)

Suppose that a serialist and a holist problem solver *both* know what is required of them, i.e., to give a canonical description of the relation and to *use* this relation. This condition was also satisfied in all of the experiments (it *can* be satisfied without difficulty because of the peculiarities of a human G.D.S. noted above).

Even so, the serialist and the holist problem solvers use quite different data. A serialist process is embarrassed by redundant data, unless it is clearly marked as redundant. Failing that, it will only succeed if it discovers and sticks to *one* irredundant description of the goal relation, and, since a canonical

---

[*]It should be noted that the TOTE hierarchy is a *post hoc* description of the activity in question.

description is to be elicited, this one must be the one the *experimenter* has in mind.

By way of contrast. a holistic process deals concurrently with many descriptions, and even if asked to give the (experimenter's) canonical account of the goal relation, it generally constructs this by cross-reference to a set of (different and redundant) descriptions.

Many of the same comments apply to the way in which both serialist and holist problem solvers *use* the goal relation in *solving* problems.

Distinctions other than *holist* and *serialist* have been drawn, and the different varieties of mentation are often called "cognitive styles." Bruner,[26] for example, discusses people's disposition to use one type of strategy over another; Witgin[27] makes a distinction between "Field-Dependent" and "Field-Independent" subjects; Kagan[28] demarcates people who are "Reflective" from those who are "Impulsive"; Elshoutt and Elshoutt[29] separate modes of problem solving in open-ended situations; Guilford[30] analyzes mental activity in terms of the coordinates "Operations" (e.g., convergent, divergent, or evaluative thinking), "Contents" (e.g., figural, symbolic, semantic), and "Products." I believe that, although each of these categories is important and bears upon the present issue, none seems to be quite so clear-cut as the holist/serialist distinction, probably because most of the categories are based on the factor analysis of massed data. The present paper is concerned with the holist/serialist distinction only.

Over an appreciable number of different problems an individual may belong to one or the other conceptual type. This is an empirical statement based on experiments with the following tasks; map learning, taxonomy learning, procedure learning, and learning the operation of a complex dynamic system. Single subjects, conceptually typed for one task, preserve that type for the others.

It is not assumed that an individual can *only* think and conceptualize in one way or the other. Rather, he has a preferred mode of thinking and conceptualizing, and this prefer-

ence will be manifest in connection with problems that are
(a) open to solution in either way or (b) large or difficult
enough to engender excessive uncertainty if tackled otherwise.*

Under these circumstances, a subject's mode of operation
becomes manifest as a strategy according to which he will
direct his attention to parts of the problem(s) under consideration. Various conversational techniques have been developed to externalize this attention-directing strategy as a
segment of discourse *about* the problem-solving process. These
techniques were used in the conduct of the experiments.

To digress slightly, there is good reason for the strategies
(and the modes of which they are symptoms) to be so remarkably distinct.

It was previously established that a trapping phenomenon,
Cognitive Fixity, exists in nearly all human cognition. Once
a subject has built up a mental organization appropriate to a
chosen strategy, he tends to stick with it. The organization
costs processing effort, and, on the whole, is only attuned to
information garnered under the strategy it was constructed
to serve. Insofar as they do not wish to waste their labors,
subjects become "fixed" with an organization they will not
discard.†

Though several canons can be employed to characterize
holist and serialist thinking and conceptualizing, only one
is isolated for the present discussion. During its operation,
either kind of process must test hypotheses about the existence
or nonexistence of relations. The serialist process picks out
(hypothetical) relations of *low* order (adicity); the holist proc-

---

*This point relies on a previously verified hypothesis that man is constrained
to regulate his uncertainty so that it is neither too high nor too low in any
operating region.

†Cognitive Fixity is an appreciable effect. Its magnitude can be estimated in
teaching situations where part of the strategy is prescribed by a teacher or a
tutorial device. Subjects (students) are often led to adopt a resultant strategy
that is quite unsuited to their conceptual type (either because the instruction is misguided or because it is misinterpreted). However, fixity still
operates to a degree that can be estimated by ascertaining how much evidence of incompatibility must be provided before a subject can be persuaded
to change strategy.

ess picks out relations of *high* order. These are the subgoal relations of the G.D.S. which are called into execution as the problems are solved.

If the hypothetical relations are described in a questioning metalanguage (as they are in the experiments of immediate interest), then their *descriptions* may often be reduced to statements about single predicates combined according to the usual connectives. In this case, low-order relations correspond to terse statements, and high-order relations to lengthy ones.

Learning is distinguished from problem solving as follows. We define a hierarchy of *control* (which must *not* be confused with a hierarchy of routines/subroutines or goals/subgoals, such as a TOTE hierarchy). Let the control hierarchy have levels L^0, L^1 . . . and let its members consist of G.D.S. or classes of them.

Any G.D.S. at L^0 is a problem solver (alias, a concept), and its domain is an environment, usually a symbolic environment described by an object language. Any G.D.S. at L^1 is also a problem solver, and its domain consists in some or all of the G.D.S. at L^0. In particular, it solves problems engendered by deficiencies in the L^0 repertoire with respect to achieving a stipulated goal (or solving a stipulated class of problems), and its solutions are obtained by modifying L^0 G.D.S. or by constructing fresh ones.

It should be emphasized that the L^0, L^1 distinction is a descriptive expedient that allows us to talk about self-referential processes *as though* self-reference did not exist. The distinction is useful and can be experimentally reified (as when a questioning metalanguage is demarcated from an object language). For all that, it is artificially *imposed* by an outside observer whose motivation is similar to that of computer theorists when they adopt an identical expedient to avoid the notion or possibility of "impure programming" (i.e., of programs that rewrite themselves).

The theory postulates that in any individual the characteristic type of L^1 process (G.D.S.) is the same as the characteristic type of L^0 process (as on page 51). Thus, individuals are typed as learning *and* problem solving in a *serialist* or *holist* fashion (rather than being demarcated as the "serialist problem solvers" and "holist problem solvers" of page 50.*

In the sequel, "memory" means organization, a form of computation and information structure. Thus memory is *not* equated with the notion of *storage* (the writing of information in registers, loci or the like). The brain, regarded as a processing machine, has many ways of storing information (specific R.N.A. and proteins, synaptic changes, reverberation, etc.). Data must be *inscribed* on the brain by almost any change of state, and evidence suggests that many sorts of inscription contribute to a trace or token. But memory has no direct connection with *storage*, which may be of many kinds and may, incidentally, involve marks on the environment just as much as marks on the brain.

The theory asserts that *memory* is the *reproduction* of an L^0 G.D.S. by an L^1 G.D.S., and that the *system* memory is isomorphic with a system of reproducing automata in Von Neuman's[6] sense, with the L^1 G.D.S. playing the part of the reproductive automaton and the L^0 G.D.S. that of the automaton which is reproduced. Von Foerster's[7] recent theory of memory constitutes a special case of this paradigm, the automata in question being finite state machines. If the reproductive process is externalized by statements in a suitable language, then a reproduction of a *concept* (a problem solver, a G.D.S.) is an *explanation* of this concept and the microstructure of the process will appear as an explanation chain, essentially a proof chain (this point is also made by Loefagren[8]).

The experiments under discussion are conversational in the sense that the subject interacts with a participant experimenter (or, more commonly, a *device* that acts as his surrogate), thereby externalizing the problem solving process as a stretch of discourse. By reversing the roles of the subject and the

*Serialist learning may be said to *chain* concepts in the behavioristic sense. While remaining uncommitted on this point, it is possible to argue that the minimal stable data structure is a TOTE hierarchy rather than a *chain*, though it is true that the two entities lead to similar behavior.

experimenter, it is thus possible to set up a situation in which the reproduction of a concept will be externalized if such a process actually occurs. The situation in question is called *"Teachback."*

The empirical findings are as follows:

1. As expected, explanation chains *do* occur in teachback.

2. The explanation chains of serialists and holists are (as predicted) quite different in kind, especially with respect to the type and referent of the hypotheses tested during the production. Here, of course, subjects have been independently characterized as serialist or holist, generally by the criterion discussed on page 52.

3. The establishment of a memory for a concept, X, may be inferred unequivocally, from the existence, in teachback, of a chain reproducing X. This memory persists for a few weeks at least (for months in all subjects tested after that interval), and there is reason to believe that the memory is indelible.

4. A concept can be reproduced internally, even if a teachback facility is provided. There is no doubt that such internal reproduction occurs when the subject matter is inherently interesting or has an affective content, but subjects can also be commanded to learn structured but clearly useless material (e.g., artificial taxonomies), and it seems unlikely that the concepts they entail would be internally reproduced.

5. After learning to solve problems, one group of subjects were tested exhaustively by questioning. They continued learning until they could achieve *full* proficiency. Another group of subjects, at the same level of proficiency, were submitted to *teachback*. After a couple of weeks, all the subjects were retested. The difference between the two groups is clear-cut to the extent that no statistical method is needed to discriminate their scores. Teachback subjects *had* a memory; test subjects did *not*.

In these circumstances it looks as though *memory* is dependent on *teachback*. As a general hypothesis, the memory of X *is* the reproduction of X (either externally, as in teachback, or internally).

The main theoretical argument can be summarized by the following general statements.

a. L^0 G.D.S. $\triangleq$ ⟨system for reproducing a relation R⟩.

b. memory of R $\triangleq$ ⟨L^1 G.D.S. for reproducing an L^0 G.D.S.⟩. Recalling that a G.D.S. is either a single G.D.S. or an ordered class of them (the problem solver), a serialist memory is characterized as follows.

a. L^0 G.D.S. named y $\triangleq$ ⟨system for reproducing relation X⟩.

b. memory of X $\triangleq$ ⟨unitary L^1 G.D.S. for reproducing y⟩.

In contrast, a holist is characterized by a many-to-one and temporally concurrent system described thus:

a. set of L^0 G.D.S. named Y $= ⟨y_1 . . y_n⟩ \triangleq$ ⟨System for reproducing a redundantly specified relation X⟩. (Each L^0 G.D.S. aims for and is under the control of one family of subgoals of R.)

b. memory of X $= ⟨$set of concurrently operating L^1 G.D.S.s for reproducing Y⟩.

Let us pause at this point to review the educational consequences of the theory.

Two (or more) major types of conceptual organization are postulated. I have referred to these elsewhere[15] as types of mental competence. Left on their own, and under propitious circumstances, individuals will solve problems and learn in a way that is compatible with their *competence* type; *i.e.*, they will tend to adopt an appropriate strategy, though they may not always succeed in doing so.

Teaching procedures (most markedly programmed instruction and CAI, but *all* teaching procedures to some extent) structure the presentation of knowledge and thereby *impose* a strategy upon the student, a tutorial strategy which may or may not be matched to the individual's competence. Insofar as the assignment of teaching materials is arbitrary or determined classwise, the probability of individual mismatch is quite high in the case of conventional instruction.

The question is, does that matter? The empirical answer to

this question is: Yes. Experiments have been run (as part of the same design as the teachback series mentioned on page 55) in which students previously assigned to the competence typed serialist (S) and holist (H) have been instructed in the problem areas of taxonomies, dynamic systems, etc., via serialist training routines (SR) and holist training routines (HR). Of the four combinations, namely

$$(A) = S \longrightarrow SR$$
$$(B) = S \longrightarrow HR$$
$$(C) = H \longrightarrow HR$$
$$(D) = H \longrightarrow SR$$

both (A) and (C) are matched, whereas both (B) and (D) are *mismatched*. Subsequently, all subjects were tested for retention and regeneration of the learned material.

Serialist subjects fare just about as well, on the average, as holist subjects (the problems were chosen to obtain this result). However, the *matched* subjects have a much higher test score than the *mismatched* subjects, so much higher that it looks as though effective learning *depends* upon securing a *matched* condition. If the size of the effect is as large as we suspect, conventional education must be grossly inefficient and an improvement of several orders of magnitude could be achieved by the (entirely practicable) expedient of matching the tutorial strategy to the competence of an individual.

The question of matching is discussed in other publications,[10–12,15,16] where it is related to analogous issues pertinent to the instruction of perceptual motor skills,[17–20] clerical training,[21,22] and the like. We shall not consider the matter any further in the present paper, but will turn, instead, to certain philosophically oriented developments of the theory.

Philosophy

In this section we comment, very briefly, on the nature of learning and the nature of an individual.

Learning

An evolutionary process is formed by an appropriate juxta-position of the following components: Reproduction, Variation, Selection, Cooperation, or Recombination.

Typical paradigms of evolution (in this, rather abstract, sense) are furnished by Fogel, Owens, and Walsh's work on simulated evolutionary systems,[23] by Myhill's abstract formu-lation,[31] and by my own work in this area.[24]

The present theory postulates that learning is a sort of evo-lution, the following entities being identified with the separate constituents of (A), (B) (C), and (D).

1. *Reproduction* is the *memory* of pages 55–56, the repro-ducible entities being G.D.S. procedures.

2. *Variation* is introduced either by encountering randomly disposed problems or via the questions which a subject is asked by the experimenter.

3. *Selection* is due to constraints upon the processor (the *brain*), chiefly, the constraint imposed by a limited *storage* capacity, in the sense defined on page 54.

4. *Cooperation* takes place in two ways: externally, by con-versational interaction with a participant experimenter (act-ing, perhaps, as a teacher); internally, by interaction between concurrently executed procedures. In the latter connection it should be noted that the possibility of internal cooperation stems from the postulate or concurrent action. It is charac-teristic of such systems that they have redundancy of potential command (as McCulloch[22] uses the phrase) and vice versa.

We are talking, of course, about the evolution of an organiza-tion (a *mind*) under the constraints afforded by a processor (a brain), and not about the evolution of a brain or a processor per se. (Recall the comments on *storage* on page 54.) To em-phasize the distinction, let us call the evolution "symbolic."

One salient characteristic of a symbolic evolution is that it automatically deals with underspecified goals (in particular, the linguistically stated goals described in the beginning of this paper) by innovative learning. Specifically, it constructs new properties, related by the goal, over and above the essential or redundant properties that are given at the outset.

Innovative behavior was often exhibited by the experimental subjects. For example, in the taxonomy learning task (one of the experimental series), the taxonomy serves to classify species of imaginary animals. But, innovative subjects invented further properties (e.g., that some animals are aggressive while others are friendly) which appeared in neither the essential nor the redundant specification. These subjects also used the invented properties in order to evaluate essential properties in the course of the test.

Individuals

Taking a rather different tack, it is not difficult to extend the definition sequence on page 56 by inquiring, "What reproduces a memory?" In other words, we proceed from

L^0 G.D.S. $\triangleq$ ⟨system for reproducing a relation, R⟩

Memory of R $\triangleq$ ⟨ L^1 G.D.S. for reproducing L^0 G.D.S. for reproducing R⟩ by writing:

Something (as yet undefined) $\triangleq$ ⟨L^2 G.D.S. for reproducing L^1 G.D.S. for reproducing L^0 G.D.S. for reproducing R⟩.

If it happens that there are at least two somethings (called A and B) which jointly understand the language in which R is stated and which both aim for R, then the last expression can be rephrased to avoid an indefinite regress (since the levels L^0, L^1, are imposed for convenience, with only the distinction of levels being essential).

$\left\{\begin{array}{l} L^0 \text{ G.D.S. (A) for reproducing } L^1 \text{ G.D.S. (B) for reproducing } L^0 \text{ G.D.S. (B) for reproducing R} \\ L^0 \text{ G.D.S. (B) for reproducing } L^1 \text{ G.D.S. (A) for reproducing } L^0 \text{ G.D.S. (A) for reproducing R} \end{array}\right.$

$\left\{\begin{array}{l} A \triangleq L^1 \text{ G.D.S. (A) for reproducing } L^0 \text{ G.D.S. (A) for reproducing } ⟨L^1 \text{ G.D.S. (B), R}⟩ \\ B \triangleq L^1 \text{ G.D.S. (B) for reproducing } L^0 \text{ G.D.S. (B) for reproducing } ⟨L^1 \text{ G.D.S. (A), R}⟩ \end{array}\right.$

We call A and B *psychological individuals* (or P-individuals), R (or some larger body of relations) their *common context*, and the ordered set [A, B, R] a stable self-reproducing system. As I understand it, Matturana's "Cognitive Domain" and my "Common Context" are identical.

P-individuals are organizations, not specific processors. They are characterized by Loefgren[8] as symbiotically self-reproducing systems (alias, self-explaining systems). While a P-individual may be highly correlated with the activity of a single brain or even a single inanimate processor which is an individual (in the biological or mechanical sense), the correspondence is not necessarily one to one, since a class of programs (such as a P-individual) may be run in various processors on different occasions.

The two types of individual, biomechanical and P-individual, are interestingly different entities. Both definitions afford legitimate units of analysis, i.e., the individuals concerned. Both have a certain range of convenience (Kelly's phrase) and a certain range of utility. Whereas the biomechanical concept of an individual has proven value in certain areas, there are other areas of study, notably in the social and psychological sciences, where it is definitely an awkward unit to work with; for example, in discussing a conversation, where do "I" end, where do "you" begin. If we are interested in theorizing about social and psychological systems, especially conversational systems, then the P-individual is an alternative unit or building block which deserves serious attention.

An Overview

The interpretations of learning as symbolic evolution (page 58) and of an individual as a P-individual (page 59) are relatively unilluminating when the analogy *mind is to program as brain is to computer* is pressed to its limit. Then, the mind is regarded as a nondeterministic program which is run in a present-generation computer and a distinction (arbitrary, but all the same conventional) is made between stored *data* and stored *operations* which periodically act upon the data. Fortunately the constraints inherent in this point of view are not mandatory, and the deliberately liberal definition of a G.D.S. gives the license required to relax them.

Most biological computation is not of the conventionally restricted type. Enzymes and their substrates (corresponding to operations and data) have a comparable status in a cell and both of them generally require reproduction if the entire organization is to persist (i.e., to be remembered). Present concern with concurrently acting parallel processors is also encouraging engineers to take a wider view of computation, and here again there is a tendency to eliminate the data/operation demarcation line and to conceive the entire system as a reproductive entity.

No adequate formal backbone existed for such notions until a year ago, when the situation was remedied by a series of papers by Chiaraviglio and Baralt,[9] An *interpretation* of their mathematical reasoning, called "Combinatomic Theory," depicts a general form of computation somewhat akin to what is known of cellular regulation. In this context, the present distinction between *storage* and *remembering* is extremely germane. It is also of interest that the serialist and holist categories of cognition, introduced as intuitively reasonable and empirically discriminable, appear as fundamentally distinct special cases of this general form.

REFERENCES

1. G. A. Miller; E. Gallenter; and K. Pribram. *Plans and the Structure of Behaviour*. Hinsdale, Ill.: Holt, Dryden, 1960.
2. A. Newell and H. A. Simon. "G.P.S.; A Programme that Simulates Human Thought." In *Computers and Thought*, ed. by E. A. Fiegenbaum and J. Feldman. New York: McGraw-Hill Book Co., 1963.
3. R. Quillian. "The Teachable Language Comprehender—A Simulation and a Model for Language." *Communications of the ACM* 20, 9 (1967).
4. W. R. Reitman. *Cognition and Thought*. New York: John Wiley & Sons, Inc., 1965.
5. Manna 2. "The Correctness of Non Deterministic Programmes." *Artificial Intelligence* 1, 1 and 2 (1970): 1–26.

62

6. J. Von Neuman. *Theory of Self-reproducing Automata.* Urbana: University of Illinois Press, 1966.
7. H. Von Foerster. "What is memory that it may have Hindsight and Foresight as well" *B.C.L. Report 153.* Urbana: University of Illinois Press, 1968.
8. L. Loefgren. "An Axiomatic Explanation of Complete Self-Reproduction." *Bull. Match. Biophysics* 30, 3 (September 1968).
9. L. Chiaraviglio and J. Baralt-Torrijos. "On the Combinatory Definability of Software." School of Information and Computer Science. Georgia Institute of Technology, 1970.
   ———. "On the Combinatory Definability of Hardware." Georgia Institute of Technology, 1970.
10. G. Pask. "Computer Assisted Learning and Teaching." In *Proceedings of the Leeds Seminar on Computer Based Learning,* ed. by J. Annett and J. Duke, pp. 50-63. NCET, September 1969.
11. ———. "Fundamental Aspects of Educational Technology (Illustrated by Principles of Conversational Systems)." *Proc. IFIP World Conference on Computer Education,* vol. I, invited papers, ed. by R. Scheepmaker. Amsterdam: IFIP, August 1970.
12. ———. "Teaching Machines." In *Modern Trends in Education,* ed. by B. Rose. London: Macmillan, 1970.
13. S. Amarel. "Representation of Problems and Goal-directed Procedures in a Computer." *Communications of ASC* 1, 2 (July 1969): 9-36.
14. W. R. Ashby. "The Constraint Analysis of Many Dimensional Relations." *Yearbook of the Society for General Systems Research* 9 (1964): 99-105.
15. G. Pask. "Strategy Competence and Conversation as Determinants of Learning." *Programmed Learning* (October 1969): 250-267.
16. ——— and B. C. E. Scott. "Learning Strategies and Individual Competence." Social Science Research Council Research Grant H.R. 983/1 (2 vols.). Richmond, Eng.: System Research Ltd., January 1971.
17. ——— and B. Lewis. "The Use of a Null Point Method to Study the Acquisition of Simple and Complex Transformation Skills." *Brit. Journal of Math. and Stat. Psych.* 21, part 1 (May 1968): 61-84.
18. G. Pask and B. C. E. Scott. "Learning and Teaching Strategies in a Transformation Skill." *Brit. Journal of Math. and Stat. Psych.,* in press.
19. G. Pask and B. N. Lewis. "The Adaptively Controlled Instruction of a Transformation Skill." *Programmed Learning* (April 1967): 74–86.
20. G. Pask; M. Elstob; and B. C. E. Scott. *An Introduction to Scripts.* Richmond, Eng.: System Research Ltd., October 1970.
21. G. Pask. Technical Information Paper on Scripts and Modular Scripts. Department of Employment and Productivity, forthcoming.
22. W. S. McCulloch. *Embodiments of Mind* Cambridge: MIT Press, 1965.

23. L. Fogel; D. Owens; and D. Walsh. *Artificial Intelligence through Simulated Evolution.* New York: Academic Press, 1966.
24. "The Computer-Simulated Development of Population and Automata." *Mathematical Biosciences.* New York: American Elsevier Publishing Co. 4 (1969): 101–127.
25. G. Pask. "The Control of Learning in Small Subsystems of a Programmed Educational System." *I.E.E.E. Transactions on Human Factors in Electronics,* vol. HFE 8, no. 2 (June 1967): 88–93.
26. J. S. Bruner; J. J. Goddenow; and G. S. Austin. *A Study of Thinking.* New York: John Wiley & Sons, Inc., 1956.
27. H. A. Witgin. "Psychological Differentiation and Forms of Pathology." *Journal of Abnormal Psychology,* vol. 70, no. 5 (1965): 317–366.
28. J. Kagan. "Developmental Studies in Reflection and Analysis." In *Perceptual Development in Children,* ed. by A. H. Kidd and J. L. Rivoire. New York: International Universities Press, 1966, pp. 487–505, 517–522.
29. T. Elshout. "The Programmed Instruction of Problem Solving." In *Programmed Learning Research,* ed. by F. Bresson and M. Montmollin. Paris: Dunod, 1969.
30. J. P. Guilford. "The Structure of Intellect." *Psychological Bulletin* 53 (1960): 267–293.
31. J. Myhill. "The Abstract Theory of Self-reproduction." In *Views on General System Theory,* ed. by M. Mesarovic. New York: John Wiley & Sons, Inc., 1964.
32. R. B. Banerji. *A Theory of Problem Solving.* New York: American Elsevier Publishing Co., 1970.

II
Artificial Intelligence
and
Robotics

The Cerebellum:
A Substrate for List-Processing in the Brain

JAMES S. ALBUS

Goddard Space Flight Center
Greenbelt, Maryland

Introduction

It is an interesting fact that almost all modern research efforts in artificial intelligence utilize some form of list-structured data base. The list-structure seems fundamental to almost all data storage systems which store items in a relational way. This fact alone might lead one to speculate that perhaps some form of list-structured data base may exist in the brain. I would like to suggest that there exists considerable anatomical and physiological evidence which supports this speculation.

A list-structured data base has as an essential feature the fact that each data-node contains information concerning the address of the next data-node or nodes in the list. Data is extracted from the contents of memory, operated on in some fashion, and then used as address information for extracting the next piece of data from memory. This looping structure is the very essence of a list-structured data base.

In the brain there exist numerous examples of looping paths. The cerebral cortex covers the brain like a canopy and is

67

connected to the thalamus as a parachute canopy is connected
to the parachutist. Many nerve cells in the thalamus receive
data from the external sensory apparatus and transmit data
to the cortex. The cortex processes this data and sends it back
to the thalamus. The thalamus in turn processes the returned
data and retransmits it back to the cortex. This looping goes on
many times. Many other loops also exist. The motor cortex
transmits to the pons which transmits to the cerebellum. The
cerebellum transmits to the thalamus and thence back to the
motor cortex. The motor cortex also has loops which go through
the striatium, the red nucleus and other subcortical motor
areas. The emotional areas of the brain form the classical
Papez's circuit, or loop.

One of the best understood loops at the micronanatomical
level is the interaction between the cerebellum and the external world via the motor effectors and sensors.

A great body of facts has been known for many years concerning the general organization and structure of the cerebellum. The regularity and relative simplicity of the cerebellar
cortex have fascinated anatomists since the earliest days of
systematic neuronanatomical observations. However, in just
the past seven or eight years the electron microscope and
refined microneurophysiological techniques have revealed
critical structural details which make possible comprehensive
theories of cerebellar function. A great deal of the recent
physiological data about the cerebellum comes from an elegant series of experiments by Eccles and his co-workers. This
data has been compiled along with the pertinent anatomical
data in book form by Eccles, Ito, and Szentagothai.[1]

Data

To credit each piece of information presented in this section
to its original source would be very tedious. Everything in this
section is taken directly either from Ref. 1 or Ref. 2. Therefore
a single reference is now made to these sources and to the
extensive bibliographies which appear in them.

Mossy Fibers

Mossy fibers constitute one of the two input fiber systems to the cerebellum. Input information conveyed to the cerebellum via mossy fibers is from many different areas. Some mossy fibers carry information from the vestibular system and/or from the reticular formation. Others carry information which comes from the cerebral cortex via the pons. The mossy fiber system which has been most closely studied relays information from the various receptor organs in muscles, joints, and skin. Mossy fibers which arrive via the dorsal spinal cerebellar tract are specific as regards modality of the muscle receptor organ, either from muscle spindles or from tendon organs, and have a restricted receptor field, usually from one muscle or a group of synergic muscles.

Mossy fibers from the ventral spinal cerebellar tract are almost exclusively restricted to Golgi tendon organ information but are more generalized as regards specific muscles than those from the dorsal spinal cerebellar tract. The ventral tract fibers seem to signal stages of muscle contraction and interaction between contraction and resistance to movement of a whole limb. Other mossy fibers carry information from skin pressure receptors and joint receptors. There are continuous spontaneous discharges on most mossy fibers, at rates between ten and thirty per second, even when the muscles are completely relaxed.

Mossy fibers enter the cerebellum and arborize diffusely throughout the granular layer of the cortex. A single mossy fiber may send branches into two or more folia. These branches travel toward the top of the folia, finally terminating in an arborization at the top of the folia. Each branch of a mossy fiber terminates in a candelabra-shaped arborization containing synaptic sites called mossy rosettes. There is minimum distance of 80–100μ between rosettes from a single mossy fiber. It is estimated that each branch of a mossy fiber entering the granular layer of the cerebellum produces from twenty to fifty or more rosettes. Thus, a single mossy fiber may produce several hundred rosettes, considering all its branches. The mossy ro-

settes are the site of excitatory synaptic contact with dendrites
of the granule cells.

The mossy fibers also send collaterals into the intracerebellar
nuclei, where they make excitatory synaptic contact with
nuclear cells.

Granule Cells

The granule cells are the most numerous cells in the brain.
It is estimated that in humans there are 3×10^{10} granule cells
in the cerebellum alone. Granule cells possess from one to
seven dendrites, the average being four. These dendrites are
from 10μ to 30μ long and terminate with a characteristic claw-
shaped ramification in the mossy rosettes. In view of the spac-
ing between rosettes on a mossy fiber, it is highly unlikely that
a granule cell will contact two rosettes from the same mossy
fiber. Thus, an average granule cell is excited by about four
different mossy fibers. Since approximately twenty granule cell
dendrites contact each rosette, this means that there are about
five times as many granule cells as mossy rosettes, and at least
100 to 250 times as many granule cells as mossy fibers. Since
a mossy fiber enters several folia, there may even be four or
five times this many granule cells per mossy fiber.

Each granule cell gives off an axon, which rises toward the
surface of the cortex. When this axon reaches the molecular
layer, it makes a T-shaped branch and runs longitudinally
along the length of the folia for about 1.5 mm in each direction.
These fibers are densely packed and are only about 0.2μ to 0.3μ
in diameter. The parallel fibers make excitatory synaptic contact with Purkinje cells, Basket cells, Stellate cells, and Golgi
cells.

Golgi Cells

Golgi cells have a wide dendritic spread, which is approximately cylindrical in shape and about 600μ in diameter (see
Fig. 1). This dendritic tree reaches up into the molecular

600 μ

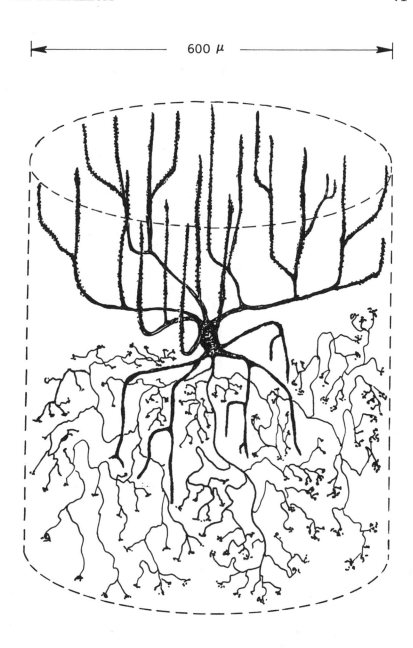

Fig. 1. A Typical Golgi Cell; Its Arborizations Extend Throughout an Approximately Cylindrical Volume 600μ in Diameter. (Reprinted with permission from the *Journal of Mathematical Biosciences.)*

layer, where it is excited by the parallel fibers, and also down into the granular layer, where it is excited by the mossy fibers. The Golgi axon branches extensively and inhibits about one-hundred thousand granule cells located immediately beneath its dendritic tree. Every granule cell is inhibited by at least one Golgi cell. The Golgi axons terminate on the mossy rosettes, inhibiting granule cells at this point. Fox states that the axon arborizations of neighboring Golgi cells overlap extensively, so that two or more Golgi cells frequently inhibit a single granule cell. Note the overlapping fields shown in Fig 2.

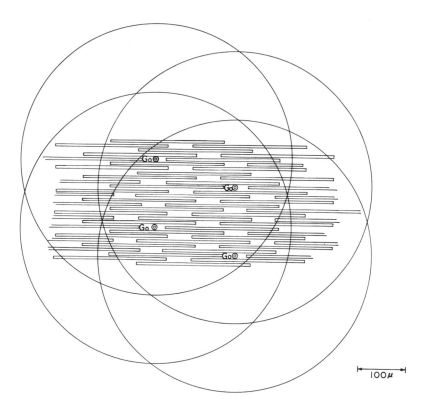

Fig. 2. View of Cerebellar Cortex Looking Down on Top of Purkinje Dendritic Trees. (Reprinted, by permission, from the *Journal of Mathematical Biosciences*.)

Note: Purkinje cells are shown here spaced approximately every 50μ in the longitudinal direction and every 60μ in the transverse direction. They are staggered so that the dendritic trees do not intermingle. Four Golgi cells are shown with the outline of their area of arborization traced. There is one Golgi cell to every nine Purkinje cells. Note the extensive overlapping of Golgi arborization. Each point on the cortex is subject to influence by about nine different Golgi cells.

This overlapping is a point of disagreement between Eccles and Fox. However, it appears that Golgi cells must overlap, considering their size and the fact that there are approximately 10 percent as many Golgi cells as Purkinje cells.

The size of the dendritic spread of the Golgi cell as shown in Figs. 1 and 2 is a point of some uncertainty. Eccles[3] states that the spread of the Golgi dendritic tree is about three times that of a Purkinje cell (i.e., 600–750μ). However, drawings by Cajal[4] and Jakob[5] and statements and drawings elsewhere in Eccles *et al.*[6] seem to indicate the dendritic spread for Golgi cells to be only slightly larger than that of Purkinje cells (i.e., 250–300μ). However, even with a dendritic spread of only 300μ, the Golgi dendritic fields would still have significant overlap, as can be shown by drawing 300μ-diameter circles around the Golgi cell bodies in Fig. 2.

Purkinje Cells

The Purkinje cell has a large and very dense dendritic tree. The dendritic tree of the Purkinje cell is shaped like a flat fan and measures on the average about 250μ across, about 250μ high, and only about 6μ thick, as shown in Fig. 3. The flat face of this fan is positioned perpendicular to the parallel fibers which course through the branches of the tree. It is estimated that around two-hundred thousand parallel fibers pierce the dendritic tree of each Purkinje cell, and that in passing virtually every parallel fiber makes a single synaptic contact with the dendrites of the Purkinje cell. At the site of a parallel fiber Purkinje dendritic synapse, the parallel fiber enlarges to about 1μ in diameter and is filled with synaptic vesicles. A spine grows out of the Purkinje dendrite and is enclosed by an invagination of the enlarged part of the parallel fiber.

A unique characteristic of the Purkinje cell is that there is virtually no intermingling of its dendritic tree with that of other cells. The Purkinje cell bodies are beet shaped and about 35μ in diameter. They are scattered in a single layer over the cortex at intervals of about 50μ along the direction of the parallel

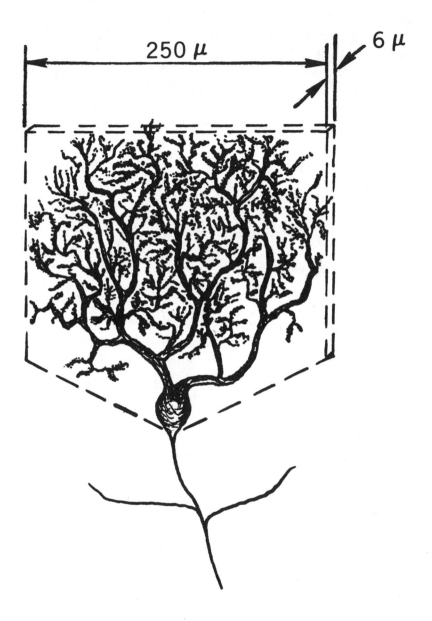

Fig. 3. A Typical Purkinje Cell; Its Dendritic Tree is Restricted to a Volume Approximately 250 X 250 X 6μ. (Reprinted, by permission, from the *Journal of Mathematical Biosciences.)*

fibers, and about 50μ–100μ in the transverse direction. Thus, the fan-shaped dendritic trees overlap in the transverse direction but are offset in the longitudinal direction sufficiently so as not to intermingle. Figure 2 shows a top view looking down on the packed Purkinje dendritic trees. The trees are about 6μ thick and are separated by about 2–4μ. Thus, a parallel fiber encounters a different synapse with virtually every Purkinje dendritic tree it passes; a 3 mm parallel fiber contacts about 300 Purkinje cells.

Purkinje cell axons constitute the only output from the cerebellar cortex. These axons make inhibitory synapses with the cells of the cerebellar nuclei and of the Deiters nucleus. In addition, Purkinje axons send recurrent collaterals to other Purkinje cells, Basket cells, Stellate cells, and Golgi cells.

Basket Cells

The Basket cells also have flat, fan-shaped dendritic trees which extend upwards in the 2–4μ spaces between Purkinje dendritic layers. Basket dendritic trees are much less dense than those of Purkinje cells but cover roughly the same area. Basket dendrites also receive excitatory synaptic contacts from parallel fibers via dendritic spines. Basket cell dendritic spines are much sparser, more irregularly spaced, longer, and thinner than Purkinje spines. They are very often hook shaped. Basket cell bodies, about 20μ in diameter, are located in the lower third of the molecular layer. Basket cells are 15 to 20 percent more numerous than Purkinje cells.

Basket cells send out axons in the transverse direction, perpendicular to the parallel fiber pathways. These axons branch and send descending collaterals which make strong inhibitory synapses around the preaxon portion of the Purkinje cells. They also send ascending collaterals into the Purkinje cell dendritic trees, where they form further inhibitory synapses. Each Basket cell inhibits about fifty Purkinje cells over an elliptical area about 1000μ x 300μ. The Basket cells do not inhibit the Purkinje cell immediately adjacent but begin their inhibitory activity one or two cells away and inhibit Purkinje cells out to about 1 mm away in the transverse direction. Thus, any parallel fiber which excites a Purkinje cell is not likely to also inhibit the same Purkinje cells via a Basket cell.

Stellate Cells

Stellate cells have dendritic aborization very similar to that of Basket cells, although somewhat smaller. On the basis of axon distribution, there are two types of Stellate cells. Stellate "a" cells send axons into Purkinje dendritic trees immediately adjacent, whereas Stellate "b" cells send their axons transversely, making inhibitory contact with Purkinje dendrites in an area similar in size, shape, and relative position to that of Basket cells. Functionally, the main distinction between Basket cells and Stellate "b" cells seems to be that Stellate "b" cells are located higher in the molecular layer and send few, if any, axon collaterals to the Purkinje preaxon, or "Basket," region. However, there are many intermediate forms, and the cell types seem to change progressively from Basket cells in the upper granular layer to Stellate "b" cells in the mid- and upper-molecular layer. Thus, in this paper the Basket cells and Stellate "b" cells will be assumed to perform roughly the same functions, which include receiving excitatory inputs from parallel fibers and transmitting inhibitory signals to Purkinje cells.

Climbing Fibers

A second type of input fiber, the climbing fibers, also enters the cerebellum. These fibers are distinguished by the fact that each Purkinje cell receives a single climbing fiber in a 1:1 fashion. They are called climbing fibers because they contact the Purkinje cell at the base of its dendritic tree and climb up the trunk of the tree, making repeated strong excitatory synaptic contacts. A single spike on a climbing fiber can evoke a complex burst of Purkinje activity. The exact nature of this activity is not entirely clear. Observations by Thach[7] seem to indicate that this complex burst of activity consists of a single Purkinje axon spike followed by several milliseconds of spike-like activity propagating throughout the Purkinje dendritic tree. This dendritic activity is accompanied by intense cell depolarization and a pause in spontaneous Purkinje axon spike activity for 15 to 30 msec. This depolarization and pause was termed the "inactivation response" by Granit and Phillips.[8]

The climbing fibers are usually thought to originate primarily in the inferior olivary nucleus and make a precise point-to-point mapping from the olivary nucleus to the cerebellar cortex. However, there is some indication from cell counts done in the olivary nucleus[9] that either each climbing fiber branches about fifteen times before reaching the cerebellum, or that the majority of climbing fibers come from other sources outside the olivary nucleus.

Information carried by climbing fibers comes from a great variety of areas. The inferior olive receives afferents from proprioceptive end organs as well as all lobes of the cerebral cortex. The inferior olive also receives a strong projection from the red nucleus and the periaqueductal gray via the central tegmental tract.

The response of climbing fibers to peripheral stimulation is quite distinct from that of mossy fibers. A climbing fiber will typically respond to pinching of the skin and deeper tissue anywhere within a receptive field, which may encompass an entire limb.[10] In monkeys performing a motor task, it has been observed that climbing fiber spikes are correlated with quick movements made in response to external stimuli but not with self-paced movements such as rapidly alternating wrist motions.[11] This evidence would seem to indicate that information carried on climbing fibers is the product of a great deal of integration through higher centers.

In addition to the precise one-for-one climbing fiber contact with Purkinje cells, climbing fibers also put out three sets of collaterals.

1. A climbing fiber sends collaterals to synapse on Basket

cells and Stellate cells in the immediate vicinity of the Purkinje cell which it contacts.

2. A climbing fiber sends collaterals to one or more Golgi cells located within an elliptical region about 1000μ x 300μ centered on the Purkinje cell which it contacts.

3. A climbing fiber sends collaterals to nuclear cells in the cerebellar nuclei and in the Deiters nucleus.

Nuclear Cells

The nerve cells of the cerebellar nuclei and Deiters nucleus are of at least two types. One type consists of large multipolar neurons, with relatively simple and irregular dendritic arborization. The axons from cells of the cerebellar nuclei go to the nucleus ventralis lateralis of the thalamus, to the Red nucleus, to the ponto-medullary reticular formation, and to the vestibular nuclei. Cells from the Deiters nucleus join the vestibulospinal stact. Thus, some of these efferents send information toward the sensimotor cortex, others toward the spinal motor neurons. The second type of nuclear neuron is smaller, with short axons, possibly a Golgi type II cell.

The cerebellar nuclei and Deiters nucleus cells receive excitatory inputs from climbing fiber collaterals and mossy fiber collaterals. They receive inhibitory inputs from Purkinje axons.

Pattern Recognition and the Perceptron

The Classical Perceptron

Again, to avoid the necessity of crediting all the many contributors to the theory of pattern recognition and linear threshold devices, the reader is referred to the review books in Refs. 12 and 13 for extensive references to the literature. These books contain mathematical proofs for most of the informal assertions made in the following paragraphs.

The Perceptron developed by Rosenblatt[14] was inspired in large measure by known or presumed properties of nerve cells.

In particular, a Perceptron possesses cells with adjustable strength synaptic inputs of competing excitatory and inhibitory influences which are summed and compared against a threshold. If the threshold is exceeded, the cell fires. If not, the cell does not fire. The original Perceptron was conceived as a model for the eye (see Fig. 4).

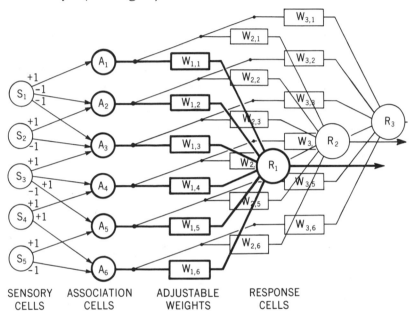

SENSORY   ASSOCIATION   ADJUSTABLE   RESPONSE
CELLS   CELLS   WEIGHTS   CELLS

Fig. 4. Classical Perceptron.

Note: Each sensory cell receives stimulus either $+1$ or 0. This excitation is passed on to the association cells with either a $+1$ or -1 multiplying factor. If the input to an association cell exceeds 0, the cell fires and outputs a 1; if not, it outputs 0. This association cell layer output is passed on to response cells through weights $w_{i,j}$ which can take any value, positive or negative. Each response cell sums its total input and if it exceeds a threshold, the response cell R_j fires outputting a 1; if not, it outputs 0. Sensory input patterns are in class 1 for response cell R_j if they cause the response cell to fire, in class 0, if they do not. By suitable adjustment of the weights $w_{i,j}$, various classifications can be made on a set of input patterns.

Patterns to be recognized or classified are presented to a retina, or layer of sensory cells. Connections from the sensory cells to a layer of associative cells perform certain (perhaps random, perhaps feature-detecting) transformations on the sensory pattern. The associative cells then act on a response cell through synapses, or weights, of various strengths. The firing or failure to fire of the response cell performs a classification or recognition on the set of input patterns presented to the retina.

Perceptron Learning

The Perceptron shows a rudimentary ability to learn. If a Perceptron is given a set of input patterns and is told which patterns belong in class 1 and which in class 0, the Perceptron, by adjusting its weights, will gradually make fewer and fewer wrong classifications and (under certain rather restrictive conditions) eventually will classify or recognize every pattern in the set correctly. The weights usually are adjusted according to an algorithm similar to the following.

1. If a pattern is incorrectly classified in class 0 when it should be in class 1, increase all the weights coming from association cells which are active.
2. If a pattern is incorrectly classified in class 1 when it should be in class 0, decrease all the weights coming from association cells which are active.
3. If a pattern is correctly classified, do not change any weights.

Four features of this algorithm are common to all Perceptron training algorithms and are essential to successful pattern recognition by any Perceptron type device:

1. certain selected weights are to be increased, others decreased;
2. the average total amount of increase equals the total amount of decrease;
3. the desired classification, together with the pattern being classified, governs the selection of the weights to be varied and the direction of variance;
4. the adjustment process terminates when learning is complete.

The Perceptron works quite well on many simple pattern sets, and, if the sensory-association connections are judiciously chosen, even works on some rather complex pattern sets. However, for patterns of the complexity likely to occur in the nervous system, the simple Perceptron appears to be hopelessly inadequate. As the complexity of the input pattern increases, the probability that a given Perceptron can recognize it goes rapidly to zero. Alternatively stated, the complexity of a Perceptron required to produce any arbitrary classification, or dichotomy, on a set of patterns increases exponentially as the number of patterns in the set. Thus, the simple Perceptron, in spite of its tantalizing properties, is not practical as a realistic brain model without significant modification.

The Binary Decoder Perceptron

This lack of power of the conventional Perceptron can be overcome by replacing the sensory-association layer connections with a binary decoder as shown in Fig. 5. It is then pos-

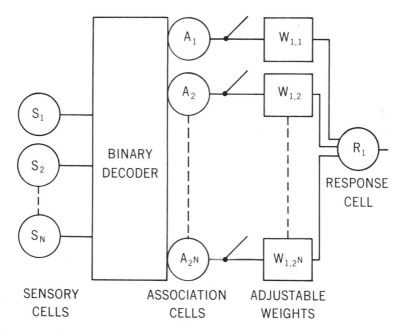

Fig. 5. Binary Decoder Perceptron. (Reprinted, by permission, from the *Journal of Mathematical Biosciences*.)

Note: Each association cell firing uniquely corresponds to one of the possible $2N$ input patterns. This type of perceptron can perform any desired classification of input patterns. However, it has no capacity for generalizing.

sible to trivially construct a Perceptron which will produce any arbitrary pattern classification. A binary decoder can be considered to be a recoding scheme which recodes a binary word of N bits into a binary word of 2^N bits. This recording introduces great redundancy into the resulting code. Each association cell pattern is restricted to a single unique association cell in the "1" condition, all other association cells in the "0" condition.

However, a binary decoder Perceptron is seldom seriously considered as a brain model for several reasons. First, the binary decoder requires such specific wiring connections that it is entirely too artificial to be embedded in the rather random-looking structure of the brain. Second, the number of association cells increases exponentially as the number of inputs. Thus N input fibers require 2^N association cells. Simple arithmetic thus eliminates the binary decoder Perceptron as a brain model.

The Expansion Recorder Perceptron

However, there does exist a middle ground between a simple Perceptron and a binary decoder Perceptron. Imagine a decoder, or rather a recorder, which codes N input fibers into 100 N association cells as shown in Fig. 6. Such a recoding scheme provides such redundancy that severe restrictions can be applied to the 100 N association cells without loss of information capacity. For example, it is possible to require that of the 100 N association cells, only 1 percent (or less) be allowed to be active for any input pattern. That such a recoding is possible without loss of information capacity is easily proven for $2^N << (\frac{100\,N}{N})$. That such a recoding increases the pattern recognition capabilities of a Perceptron is certain, since the dimensions of the decision hyperspace have been expanded 100 times. The amount of this increase under conditions likely to exist in the nervous system is not easy to determine, but it may be enormous. It can be shown that $(\frac{100\,N}{N}) > 100^N$. Thus 2^N possible input patterns can be mapped onto 100^N possible association cell patterns. If this is done randomly, the associa-

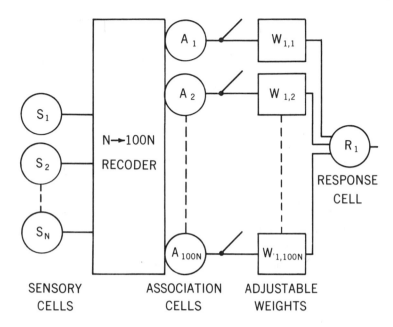

Fig. 6. N 100N Expansion Recoder Perceptron. (Reprinted, by permission, from the *Journal of Mathematical Biosciences.*)

Note: The association cell firing is restricted such that only 1 percent of the association cells are allowed to fire for any input pattern. This perceptron has a large capacity and fast learning rate, yet it maintains the number of association cells within limits reasonable for the nervous system.

tion cell patterns are likely to be highly dissimilar and thus easily recognizable. The ratio $\frac{100^N}{2^N} = 50^N$ rapidly increases as N becomes larger.

The restriction that only one percent of the association cells are allowed to be active for any input pattern means that any association cell participates in only one percent of all classifications. Thus, its weight needs adjusting very seldom and there is a fairly good probability that its first adjustment is at least in the proper direction. This leads to rapid learning.

List Processing in the Cerebellum

The Cerebellum as a Perceptron

A theory by Albus[15] details an analogy between the cerebellum and the expansion recorder Perceptron.

In this theory, the Purkinje cells are hypothesized to be analogous to the Perceptron response cell as shown in Fig. 7.

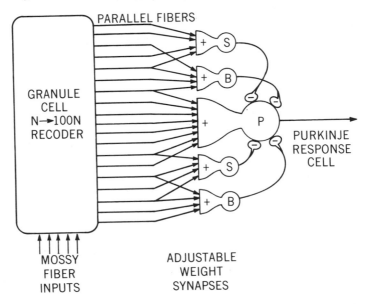

Fig. 7. Cerebellar Perceptron: P, Purkinje cell; B, Basket cells; S, Stellate "b" cells; each Purkinje cell has inputs of the type shown above. (Reprinted, by permission, from the *Journal of Mathematical Biosciences*.)

The mossy fiber input to the cerebellum is suggested to convey the pattern to be classified, or recognized. The mossy rosette, granule cell, Golgi cell network is hypothesized to perform an expansion recoding which greatly expands the Purkinje cell's ability to distinguish mossy fiber input patterns and respond to them in the proper way. Climbing fiber input to the Purkinje cells is hypothesized to act as an unconditional stimulus forcing the Purkinje into the correct response. A scheme of error correcting synaptic weight adjustment is suggested as the learning mechanism. The mossy fiber input patterns are suggested to act as a conditional stimulus. After learning is complete, the mossy fiber input will elicit the associated climbing fiber response. A Purkinje cell climbing fiber response is then considered to be stored on, or in association with a mossy fiber pattern. The stored climbing fiber response is thus analogous to the contents of a memory location, and the associated mossy fiber pattern is analogous to the address.

One of the unique features of this theory is that synaptic weights are hypothesized to be adjusted by weakening incorrect responses rather than by strengthening correct ones. The principal response of a Purkinje cell to climbing fiber activity seems to be to pause (Ref. 8, 11, and 16) rather than to fire a burst of spikes (Ref. 1).

Motor Sequence Generation

It is reasonably certain that patterns of activity on mossy fibers represent to the cerebellum the position, velocity, tension, etc., of the muscles, tendons, and joints. This is feedback information necessary to generate the next command in a sequence of muscle commands in order to produce sequential motor activity at a subconscious level.

Assume, for example, that the red nucleus sends a command C_1 through the inferior olive and thence via climbing fibers through Purkinje cells and nuclear cells to the muscles. At this time the muscles and joints in their resting state are sending pattern M_1 to the cerebellum via mossy fibers. Thus C_1 is imprinted on M_1. Now when C_1 reaches the muscles, they respond by moving to a new position. This generates a new mossy fiber pattern M_2. By this time a second command C_2 is sent from the red nucleus. C_2 will be imprinted on M_2. In a similar manner C_3 is imprinted on M_3, C_4 on M_4, etc. This process may be continued for a lengthy sequence of motor commands C_1 C_2 C_3 . . . and resulting body positions M_1 M_2 M_3. . . . Upon repetition of the sequence of motor commands C_1 C_2 C_3 . . . , the signals from the red nucleus will be reinforced at the nuclear cells by output from Purkinje cells responding to feedback mossy fiber patterns M_1 M_2 M_3. . . . Upon each repetition, more and more of the muscle control can be assumed by the output of the Purkinje cells, and less attention is required by higher motor centers.

Once learning is complete, the sequence of motor commands C_1 C_2 C_3 C_4 can be elicited entirely from the Purkinje cells via the mossy fiber input patterns M_1 M_2 M_3 M_4. . . . Little input is required from higher centers except perhaps to initiate and/or terminate the sequence.

A sequence of muscle commands is nothing more or less than a linear list. The command C_1 can be considered to be the contents of address M_1. Since C_1 causes an event which produces address M_2, the address M_2 corresponds to a link, or pointer. C_1 causes M_2 which addresses C_2 which causes M_3 and so on down the list.

Consider now Fig. 8. The planar array corresponds to an array of Purkinje cells. The IN fibers are climbing fibers. The OUT fibers are Purkinje axons. Inputs to the N 100 Recoder are mossy fibers, outputs are parallel fibers. All the Purkinje

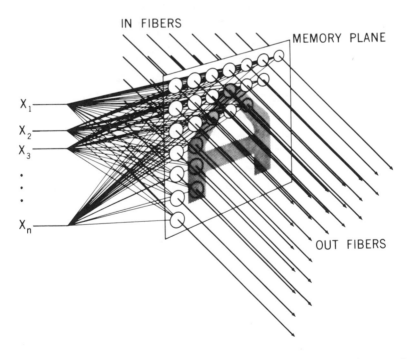

Fig. 8. An idealized array of Purkinje cells. IN fibers correspond to parallel fibers. OUT fibers correspond to Purkinje axons. Cells in the A shaped area are pausing in response to an A shaped pattern of IN fibers firing. (Reprinted, by permission, from the *Journal of Mathematical Biosciences*.)

cells are assumed to be firing at a rather uniform rate because of parallel fiber activity. Choose now a time when a particular mossy fiber pattern M_1 is stimulating a particular small subset of the parallel fibers. If at this instant a climbing fiber pattern C_1 arrives, all the Purkinje cells in the "A" outlined area will pause. The principle response of Purkinje cells to climbing fiber activity seems to be a pause in spontaneous firing (Refs. 7, 8, 11, 16), rather than a burst of spikes as commonly supposed (Ref. 1). On these cells which are pausing, any parallel fiber synapse which is encouraging the Purkinje to fire rather than pause is a candidate for being weakened. Any Purkinje which fires too soon after the pause signal is in error. Any parallel fiber input contributing to this error is weakened. This is the process of data storage. The pattern A can be considered to have been stored in the address M_1. Thereafter, when M_1 appears on the mossy fiber inputs, the same subset of parallel fibers will be active as was active previously, when the A pattern was stored. All of these parallel fiber inputs to the Purkinje cells were weakened when the pattern A was stored. Therefore, all the Purkinje cells within the A area receive less excitation when the M_1 pattern occurs. This reduction in excitation causes these particular Purkinje cells to pause. Thus, the appearance of mossy fiber pattern M_1 causes pattern A to appear on the Purkinje axon output. A is therefore said to be stored in address M_1.

Thalamocortical Relationships

As suggested earlier, the looping structure which exists between the cerebellum and periphery also exists between the cerebellum and motor cortex and in many other parts of the brain. One of the most interesting loop structures is the relationship between cerebral cortex and thalamus.

The thalamus is the principal relay center for information entering the cortex. Anatomical relationships between the reticular formation, the medial lemniscus, the thalamus, and the cortex is given in two Golgi studies by Scheibel and Scheibel.[17,18]

Medial Lemniscal Terminations in Mice

The medial lemniscus sweeps laterally and around so as to enter the neutral basal nucleus (VB) of the thalamus from a lateral and somewhat posterior neutral direction. Each medial lemniscal fiber terminates in a dense, conical-shaped arborization which makes repeated axodendritic contacts with thalamic bush cells. A single-fiber arbor may encompass three to ten Bush cells in the mouse and rat, twenty to fifty in the monkey.

The conical lemniscal fiber terminations are arranged somatopically in concentric layers.

Bush Cells

The bush cells have dendrites which branch in all directions for about 250$^{\mu}$. This implies that any single bush cell contacts the arborization of several lemniscal arborizations, although probably one lemniscal arborization predominates. Axons from bush cells run rostrally and terminate in the cortex as specific afferents. Axons from adjacent bush cells tend to run in bundles on their way to the cortex. These axons put out collaterals as they pass through the thalamic reticular nucleus which forms a thin layer over the rostral end of the thalamus.

Spinothalamic Fibers

Terminations from the spinothalamic fibers are diffuse and form a moderately dense, apparently random neuropile throughout the VB nucleus. Spinothalamic fiber collaterals make bouton contact with both dendrites and cell bodies of bush cells, but the contacts are much less localized and intensive than those of medial lemniscal fibers.

Ascending Reticular Fibers

Long ascending reticular fibers enter the VB nucleus and form a diffuse plexus of synaptic contacts on bush cells. In the VA and VL nucleus, the long reticular fibers, in conjunction with additional input fibers from the bracium conjunctivum and the basal ganglia, form a dense plexus of fiber terminations.

Descending Cortico-Fugal Fibers

a. Large caliber fibers from the cortex terminate in VB in flat, disc-shaped arborizations. These disc-shaped arborizations extend throughout the entire nucleus in the mediolateral and dorsoventral directions but are very restricted in the rostrocaudal direction.

b. A second category of corticothalamic fibers terminate diffusely over extremely large fields.

c. A third category of fibers are fine caliber collaterals from the median forebrain bundle which terminate diffusely without extensive ramification. Some of these fibers may make presynaptic axon-axon contact with the lemniscal bush arborization.

Long-axoned Integrator Cell

A second type of cell in the VB nucleus is the large integrator cell, which has extremely long dendrites extending throughout the VB nucleus. Its axon makes several bifurcations and runs long distances both rostrally and caudally. This cell is rather rare, being only one percent as numerous as the bush cells.

Short-axoned Internuncial Cells

These cells are about the same size as the bush cells but their axons arborize near the cell body. They do not seem to occur in small rodents.

Recurrent Fibers from Thalamic Reticular Nucleus

Cells in the thalamic reticular nucleus are contacted by collaterals from bush cell axons. These cells send their axons back to synapse on neurons and in other nonspecific thalamic nuclei. This arrangement may give rise to the rhythmic firing patterns exhibited by both specific and nonspecific thalamic nuclei.

Thalamic Rhythms

Eccles[19] and Anderson[20] suggest the rhythmic activity of the thalamus is caused by internuncial cells such as the short-axoned ones reported in Ref. 17. However, since such cells do not seem to exist in small rodents (and the rhythms do), the recurrent fibers from the thalamic reticular nucleus seem a more likely source.

Rhythmic activity in the thalamus occurs in both specific and nonspecific nuclei. It is a phenomenon internal to the thalamus, since animals with their cortices removed still exhibit thalamic rhythms. Single cells within the thalamus are seen to fire in a manner correlated with the rhythmic evoked potentials. In fact, the internal voltage fluctuation caused by IPSPs and EPSPSs is seen to be correlated with the EEG records of rhythmic activity.

A Hypothesis

The thalamic bush cells have two principal types of input: specific input from medial lemniscus fibers and general diffuse input from spinothalamic, corticothalamic, and reticulo-thalamic fibers. This is logically similar to the structure in the cerebellar cortex where the Purkinje cell receives diffuse input from parallel fibers and basket cells and receives specific input from climbing fibers. Continuing the cerebellar analogy, one might hypothesize that the bush cells receive an unconditional stimulus (US) from medial lemniscal fibers which cause them to fire with an unconditional response (UR). The conditional stimulus (CS) is the diffuse input from all parts of the brain, cortex, RF, and cord. The bush cells could then be thought to store patterns of medial lemniscal fiber firing in association with the state of the animal at the time when the medial lemniscal pattern occurred.

One might speculate that the input from the median forebrain bundle somehow dictates the patterns to be stored and those to be allowed to pass through without being stored.

Recall of a sensory experience might then be effected by duplicating the same pattern of inputs from the cortex, RF, and cord as existed when storage occurred. The feedback loop through the cortex makes possible storage and recall of sequences of experiences. If somewhat similar storage capabilities exist in the cortex, it is then possible for present specific input to the bush cells to be modified (either enhanced or inhibited) as a result of past experience stored in the cortex.

This type of memory mechanism would appear capable of producing simple functions, such as habituation, in rather simple structures of rats and mice, yet capable, too, of much more complex functions in higher forms, where the basic structure is more elaborated.

The rhythmic activity might correspond roughly to a memory cycle time. In other words, the bush cells send a pattern to the cortex; they then pause to wait for that pattern to access memory in the cortex and to return the contents of cortical memory before they compare the cortical information with lemniscal information and produce another pattern to send to the cortex.

The Cerebral Cortex

The specific connections in the cerebral cortex are not known in anywhere near as much detail as are those in the cerebellar cortex. Colonnier[21] suggests that the intercellular relationships in the cerebral cortex are similar in many ways to those existing in the cerebellar cortex. A major structural difference exists in that the cerebrum is organized in vertical columns whereas the cerebellum is organized horizontally along the folical ridges. However, many features of the large pyramidal cells are analogous to Purkinje cells. Pyramidal cells receive input from parallel running vertical columns of axons via dendritic spines. They receive other inputs via basketlike arborizations on their cell bodies from basket cells whose axons run for considerable distances in the horizontal direction. They also receive repeated contacts of the "climbing fiber" type from fusiform stellate cells. Pyramidal cell axons provide the output from the cerebral cortex. Several other types of cells, small pyramidal and stellate ones appear to correspond in many respects with the inter-neurons of various types in the cerebellum.

Thus, it appears that the cerebral cortex, while undoubtedly structured to do many other complex processing tasks, might also perform a pattern storage-recall function similar in some respects to that performed in the cerebellum. Such a capability would make the looping re-entry pathways between the thalamus and the cerebral cortex an ideal substrate for list-structured storage. The anatomy of the brain indicates no restrictions on the type of list structures which might be possible. The thalamus has the capability to access many areas of the cortex simultaneously in parallel fashion. The resulting list structures could have any type of logical tree of graph form.

Implications

The implications of list structure in the brain are extensive. It implies that data processing in the brain is not compartmentalized, but rather that the significant features of brain function involve repetitive interaction between widely separated brain nuclei. It implies that brain function must be studied as a systems problem, and that single-cell recording with microprobes frequently will produce extremely ambiguous and/or apparently random data. Finally, list structure in the brain implies that the fields of computer science and neuroscience may not be so widely separated after all.

REFERENCES

1. J. C. Eccles; M. Ito; and J. Szentagothai. *The Cerebellum as a Neuronal Machine*. New York: Springer-Verlag, 1967.
2. F. A. Fox *et al.* "The Primate Cerebellar Cortex: A Golgi and Electron Microscope Study." In *Progress in Brain Research,* vol. 25, ed. by C. A. Fox and R. S. Snider. New York: American Elsevier Publishing Co., 1967.
3. J. C. Eccles *et al. The Cerebellum as a Neuronal Machine.* p. 205 and fig. 116.
4. R. S. Cajal. *Histologie du Système Nerveux de l'Homme et des Vertebres,* tome II. Paris: Maloine, 1911.
5. A. Jakob. "Das Kleinhim." In *Handbuch der Mikroskopischen Anatomie des Menschen* IV/I, ed. by W. V. Mollendort. Berlin: Springer, 1928.
6. J. S. Eccles *et al. The Cerebellum as a Neuronal Machine,* p. 60 and fig. 13.
7. W. T. Thach, Jr. "Somatosensory Receptive Fields of Single Units in Cat Cerebellar Cortex." *J. Neurophysiol.* 31 (1967): 785–797.
8. R. Granit and C. G. Phillips. "Excitatory and Inhibitory Processes Acting upon Individual Purkinje Cells of the Cerebellum in Cats." *J. Physiol., London* 133 (1956): 520–547.
9. A. Escobar; E. D. Sampedro; and R. S. Dow. "Quantitative Data on the Inferior Olivary Nucleus in Man, Cat, and Vampire Bat." *J. Comp. Neurol.* 132 (1968): 397–403.
10. W. T. Thach. "Discharge of Purkinje and Cerebellar Nuclear Neurons during Rapidly Alternating Arm Movements in the Monkey." *J. Neurophysiol.* 31 (1968): 758–797.
11. W. T. Thach. "Discharge of Cerebellar Neurons Related to Two Maintained Postures and Two Prompt Movements. II Purkinje Cell Output/and Input," *J. Neurophysiol.* 33 (1970): 537–547.
12. N. J. Nilsson. *Learning Machines: Foundations of Trainable Pattern Classifying Systems.* New York: McGraw-Hill Book Co., 1965.
13. M. Minsky and S. Papert. *Perceptrons: An Introduction to Computational Geometry.* Cambridge: MIT Press, 1969.
14. F. Rosenblatt. *Principles of Neurodynamics: Perceptrons and the Theory of Brain Mechanisms.* Washington, D.C.: Spartan Books, 1961.
15. J. S. Albus. "A Theory of Cerebellar Function." *J. Math. Biosciences,* in press.
16. C. D. Bell and R. J. Grimm. "Discharge of Purkinje Cells Recorded on Single and Double Microelectrodes." *J. Neurophysiol.* 32: 1044–1055.
17. M. E. Scheibel and A. B. Scheibel. "Patterns of Organization in Specific and Nonspecific Thalamic Fields." In *The Thalmus,* ed. by D. P. Purpura and M. D. Yahr, New York: Columbia University Press, 1966.

18. M. E. Scheibel and A. B. Scheibel. "Anatomical Basis of Attention Mechanisms in Vertebrate Brains." In *The Neurosciences: A Study Program*, ed. by G. C. Quarton, T. Melnechnk, and F. O. Schmitt. New York: The Rockefeller University Press, 1967.
19. J. C. Eccles. "Properties and Functional Organization of Cells in the Ventrobasal Complex of the Thalmus." In *The Thalmus*.
20. P. Anderson. "Rythmic 10/sec Activity in the Thalmus." In *The Thalmus*.
21. M. L. Colonnier. "The Structural Design of the Neocortex." In *Brain and Conscious Experience*, ed. by J. C. Eccles. New York: Springer-Verlag, 1966.

ADDITIONAL READINGS

Cover, T. M. "Classification and Generalization Capabilities of Linear Threshold Units." *Rome Air Development Center Technical Report RADC-TDR-64-32* (1964).
Hubel, D. H. and Wiesel, T. N. "Receptive Fields, Binocular Interaction, and Functional Architecture in the Cat's Visual Cortex." *J. Physio.* 160 (1962): 106–154.
Jakob, A. "Das Kleinhim." *Handbuch der Mikroskopischen Anatomie des Menschen* IV/I, ed. by W. V. Mollendort. Berlin: Springer, 1928.
Marr, D. "A Theory of Cerebellar Cortex." *J. Physiol.* 202 (1969): 437–470.
Mettler, F. A. In a discussion following a paper by J. C. Eccles. *Neurophysiological Basis of Normal and Abnormal Motor Activities*, ed. by M. D. Yahr and D. P. Purpura.
Ruiz-Marcos, A. and Valverde, F. "Temporal Evolution of the Distribution of Dendritic Spines in the Visual Cortex of Normal and Dark Raised Mice." *Exp. Brain Research* 8 (1967): 785–797.

How a Bug's Mind Works

WALTER JACOBS

American University
Washington, D.C.

Introduction

This paper will discuss a general model for the design of a
system that interacts continually with a task environment.
The system has no direct internal representation of this environment; either the relevant details are too variable to be
handled concisely, or the tools to form and store an internal
"map" are not present. The first of these possibilities is exem-
plified by a robot chauffeur to drive a car in traffic, the second,
by a living creature with a limited nervous system.

The model to be presented is called a *purposive system.*[1]
A device of this type has a hierarchical organization that provides a *task-oriented* context for its interactions. A number of
its features may help to overcome some of the obvious problems that arise with systems operating in a complex environment. Among these features are the way memory is organized
as a highly associative list structure, the narrow contexts in
which recognition processes operate, the sophisticated learning
processes that are integral to the structure, and the direct
relation between the task-oriented behavior of the system and
the task-oriented language of its internal program.

To explain how a purposive system produces its behavior
requires a long description, even though its structure is relatively simple by comparison with the complexity of that be-

havior. This is because the production is decentralized; decisions are made at a high level, interpreted through some intervening levels, and acted on at the lowest level. Thus, the hierarchy of organization must be explained, as well as the system of communication that coordinates the activity at the several levels.

In presenting this structure, it will be useful to look at an example that has been simulated on a computer. The simulation that will be described represents a robot, PERCY, whose behavior is like that of a nest-building creature. PERCY operates in an environment that is rather uncomplicated. At the same time, it possesses all of the structure of the purposive system, dealing with a varied set of tasks in a rich environment.

PERCY's task was adapted from that of L. Friedman's ADROIT.[23] There are also superficial resemblances in structure. But the crucial feature of a decision-making system is the way information is processed as it flows through the system, and here PERCY is quite different from ADROIT as well as from other approaches to robot design. The knowledge that PERCY uses to guide its behavior has a special form which allows it to make decisions with a brief evaluation of a few alternatives. The structure requires very little modification to provide for learning.

PERCY's Environment and Task

PERCY's environment contains its *nest*, several clumps of nest-building *material*, and its *food*; food, like PERCY, moves around, and must be pursued and captured. The environment contains some *walls*, which are *obstacles* to PERCY's movements, and the nest itself is an obstacle that PERCY must get around when heading for something beyond. The remaining elements in the environment are *landmarks*, which also play a basic role in PERCY's activities. They can be seen at any distance when they lie within PERCY's angle of vision and there is no intervening wall; PERCY must use landmarks in locating food, material, or its nest.

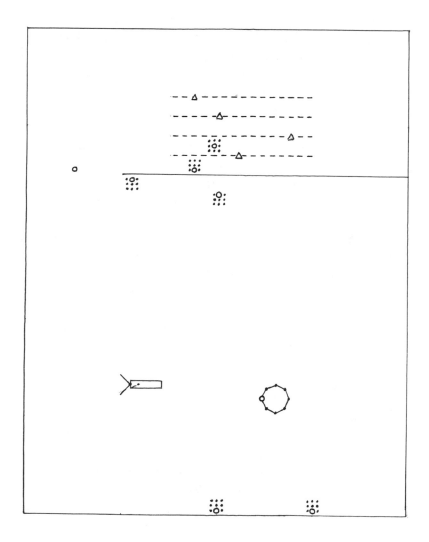

Fig. 1.   Percy's Environment.

Figure 1 shows a diagram of the environment, including
the elements that have been mentioned. PERCY's world is
enclosed by walls, and an additional wall divides it into a
lower area and an upper area. The lower area contains the
nest—the octagonal shape whose vertices represent *nest sites*.
It also contains several clumps of material. In the upper area

are found food, moving along the dotted lines shown in that area, and two additional locations of material. The small circles are the landmarks—one at the nest site, one in each material cluster, and one at the *doorway* between the upper and lower area. The small rectangle represents PERCY, and an *eye, center,* and *arm* can be seen. Also, PERCY's *angle of vision* is indicated by the dashed lines issuing from its eye.

The task is to build a nest, which means locating material, bringing it back to the nest, and placing it at an unfilled nest site. Eight repetitions are needed to complete the nest. But PERCY must get enough food while making headway with the building of its nest. These two needs are in conflict, because time spent in getting food interferes with progress on the nest. PERCY gets hungry slowly enough so that it does not have to find food on every trip, but unless it makes good decisions about when and where to look for material and food, it will not be successful in its task.

Success is measured by *satisfaction,* an internal measure that decreases when PERCY is hungry or is behind schedule with its nest. Its decisions are made so as to try to sustain or increase satisfaction. But it has no internal representation of its environment on which to test out these decisions. It must rely on measures showing how the possible decisions have worked out in the past. Not only is specific knowledge about the environment lacking, but PERCY has no way of recalling information about sequences of decisions that it made in prior instances of the task. A major objective of the simulation is to test whether PERCY can learn to string together good sequences of decisions while operating under these constraints.

A Sample of PERCY's Behavior

When PERCY is born into the environment described, it begins its activity and continues without any command or direction until its nest has been completed. As yet, nest-building is the only task provided for in the simulation; under the present arrangement, as soon as the task is done, the nest is returned to its beginning state and PERCY begins to build it again. This setup will give an adequate opportunity to test out some of the learning features available in the purposive system.

A part of PERCY's behavior during a trial of its task is shown schematically in Fig. 2, which gives a close-up of the

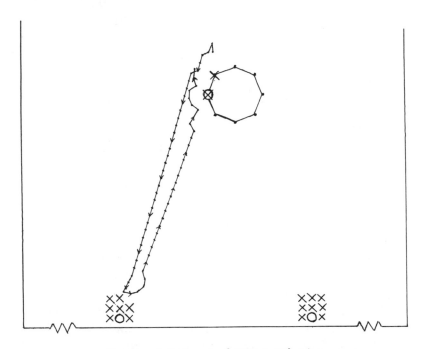

Fig. 2.   A Segment of Percy's Behavior.

nest and vicinity. Just before the time at which this activity starts, PERCY had placed material at the nest site near which it stands in the diagram. This material had been picked up not far from the doorway, after which PERCY had moved into the upper area, captured and eaten some food, and returned to the nest to place the material it had been carrying.

The behavior that follows the trip just recounted is indicated by the path marked out by the small arrows. Each arrow indicates the movement of PERCY's eye during a single *cycle* of behavior that takes one unit of time. Thus, the total activity represented in the figure covers more than eighty cycles. To an observer, this sequence clearly divides into phases, more or less like those used in the following account.

a. PERCY backs away once from the site it faces.

b. It begins to sidle around the nest, keeping its body pointed directly toward the landmark for which it is about to head. As soon as it has passed far enough around the nest so that no nest site lies within its angle of vision, it takes off directly for that landmark. It moves at a uniform rate (four units of distance per cycle) until it comes within sixteen units of an element of material.

c. It now turns abruptly and advances to a point at arm's length (four units) from the material, meanwhile extending its arm. The material is picked up, held at the tip of the arm, and moved to PERCY's back by a return of the arm to rest position.

d. The creature now turns about its center a number of times, until the nest landmark comes within its angle of vision.

e. It heads for the landmark until it arrives near (within sixteen units of) one of the nest sites. PERCY once again uses a crablike motion, keeping away from the nest as it moves and continually facing the landmark. This continues until it comes near the nest landmark.

f. It now begins an odd little "dance" that is repeated at each nest site that is already filled with material. (This is ended in the diagram at the second nest site, to keep the picture from becoming confused, but the account continues to describe the behavior beyond the point where it is plotted.) This ritual consists of one step toward the site, followed by a turning away and a circling of the same site. The movement brings it near the next site, and if that is filled, the same steps occur again. Eventually, this process brings PERCY near to the first site. Here it begins to advance to that site, meanwhile extending its arm with the material that it has been carrying since the end of phase c. As it arrives at arm's length from the site, it places the material there and remains where it is while returning its arm to the rest position. It now turns once to the left, so that the next site comes within its angle of vision.

Several aspects of this description are worthy of comment before an explanation is given of the way it is produced. PERCY interacts with its environment in accordance with an internal "context" that is based directly on its task. As might be guessed, this context underlies the way chosen above to divide the sequence of actions into phases. The interaction is obviously purposeful and nontentative, and the observer has no difficulty in understanding how it relates to the task PERCY is carrying out. There are little oddities, such as the dance that precedes placing material at the nest. This type of thing, which is reminiscent of phenomena commonly observed in animal behavior, appears in PERCY's case solely because it can be eliminated only by needlessly complicating PERCY's program.

Phases similar to those described can be observed again and again as PERCY continues its task. Of course, they are never exactly the same twice, because they are always conditioned by the environment as it happens to be encountered. The way the phases unite to make up round trips to the nest is also fairly evident. But the observer must watch PERCY's behavior for a number of trips to begin to see the principle on which the changing scenario is founded. For example, the trip following the one described begins with PERCY turning away from the nest until the door landmark comes into view. PERCY then heads for that landmark, turns until it spots food, and chases the food. Material is picked up on the way back to the nest. Evidently PERCY was hungry as that trip started, but was not when it decided how to go about the trip pictured in Fig. 2.

How the Behavior Is Controlled

A purposive system uses four levels of control in organizing its task behavior. These levels, each of which is dealt with by a separate *component* of the system, represent successively higher degrees of abstraction from the specific conditions being met in the environment. Figure 3 shows the names assigned to the components, their variables of state, and the communications that pass between them.

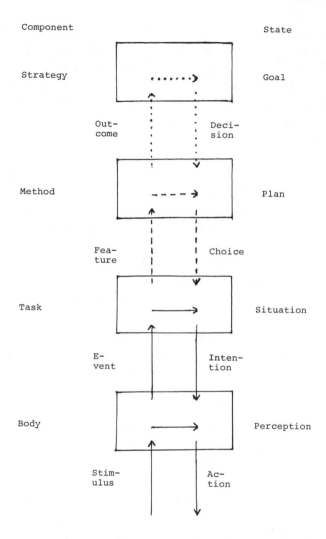

Fig. 3. Components and Communications of a Purposive System.

It will help in understanding these terms to show how they provide the context, the control, and the communications for the sample of PERCY's behavior just described. Figure 4 describes (in meaning, not in syntactical form) the communications and the states that underlie the very first cycle of the segment of behavior shown in Fig. 2. The table is best understood by thinking of a series of reports progressing from

	Preceding State and Upward Communications	New State and Downward Communications
Goal	Add M to nest, using LN and LD as landmarks	Get just M this trip, using LL
↑ Outcome Decision ↓	↑ Submethod done LD and LN used, M placed, task continues	↓ *Get M*, use LL
Plan:	*Add-to-Nest* done Continue	Begin getting M. Search for M or LL
↑ Feature Choice ↓	↑ Subtask done Continue	↓ *Seek* M or LL
Situation	*Place M* done Continue	Begin seeking M or LL by moving about
↑ Event Intention ↓	↑ New nest site empty	↓ *Move*, no target, Report if M or LL sighted
Perception	No target, Obstacle N, New N empty, Arm condition—none	No target, Obstacle N, Alternative LL, Arm condition—none
↑ Stimulus Action ↓	N at right filled, at left empty. Two LL's visible.	Back away from N at left

Abbreviations: M—material, N—nest site,
                 LL —lower material landmark,
                 LN —nest landmark,
                 LD—door landmark

Fig. 4. Communications and States in a Cycle of Behavior.

the lowest levels of an organization to the top administration and a resulting set of directives passing back down. The report at each level is about information relevant to that level and in an appropriate format. It is easy to verify that the higher one goes, the more detached and long-range is the context— even though every level is concerned with the current status of the task.

Each cycle that occurs during the lifetime of the system is marked by a flow of information upward and a flow of responses downward. But in most cycles, the flow never goes above the second level. Only when a *subtask* is ended (for example, *Place M* in the table) does the flow go to the third level, to induce the *choice* that indicates the new subtask (*Seek* M or LL in that case). And only when a *submethod* is complete (*Add-to-N* in the table) does the flow reach the top and elicit a *decision* about the new submethod *(Get M)*.

PERCY uses only three types of submethods: *Get M, Hunt F* (food), and *Add-to-N*. Also, there are only five kinds of subtasks: *Seek V* (V standing for a list of targets), *Go to L* (L is a designated type of landmark), *Take M, Place M*, and *Chase F*. Each of the six phases of the behavior described in the preceding section corresponds to a single subtask.

Figure 5 describes the communications and state changes for about half of the cycles plotted in Fig. 3, beginning with the one just mentioned. It uses a more concise syntax, which should nevertheless be easy to follow. (Use the clues obtained by comparing the first two lines with Fig. 4, representing the same cycle. Leftward in Fig. 5 corresponds to upward in Fig. 4.)

Each pair of rows in Fig. 5 denotes one cycle, and the flow for the cycle is indicated by the arrows. The entries for many cycles have been omitted, as indicated by the dashed lines in columns 6 and 7. This is because they exactly duplicate the entries found in the last two columns of the pair of rows immediately preceding the dashed line. In other words, the first change in perception is shown.

A line extending across the last three columns marks a change in the situation. One extending across the last five columns denotes completion of a subtask, accompanied by a change of plan. And finally, a line crossing all seven columns signals the finish of a submethod, with a new goal and corresponding decision needed.

The system of communications reflected in the table, together with the task *knowledge* to be described shortly, makes it possible for a single decision to cover a sequence of forty or more actions, each of which is responsive to the perception that accompanies it. The explanation of the process that coordinates the activity from top to bottom will begin by discussing actions and perceptions, continue by showing what supports the flow of information between neighboring levels of the system, and wind up by examining the way decisions are made. In addition to this, it will be necessary to examine the various kinds of learning that must be present in a system that is born without specific information about the environment in which it must operate.

Actions and Perceptions

In a purposive system, an action is an operation by the body component, trying to affect the environment in a desired way. Thus, PERCY in the nest-building task makes use of six actions:

1. *advancing* toward a visible target, while at the same time avoiding an obstacle if one is *near* (at a distance of less than sixteen units);

2. *circling* past the nest by maintaining a fixed angle with the nearest nest site (and therefore a fixed distance from it);

3. *moving* when no target is visible; PERCY can look in every direction by repeating this action a number of times;

4. *extending* its arm while moving to within arm's length of a target, either to pick up food or material or to place material at a nest site;

5. *eating* food after it is seized;

6. *retracting* the arm to its rest position.

Both the perception and the intention for a particular cycle must be used by the body in carrying out the action for that cycle. The intention specifies the type of action and the kind of target to which it is directed; the perception identifies the particular target perceived, as well as any obstacle to be avoided while the action is carried out. If the intention signals an advance toward food, the food element just perceived is the one meant. Thus, the task and higher components need only be concerned with abstractions of the outside world; the body component focuses these abstractions on the perceived elements to which they allude.

Actions are carried out by the system's motor apparatus. The other aspect of its interface with the environment is the set of sensors. But the body component does more than simply

Goal	Decision → ← Outcome	Plan			Choice → ← Feature
		Type	List	Hist.	
Add to N	←Done(LD,LN,CON)	Aϕ	(LD,LN,CON)		←Done (CON)
Get M only	Get M(LL) →	M1(M,LL)		ϕ	Seek (M,LL) → ←Done(LL)
		M2(LL,M)		LL	Go to(LL,M) → ←Done (M)
		M3	ϕ	LL,M	Take (M)→
	←Done(LL,M)	Mϕ	(LL,M)		←Done(ϕ)
Add to N (use LN)	Add to N(LN) →	A1	(LN)	ϕ	Seek(LN) → ←Done(LN)
		A2	(LN)	LN	Go to LN(ϕ) ←Done(LN)
		A3	(N)	LN	Place M(ϕ)

Situation			Intention →	Perception			
Type	Targ.	List	← Event	Targ.	Obst.	Alt.	Arm
Pφ	φ	(CON)	← Alt = e	φ	N	e	φ
S1	φ	(M,LL)	Move(φ,(M,LL)) →	φ	N	LL	φ
Sφ	LL		← Alt = LL				
G1	LL	(M)	Advc.(LL,(M)) →	LL	N	φ	φ
			← Targ. = LL, Alt. = φ				
			Advc.(LL,(M)) →	LL	N	φ	φ
			← Targ. = LL, Alt. = φ				
			Advc.(LL,(M)) →	LL	φ	φ	φ
			← Targ. = LL, Alt. = φ				
			Advc.(LL,(M)) →	LL	φ	M	φ
Gφ	M		← Targ. = LL, Alt. = M				
T1	M	(Arm)	Ext.(M,Arm) →	M	φ	φ	φ
			← Targ. = M, H = φ				
			Ext.(M,Arm) →	M	φ	φ	M
			← Targ. = M, H = M				
T2	φ	(Arm)	Retr.(φ,Arm) →	φ	φ	φ	x
			← Arm Pos. = x				
			Retr.(φ,Arm) →	φ	φ	φ	φ
Tφ	φ		← Arm Pos. = φ				
S1	φ	(LN)	Move(φ,(LN)) →	φ	φ	φ	φ
			← Alt. = φ				
			Move(φ,(LN)) →	φ	φ	LN	φ
Sφ	LN		← Alt. = LN				
G1	LN	φ	Advc.(LN,φ) →	LN	φ	φ	φ
			← Targ. = LN				
			Advc.(LN,φ)	LN	N	φ	φ
			← Targ. = LN				
			Advc.(LN,φ)	n	N	φ	φ
Gφ	LN	φ	← Targ. = near				
P1	N	φ	Advc.(N,φ)	f	N	φ	φ

Fig. 5. Communications and States Underlying Behavior of Fig. 2.

sense incoming stimuli. It also discards all sensations that are not needed in the current situation. The perception is the information that remains.

For example, when PERCY is carrying material, it never perceives any of the landmarks it uses in locating material. Conversely, when it has just placed material at the nest, it ignores the nest landmark and is interested in the landmarks that help it to locate food or material. The targets of current interest are contained in the intention issued in the cycle just completed.

Figure 5 has already indicated the format of an intention:

> Action type: Advance
> Target type: Door landmark (LD)
> Alternatives: Material (M), Food (F).

This communication tells the body component to advance toward the door landmark just perceived and then to report on the visibility of the same landmark. Further, if either food or material is visible, that fact is to be reported. And if any obstacle is near, avoiding it is part of the action "Advance."

Perception is actually a three-phase process. First, sensations are received from the environment; an object can be seen only when it lies in PERCY's angle of vision, is not hidden by a wall in between, and, except in the case of food and landmarks, is near. Second, any object other than an obstacle is ignored unless it is of a type mentioned in the intention. And finally, if more than one target of a given type is seen, or more than one alternative target, or more than one obstacle, a priority rule is applied to pick out a single representative of its category. In addition, when the intention concerns PERCY's arm, the perception must supply information about the status of the arm and what, if anything, is held by it.

As already noted, the perception is then reported to the task component and retained to the end of the cycle for use in carrying out the intended action. Thus, it acts as the very-short-term memory of the system.

The Production of Behavior

The perception that is formed must be related to the current task for the ensuing action to be responsive. The operations involved in this coordination are depicted in the flow-diagram of Fig. 6. The large rectangles—PERCEIVE, ACT,

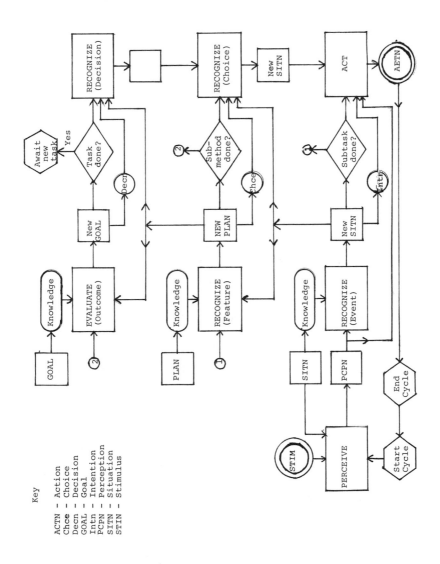

Fig. 6.   Flowchart of Processing in a Purposive System.

RECOGNIZE, EVALUATE—are the operations of the system; the small squares—perception, situation, plan, goal—are the state variables; and the circles are the communications that form the inputs and outputs of the operations. The arrows mark out the possible sequences of operations in producing one cycle of behavior.

Note that nothing in the chart is specific to PERCY or its task; only the general organization of the purposive system is indicated. What specializes the system to PERCY are the content of knowledge and the details of the PERCEIVE, ACT, and EVALUATE blocks.

The following is the sequence of operations and the flow of information during a cycle of behavior.

a. The cycle begins with the body component performing the PERCEIVE operation to derive the *perception* for the cycle. This operation senses the incoming *stimulus*, and uses the *intention* produced in the preceding cycle to indicate what elements in the resulting sensation are of interest at the current stage of the task.

b. The perception is communicated to the task component, where the RECOGNIZE operation is executed. RECOGNIZE uses the entry in *knowledge* that corresponds to the type of *situation* arrived at in the preceding cycle, and it determines the *event* that corresponds to the perception. The event "identifies" the new situation, and its knowledge entry replaces that of the preceding situation.

c. If the new situation indicates that the subtask is done, that situation is communicated to the method component, and the process continues as in step e. Otherwise it continues with step d.

d. The intention corresponding to the new situation is sent back to the body component, and the ACT operation is initiated. This operation is guided by the perception, and it produces the *action* that completes the cycle.

e. When the subtask is over, the submethod component parrots the operation of the task component described in step b. RECOGNIZE is applied, using the knowledge entry for the *plan* in effect, to determine the *feature* that corresponds to the situation that is being reported. This identifies the new plan, and its knowledge entry replaces the one just used.

f. If the new plan indicates that the *submethod* is done, that plan is communicated to the strategy component, and the process continues as in step h. Otherwise, step g is applied.

g. The new plan is sent back to the task component, and the choice contained in it is recognized. That choice brings about a new situation to replace the one arrived at in step b. The corresponding entry in knowledge is called on, and the process continues as in step d.

h. The *history* contained in the new plan determines the *outcome* of the *goal* that has been in effect since the last decision. The new decisions open under this outcome are *evaluated,* and the one that yields the highest *expected satisfaction* is selected; the *satisfaction constant* associated with the outcome is then revised. The decision, which defines the new goal, is communicated to the method component. Here it is recognized, a new plan is determined, its knowledge entry becomes operative, and the process continues as in step g.

i. If the outcome indicates that the task has been completed, the new goal, plan, and situation arrive at waiting states, until an incoming stimulus indicates the new task to be undertaken.

This summary underlines the central role of the operation RECOGNIZE. It is often hard to design recognition processes so that they give reliable results. But in the purposive system, recognition takes place in a narrow context and with relatively few categories among which to assign the input. The examples of Figs. 7 and 8 show PERCY's knowledge for the subtask *Place M* and the submethod *Add-to-N*, respectively; the small numbers of events or features possible are typical of all PERCY's knowledge. (The complete knowledge, covering all five subtasks and three submethods, is given in the Appendix.)

As Fig. 7 shows, the knowledge for a subtask consists of entries, one for each type of situation that can occur. Each entry includes the intention, together with a list of rows. The information in a row consists of a definition of the corresponding event as a class of perceptions, the probability assigned to

Situation		Perception Categories		New Situations		
Type	Intention	Target	Alternate	Prob. Type	Target	Alternate
P1	Advance, Nest, ϕ (At nest, checking first site)	N empty N filled N not seen	ϕ ϕ ϕ	P3 P2 Pϕ	Nest ϕ (Illegal)	Hand Nest
P2	Circle, ϕ, Nest (Circling nest, looking for empty site)	ϕ ϕ ϕ	New N not seen New N filled New N empty	P2 P2 P3	ϕ ϕ Nest	Nest Nest Hand
P3	Extend, Nest, Hand (Advancing to N while extending arm)	N filled N empty (Other)	Holding ϕ Holding M	P4 P3 Pϕ	ϕ Nest (Illegal)	Arm Hand
P4	Retract, ϕ, Arm (Returning arm)	ϕ ϕ	Arm back Arm not back	P5 P4	ϕ ϕ	Nest Arm
P5	Circle, ϕ, N (Circling to next N and checking)	ϕ ϕ ϕ	New N not seen New N empty New N filled	P5 Pϕ Pϕ	ϕ (Continue) (Finished)	Nest
Pϕ	Done, Feature, ϕ (Subtask ended)	Seek Other	V	S1 (next task)	ϕ	V

Fig. 7. Knowledge for *PLACE M*.

Plan		Situation Categories		New Plans	
Type	Choice	Last Target	Prob. Type	Targets	History
A1	Seek V; H	Food sighted Material sighted Landmark sighted	Aϕ Aϕ A2	Food Material L, V'	H, F H, M H, L
A2	Go to L, V; H	LD sighted Food sighted Material sighted LN sighted	A1 Aϕ Aϕ A3	LN Food Material LN	H, LD H, F H, M H, LN
A3	Place M, ϕ; H	Continue Done	Aϕ Aϕ	CON DONE	H, N H, N
Aϕ	Done, H	Get material, V Get material, ϕ Hunt food, V Hunt food, V	M1 M3 F1 F3	V ϕ V V	ϕ ϕ ϕ ϕ

Fig. 8. Knowledge for *Add-to-N* Submethod.

that event, and the new situation that will replace the present one when that event is recognized as occurring.

Furthermore, there is one entry for each type of situation, even where the intention can be variable. (This property of knowledge is not exhibited in Place M, since all intentions are fixed. Figure 8 illustrates the use of variables.) In this way, generalization of an important kind is introduced into the system, and the consequence is that a single subtask (such as Seek V, or Go to L) can be used in different submethods or even in different tasks.

Since each entry in knowledge identifies (i.e., points to) every entry that can replace it during the production of behavior, knowledge has the organization of a list structure. This organization means that it is usually unnecessary to search memory. Consequently, neither the time nor the difficulty of recall should be appreciably greater with large quantities of knowledge than with small quantities.

The column marked "probabilities" in the knowledge table calls for comment. In the present simulation, perceptions are coded in discrete form, and recognition is certain. In a real application, the event recognized is the one that is most probable, given the perception and the prior probabilities contained in the knowledge entry. Moreover, each time an event is recognized, its prior probability is thereby increased. This adjustment of probabilities constitutes the simplest kind of learning used by a purposive system. The learning aspects of such systems will be examined later.

Figure 8 brings up two additional points. First, there are variable elements, as already noted, and these appear in the choice for the new plan as well as in the choice for the current plan. The Recognize routine that identifies the new plan during a cycle must also fix the identity of the variable list of targets if one is present In many cases, the variable simply takes the same value that it has in the current plan. Otherwise there are simple rules for modifying that value; for example, a target that is sighted is dropped from the list of alternative targets. Similar remarks apply to a subtask for which the knowledge has variable targets.

The second point is the presence of a *history* as part of a plan. The history is the system's short-term memory. It simply accumulates a summary of the targets that have been sighted since the last decision. When the submethod is done, the history is reported to the strategy component. Here the information it contains is used in the decision-making and learning process that takes place in that component, in a manner that will be described below.

The Making of Decisions

So far, we have explained how a decision governs a sequence of actions that extends until the *outcome* of that decision is determined. It remains to describe how decisions are made. There are two aspects to this: the notion of the task *strategy* and the process of evaluation.

A strategy is represented by its knowledge, which somewhat resembles in format the knowledge for a subtask or a submethod. The similarity is apparent in Fig. 9, where the strategy for PERCY's task is given. However, there is an important difference: an outcome does not lead to a unique new goal when it is recognized. Rather, as the figure indicates, an outcome brings up a list of goals. Then PERCY's strategy component *evaluates* these to find out which ought to bring the greatest satisfaction and selects that as the new goal.

For example, when PERCY has completed the Type 1 goal, *Add-to-N*, by placing M at a nest site, and the task is still not done, it must select among three types of goals, one of which offers two alternatives for target landmark. Thus, there are four possibilities to choose from. (The difference between goals of Type 2 and Type 3 is that those of the former are used when PERCY is not carrying material, of the latter type when material is already carried. In a goal of Type 4, it is necessary to pass through the doorway into the upper area, while in one of Type 5, PERCY does not change areas.)

The satisfaction S on which PERCY bases its decisions is a function of the outcome i just reached and of two other vari-

	Goal	Outcome	New Goals	
Type	Decision	Type	Prob. Type	Decision
1	Add to N (LN) or (LN, LD)	M placed at N, task continues	2	Hunt F (M, LD)
			4	Get M (F, LD, LU)
			5	Get M (LL) or (LM)
		M placed, task done	φ	Identify new task
2	Hunt F (φ) or (M, LD)	F eaten, φ carried	5	Get M (LL) or (LM) or (LU)
		M sighted at LU	5	Get M (φ)
3	Hunt F (φ) or (LD) or (LN, LD)	F eaten, M carried	1	Add to N (LN, LD)
		LN sighted	1	Add to N (LN)
			3	Hunt F (φ)
4	Get M (F, D, LU)	M taken at LU	1	Add to N (LN, LD)
			3	Hunt F (φ)
		F sighted	2	Hunt F (φ)
			5	Get M (LU)
5	Get M (φ) or (LL) or (LM) or (LU)	M taken at LL	1	Add to N (LN)
			3	Hunt F (LD) or (LN, LD)
		M taken at LM	1	Add to N (LN)
			3	Hunt F (LD) or (LN, LD)
		M taken at LU	1	Add to N (LN, LD)
			3	Hunt F (φ)
φ	Identify task			

Fig. 9. Knowledge for Nest-building Strategy.

ables. The first of these, denoted by h, measures how hungry PERCY is. Apart from a reservation to be mentioned shortly, h is simply the number of cycles that have elapsed since the last time PERCY ate. The second variable, v, is the number of cycles since the previous addition to the nest.

Moreover, the satisfaction S_i at the point where outcome i is reached is an average of two quantities:

$$S_i(h,v) = \alpha U_i(h,v) + (1-\alpha)V_i(h,v). \qquad (1)$$

The first quantity, U_i, is a measure of immediately past satisfaction, directly related to the values h and v. The second quantity, V_i, can be thought of as expected satisfaction associated with the outcome to follow the current one. Thus, U_i is low when PERCY has just eaten, because it was hungry till then, but V_i is high because it expects not to be hungry when the next outcome is reached. Finally, α is a "PERCYnality" factor that indicates the relative importance placed on the immediate past and future.

In describing the evaluation process, it is useful to rearrange the information in Fig. 9 into the form of Fig. 10. This lists the various outcomes i of the nest-building task and the decisions d that are open at the point where the outcome occurs. For each such decision and corresponding goal, the possible outcome j are shown. Then

$$V_i(h,v) = \max_d \sum_j p_d(ij)U_j(h' + t_{ij}, v' + t_{ij}). \qquad (2)$$

Here

$$h' = (h - 450)^+ \qquad \text{if} \quad i = 2,3$$
$$ = h \qquad\qquad\quad \text{otherwise;}$$
$$v' = 0 \qquad\qquad\quad \text{if} \quad i = 1$$
$$ = v \qquad\qquad\quad \text{otherwise.}$$

(In words, v is reduced to 0 when *Add-to-N* is done, and h is reduced to the larger of 0, h − 450 when F is eaten, i.e., PERCY does not remove its hunger completely if it waits too long for food.) Also

$p_d(ij)$ is the probability, based on past experience, that outcome i will be followed by outcome j if decision d is made

t_{ij} is the average time for the goal corresponding to d to end with outcome j.

	Outcome (Goal Type)	New Goal, Decision	Possible Outcomes
1.	M placed at N (1)	2, Hunt F (M, LD)	2, 7
	continue task	4, Get M (F, LD, LU)	6, 8
		5, Get M (LL)	4
		5, Get M (LM)	5
2.	F eaten, ϕ carried (2)	5, Get M (LL)	5
		5, Get M (LM)	5
		5, Get M (LU)	6
3.	F eaten, M carried (3)	1, Add to N (LN, LD)	1
4.	M taken at LL (5)	1, Add to N (LN)	1
		3, Hunt F (LD)	3
		3, Hunt F (LN, LD)	3, 9
5.	M taken at LM (5)	1, Add to N (LN)	1
		3, Hunt F (LD)	3
		3, Hunt F (LN, LD)	3, 9
6.	M taken at LU (4 or 5)	1, Add to N (LN, LD)	1
		3, Hunt F	3
7.	M sighted (1)	5, Get M	6
8.	F sighted (4)	2, Hunt F	2
		5, Get M (LU)	6
9.	LN sighted (3)	1, Add to N (LN)	1
		3, Hunt F	3

Fig. 10. Evaluation Table for Nest-building Strategy.

The form of $U_i(h,v)$ is as follows.
$$U_i(h,v) = S_i - (h - 300)^+ - (h - 450)^+ - (v - 100)^+ \quad (3)$$
S_i is a *satisfaction constant* for the outcome i, and the other terms express U as a piecewise linear function of h and v. Equations (1), (2), and (3) implicitly define an evaluation function that is used in the following way.

1. PERCY maintains a 9 x 9 matrix showing, for each outcome pair (i,j), the number of times n(i,j) that i has been followed by j in its past efforts on the task, and the

total time $T(i,j)$ that has been consumed in those cases. Then

$$t_{ij} = T(i,j)/n(i,j).$$

Also, there is a vector $(S_1, \ldots, S_9)$ of satisfaction constants.

2. When outcome i occurs and the parameters have the values h and v, $V_i(h,v)$, as given by (2) and (3), is evaluated. This calculation yields a decision and at the same time provides an estimate of $S_i(h,v)$ using (1).

3. If the new value of $S_i(h,v)$ is substituted for $U_i(h,v)$ in (3), a new value of S_i is obtained for use in later decisions. To make this adjustment is equivalent to the assumption that if appropriate values of the $S_1, \ldots, S_9$ are used, $S_i(h,v)$, $U_i(h,v)$, and $V_i(h,v)$ will all be nearly equal; in other words, the satisfaction constants S_i approximately measure how immediate satisfaction should be adjusted to allow for the future course of the task.

4. Finally, the number of cycles it took to arrive at outcome i is used to reestimate the corresponding average time t_{ij}.

There is reason to expect that this procedure will, with repeated executions of the task, lead to values of the constants S_i that give rise to good decisions. Tests of the procedure are to be undertaken shortly.

Learning

The iterative adjustment of the satisfaction constants is PERCY's method of using past experience to arrive at good decisions. More specifically, these constants substitute for search of the decision tree implicit in PERCY's task. In effect, PERCY *learns* how to respond to the more urgent of its two drives and still be favorably situated with respect to the other one.

In addition to this form of learning, there are three other and quite distinct aspects of the purposive system that also correspond to accepted meanings of the word: namely, *adapta-*

tion, conditioning, and *imprinting.* A fifth and very important denotation of "learning"—namely, the acquisition of new tasks —is not possible in the purposive system, since reprogramming to change the knowledge produces a distinct instance of the system. The system is said to acquire a new task only if there is a *learning task* that causes changes in the knowledge of other tasks by operating on perceptions of the environment. But this will call for an extension of the system to produce a "teachable" machine. The flow diagram of Fig. 5 contains no operation that can change task knowledge, except for the probability values and the satisfaction constants.

The learning that is produced by adjustment of probabilities has already been mentioned on page 109; it is referred to as adaptation. By the adjustment, the system learns to expect regularities in the environment and to use them in recognition. It can also adjust its behavior to take account of slow changes in the outer world. But there is a penalty paid for this kind of learning: as the system gets older and "set in its ways," it may reach the stage of perceiving events that do not correctly reflect the stimuli, because its prior probabilities overbalance the information contained in the perception (analogous to the way the human eye is sometimes "fooled").

Another, somewhat related kind of learning takes place in the probabilities associated with the "downward communications" of the system: the choices and decisions. The prior probability that a particular new subtask will follow a given terminal situation may get to be very high. The system in that case may jump the gun and initiate the new subtask without waiting for the actual choice. This form of learning is called *conditioning.* By means of it, a sequence of subtasks that are distinct during the early part of the system's lifetime can be strung together to form a single subtask. (This feature has not yet been provided in PERCY, because it is useful primarily for the teachable machine.)

Finally, imprinting is a process that takes place in the early stages of the system's lifetime, when it learns to identify certain patterns of sensation with internal concepts. For example,

PERCY cannot be born with the ability to distinguish specific landmarks. The association of some stimulus with the target "nest landmark" should take place during an *imprinting task* and be used by the PERCEIVE operation thereafter. (This task also has not been worked out in PERCY. It calls for attention to the sensory process, which has been ignored in the actual simulation.)

Concluding Remarks

The structure of the purposive system has now been described, with the help of an explicit example to hopefully pull together the many parts of the exposition into a coherent account. (Acknowledgment of the invaluable programming assistance of Walter Bilofsky must be made here; this paper has depended heavily on the specific insights gained by following the adventures of the "bug" as actually computed.)

Necessary as PERCY has been in explaining the system, it is now important to pursue useful applications. There is little to be gained in using the purposive system for tasks that can be readily carried out by conventional programs. Its applications will be found in problems for which conventional programs are developed with great difficulty.

Even so, it will be valuable to try to add new tasks to PERCY, provided that the addition is handled in a manner to throw light on the problem of the teachable machine.

By adding a lady bug to PERCY's environment, a courting task can be created. One can observe how existing knowledge is modified and extended to support the new task, and how satisfaction in the new task is related to that gained in eating or building a nest. It may then be possible to devise an extension of structure and a learning task so that PERCY can be taught how to behave toward the opposite sex.

To conclude this chapter, some remarks on its title are appropriate. It should be clear that the purposive system provides an explicit model of the workings of the central nervous system, at least in creatures whose behavior is purely instinctive. The model may be a crude one, but it appears to go well beyond what has been attempted elsewhere.

The hope that the model will have substantial use in psychology is encouraged by the fact that it extends the Hebb[4] model and suggests an explicit theory of neuronal function. The individual entry in knowledge can be represented as a cluster of neurons firing together. The direction in which the cluster transmits its excitation is determined by the simultaneous firing of other clusters; this latter firing forms the communication that is thereby "recognized." The synaptic facilities that accompanies the firing represents the change in prior probability of the corresponding row in the knowledge entry.

Furthermore, the situation in effect during a cycle of PERCY's behavior describes the *meaning* of the action that takes place; a short English phrase can be assigned to each situation that "names" the action it controls. In the same way, the plan and goal give the meaning of longer sequences of action. The natural-language character of these components of PERCY's task knowledge throws new light on the role of language in cognitive processes.

Appendix

KNOWLEDGE FOR THE NEST-BUILDING TASK

	Situation	Perception Categories		New Situations		
Type	Intention	Target	Alternate	Prob. Type	Target	Alt.
P1	Advance, Nest, φ	N empty	φ	P3	Nest	Hand
	(At nest, checking	N filled	φ	P2	φ	Nest
	first site)	N not seen	φ	Pφ	(Illegal)	
P2	Circle, φ, Nest	φ	New N not seen	P2	φ	Nest
	(Cirling nest,					
	looking for	φ	New N filled	P2	φ	Nest
	empty site)	φ	New N empty	P3	Nest	Hand
P3	Extend, Nest, Hand	N filled	Holding φ	P4	φ	Arm
	(Advancing to N	N empty	Holding M	P3	Nest	Hand
	while extending					
	arm)	(Other)		Pφ	(Illegal)	
P4	Retract, φ, Arm	φ	Arm back	P5	φ	Nest
	(Returning arm)	φ	Arm not back	P4	φ	Arm
P5	Circle, φ, N	φ	New N not seen	P5	φ	Nest
	(Circling to nest	φ	New N empty	Pφ	(Continue)	
	N and checking)	φ	New N filled	Pφ	(Finished)	
Pφ	Done, Feature, φ	Seek	V	S1	φ	V
	(Subtask ended)	(Other)		(nest task)		
C1	Advance, Food, V	F near	φ	C2	F	Hand
	(Advancing	F seen	φ	C1	F	V
	toward food)					
		—	M sighted	Cφ	M	φ
		Nothing seen	φ	Cφ	φ	φ
C2	Extend, Food, Hand	F near	Holding φ	C2	F	Hand
	(Advancing	—	Holding F	C3	φ	Arm
	toward food,	F not seen	Holding φ	Cφ	φ	φ
	extending arm)					
C3	Eat, φ, Arm	φ	Holding F	C3	φ	Arm
	(Eating food)	φ	Holding φ	C4	φ	Arm

	Situation	Perception Categories		New Situations		
Type	Intention	Target	Alternate	Prob. Type	Target	Alt.
C4	Retract, φ, Arm (Retracting arm)	φ	Arm not back	C4	φ	Arm
		φ	Arm back	Cφ	F	φ
Cφ	Done, T, φ	Take M	φ	T1	M	φ
		Seek	V	S1	φ	V
T1	Extend, M Hand (Advancing toward M while extending arm)	M	Holding φ	T1	M	Hand
		φ	Holding M	T2	φ	Arm
T2	Retract, φ, Arm (Retracting arm)	φ	Arm not back	T2	φ	Arm
		φ	Arm back	Tφ	M	φ
Tφ	Done, M, φ	Seek	V	S1	φ	V
S1	Move, φ, V (Moving to search for V)	φ	Nothing seen	S1	φ	V
		φ	Target seen	Sφ	T	φ
Sφ	Done, T, φ	Take M	φ	T1	M,	Hand
		Chase F	V	C1	F,	V
		Go to L	V	G1	L,	V

	Situation	Perception Categories		New Situations		
Type	Intention	Target	Alternate	Prob. Type	Target	Alt.
G1	Advance, L, V (Advancing toward landmark)	L near	φ	Gφ	L	φ
		L seen	φ	G1	L	V
		L seen	L' seen	G1	L'	V'
		L seen	M seen	Gφ	M	φ
		L seen	F seen	Gφ	F	φ
		φ seen	φ seen	Gφ	(Illegal)	
Gφ	Done, T	Place M	φ	P1	N	φ
		Take M	φ	T1	M	φ
		Chase F	φ	C1	F	φ
		Seek	V	S1	φ	V

Plan		Situation Categories		New Plans	
			Prob.		
Type	Choice	Last Target	Type	Targets	History
A1	Seek V; H	Food sighted	Aϕ	Food	H, F
		Material sighted	Aϕ	Material	H, M
		Landmark sighted	A2	L, V'	H, L
A2	Go to L, V; H	LD sighted	A1	LN	H, LD
		Food sighted	Aϕ	Food	H, F
		Material sighted	Aϕ	Material	H, M
		LN sighted	A3	LN	H, LN
A3	Place M, ϕ; H	Continue	Aϕ	CON	H, N
		Done	Aϕ	DONE	H, N
Aϕ	Done, H	Get material, V	M1	V	ϕ
		Get material, ϕ	M3	ϕ	ϕ
		Hunt food, V	F1	V	ϕ
		Hunt food, V	F3	V	ϕ
F1	Seek, V; H	Food sighted	F3	F, V'	H, F
		Material sighted	Fϕ	M	H, M
		Landmark sighted	F2	L, V'	H, L
F2	Go to L, V; H	Near landmark	F1	V	H, L
		Food sighted	F3	F, V'	H, F
		Material sighted	Fϕ	M	H, M
		Nest sighted	Fϕ	LN	H, LN
F3	Chase F, V; H	F eaten	Fϕ	F	H, F
		F lost	F1	F	H
		Material sighted	Fϕ	M	H, M
Fϕ	Done, H	Get material	M3	ϕ	ϕ
		Add to N	A2	LN	ϕ
		Hunt F, V	F1	V	ϕ
		Get Material, V	M1	V	ϕ
		Add to N, V	A1	V	ϕ
M1	Seek V; H	M sighted	M3	M	H, M
		L sighted	M2	L, V'	H, J
		F sighted	Mϕ	F, V'	H, F
M2	Go to L, V; H	M sighted	M3	M	H, M
		F sighted	Mϕ	F, V'	H, F
M3	Take M, ϕ; H	M taken	Mϕ	M	H, M
Mϕ	Done, H	Add to N, V	A1	LN, V	ϕ
		Hunt F, V	F1	F, V	ϕ

Outcome (Goal Type)	New Goal, Decision	Possible Outcomes
1. M placed at N (1) continue task	2, Hunt F (M, LD)	2, 7
	4, Get M (F, LD, LU)	6, 8
	5, Get M (LL)	4
	5, Get M (LM)	5
2. F eaten, ϕ carried (2)	5, Get M (LL)	5
	5, Get M (LM)	5
	5, Get M (LU)	6
3. F eaten, M carried (3)	1, Add to N (LN, LD)	1
4. M taken at LL (5)	1, Add to N (LN)	1
	3, Hunt F (LD)	3
	3, Hunt F (LN, LD)	3, 9
5. M taken at LM (5)	1, Add to N (LN)	1
	3, Hunt F (LD)	3
	3, Hunt F (LN, LD)	3, 9
6. M taken at LU (4 or 5)	1, Add to N (LN, LD)	1
	3, Hunt F	3
7. M sighted (1)	5, Get M	6
8. F sighted (4)	2, Hunt F	2
	5, Get M (LU)	6
9. LN sighted (3)	1, Add to N (LN)	1
	3, Hunt F	3

REFERENCES

1. W. Jacobs. "Help Stamp out Programming." In *Theoretical Approaches to Non-Numerical Problem Solving*. Berlin: Springer-Verlag, 1970.
2. L. Friedman. "Instinctive Behavior and its Computer Synthesis." *Behavioral Science*, 12, 2 (1967).
3. ———. "Robot Control Strategy." In *Proc. Intern. Jt. Conf. on Artif. Intell.* Bedford, Massachusetts: The Mitre Corp., 1969.
4. D. O. Hebb. *The Organization of Behavior.* New York: John Wiley & Sons, Inc., 1949.

A Model of the Brain's Hippocampal Computer*

WILLIAM L. KILMER

Michigan State University
East Lansing, Michigan

and

TURNER McLARDY

Boston State Hospital
Boston, Massachusetts

Introduction

To help understand a complicated process one will often mentally construct an operational model. The biological data and the modeling described here are intended to help clarify various ideas about what the hippocampus of the brain really does and how it does it.

From 1963 until Dr. Warren McCulloch's death in 1969, Kilmer and McCulloch, and occasional others[1] worked on a theory of the core of the vertebrate nervous system, the reticular formation. Its basis was McCulloch's hypothesis that the

*This work was supported by Contract AFOSR-1023-67B. Grateful acknowledgment is due Mr. Duane Leet, Ph.D. candidate in electrical engineering and systems science at Michigan State University. Mr. Leet did all the programming for this project on the university's CDC 6500 computer.

127

main function of the core of the reticular formation is to commit the organism to one or another gross mode of behavior. Examples of gross modes are sleeping, mating, fleeing, fighting, hunting, urinating, defecating, grooming, giving birth, building and locating a nest, caring for offspring, hoarding, gnawing, migrating, and hibernating. When an animal is fully committed to a mode, that mode is incompatible with all others. This prevention of simultaneous commitments to more than one mode maximizes chances of survival. (Simultaneous commitments *can* happen where little urgency is associated with the animal's activities, for example, in play.)

As work on the reticular formation progressed, the question of which brain structures decide on acts within modes arose. To explain what is meant by "act," the following examples are presented. If a cat committed to the fleeing mode comes to a trail fork with very different, but familiar, landscapes down the two forks, whether he goes left or right is an act decision. If he then comes to a climbable tree, whether he climbs it or passes on is another act decision. If he next comes to a stream, whether he veers left or right, dives in, or tries to jump the water is also an act decision. Similarly, if he heads for a thicket and freezes, that is an act. Again, consider a wolf in the hunting mode. His acts may include stalking, lying in ambush, driving a herd of prey, running to the attack, rejoining his pack, digging for mice, and so on. Acts, then, are well-motivated, species-typical, intramodal behaviors that are based on an animal's instincts but which are usually decided on partly as a function of reinforced past individual experience.

During 1969, using the above notions of modes and acts, McLardy and Kilmer reworked some previous ideas of McLardy's[2] and hypothesized that one main function of the CA3 sector of the mammalian hippocampus is to help select act decisions and activate them via signals over the precommissural fornix into the motor circuits of the medical forebrain bundle (see Figs. 1, 2, and 3). Special emphasis was placed upon the behavior-formative period, because during this time most acts must be utilized and sophisticated by elaboration

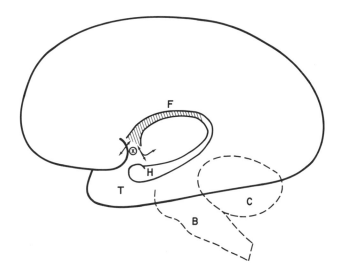

Fig. 1. Mesial View of the Right Half of the Human Brain, Showing Location of the Hippocampus, H, and It's Main Output Pathway, the Fornix, F; T is the Temporal Lobe; X is the Anterior Commissure.

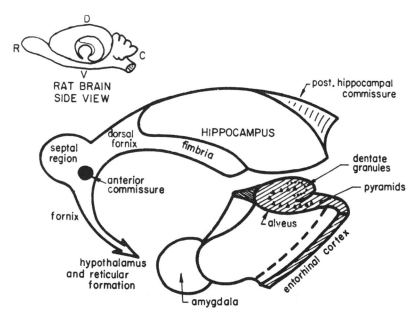

Fig. 2. Schematic Diagram of a Mesial View of the Hippocampal Complex in the Rat, with Section Through Its Middle Portion. (Reprinted, by permission, from Douglas, "The Hippocampus and Behavior," *Psychological Bulletin*, vol. 67, no. 6, pp. 416-442, 1967, Fig. 1.)

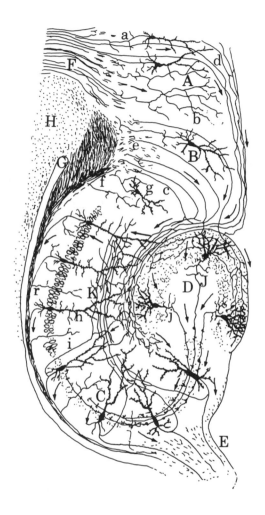

Fig. 3.   Cajal Drawing of Traverse Section of Mouse Hippocampus (Corresponding to the Section in Fig. 2). (Reprinted, by permission, from Cajal, *Histologie du système nerveux de l'homme et des vertébrés*, vol. II (Paris: Maloine 1911.)

Note: The Dentate gyrus is centered around D; the mossy fibers pass (downward) into the CA3 field marked C. Each CA3 pyramidal neuron gives rise to a bifurcating axon; one branch entering the fimbria-fornix at E and the other crossing upward to form the pathway marked K. The latter consists of the Schaffer collaterals passing into the CA1 apical dendritic field. The entorhinal region is shown at A, and the subiculum, a transition zone, at B. Hippocampal basket cells are not shown.

in both the perceptual and the motor domains. The neocortex is presumably not yet well developed or well programmed, so that the allocortex, or "limbic system," which includes the hippocampus, must dominate the control of act behavior during this period. This presumption concords with accumulating evidence that a major concern of the limbic system as a whole is with self- and species-preservatory behavior at about the act level.[3]

Since our approach to the problem of explaining *how* the hippocampus operates requires the sharpest possible appreciation of *what* the hippocampus does, pointers toward physiological functions occupy the first part of our presentation. The second part describes how the hippocampal circuitry can be computer-simulated, and how the hypothetical CA3 functioning can be investigated in the resulting circuit model by working out high-order logical effects of various operational combinations of circuit parameters.

Pointers to What Hippocampus Does

1. The hippocampal complex has long been judged to be heavily concerned with olfactory information as well as with somatic inputs and with feeding and mating, in which there is a strong affective component.[4] Since affects have long been considered to largely determine types of conduct, it became natural to think that the hippocampal complex was heavily involved in determining what an animal does at the act level. It was also noted early that in terrestrial mammals the hippocampal complex is generally largest, relative to the rest of the brain, in those that rely most heavily on rich instinctive organization of behavior.

2. Almost all of CA3's extrahippocampal output passes over the precommissural fornix into the head end of the basal forebrain motor circuitry[5,6] (see Fig. 4). Electrical stimulation in the latter has elicited, in rats, cats, and primates, many of, and generally only, the behaviors we call acts.[7] The septal input to CA3 and the fascia dentata generally originate in regions[8] where Olds[9] and others have demonstrated high reinforcement potentials.

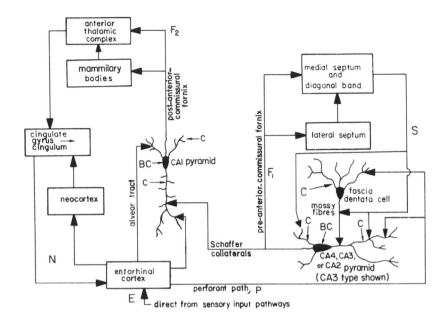

Fig. 4.   Schematic Diagram of the Long-Axoned Cell Types in the Hippo-campus and Their Principal Connections. (Reprinted, by permission, from Raisman *et al.*, *Brain*, vol. 89, pp. 83-108, 1966.)

Note: All C inputs are commissural, probably from mirror image points across the midline [except in the case of fascia dentata, where commisural connections appear scrambled in this respect (Raisman, personal communication)]. The BC inputs to pyramids are from inhibitory basket cells. It is assumed that the main input to the fascia dentata/CA 3 complex in the hippocampus occurs over P, since S is small in quantity. The P input is assumed to be derived from E.

It is hypothesized that the main function of F_1 is to help decide on acts, such as turn right, climb, swim, and freeze, within overall modes of behavior, such as flee, the latter being commanded by the core of the reticular formation. The F_2 hippocampal output is hypothesized (elsewhere) as being mainly a thalamocortical relevance-weighter and attention-setter.

Not shown are Cajal's CA1 pyramidal axon pathway into the medial entorhinal region, the alvear pathway, the diagonal band and septal connections with the basal ganglionic motor systems, and other less prominent connections.

At least in the rat, the above figure is a good approximation for dorsal hippocampus.

3. The hippocampal 3-7 Hertz theta EEG rhythm depends almost entirely upon the integrity of the septo-hippocampal connections. In the awake animal, theta waves emerge most prominently in the septo-hippocampal circuit and are especially pronounced in animals, such as the rabbit and opossum, whose behavior consists largely of species-typical acts. Permeggiani[10] claims that in cats, theta waves appear most prominently when an animal is about to undertake a well-motivated, species-typical (but not automatized) motor act that is dependent upon past experience—that is, in our terminology, an *act*. Bennett[11] correlates theta amplitude with the investigative or attentional components of exploratory behavior in cats, as does Adey.* Several authors[4,12-14] have noted a probable behavior inhibitory role of the hippocampus under high theta conditions, suggesting to us that these conditions are correlated with the inhibition of all acts long enough for one to be optimally decided upon. Noda *et al.*[15,16] have data suggesting that the hippocampus usually idles during low theta amplitude and works during high theta amplitude. Adey cautions against too simplistic a view of theta phenomena, noting that theta signatures vary nearly as much as do the whole animal's behaviors. In general, however, theta rhythm phenomena seem strikingly correlative with act decisions.

4. Bilateral experimental lesions of the hippocampus in adult animals yield three types of effects, all of which tend to point to concern with act decision-making:

> a. The animals are slow to initiate actlike behavior, their attention to stimuli that normally provoke acts seemingly being impaired. Also, they do not habituate to environmental effects as well as normals. Apparent attentional aberrations occur in both approach and withdrawal behavior;[13,17]

> b. The animals are deficient in inhibiting innate or previously learned responses when such are no longer

---

*In a personal communication summarizing several observations reported in a large collection of papers.

appropriate. Their open-field activity levels change, usually increasing. They tend to perseverate, and, judging from DRL tests, they do not regulate their transition tempo from act to act within act sequences as well as do normals;[14]

c. The animals rarely succeed in reversing previously learned responses, apparently because of a reduced capacity for retraining act decisions.[13]

Bilateral fornicotomies (cutting the main hippocampus output pathway) in neonate rats did not discernibly affect laboratory behavior until, later in life, these animals were called upon to integrate an ongoing act with latent-learned knowledge for the first time.[18] There are, however, some difficulties in the interpretation of this. The investigation of Isaacson et al.[19] of sequelae to infant limbic lesions in rats and cats makes it probable that some normal adult hippocampal functions can be transferred to other structures if the hippocampus is lesioned early enough. Also, Glickman's study[20] of barn owls and hippocampally lesioned mice suggests that ethological studies of lesioned animals might often reveal deficits that are not detectable in the laboratory animals. At present, one guide for such research is Cadell's observation[21] that fornicotomy affects play and social behavior in young rhesus monkeys.

5. Olds and Hirano[22] have recorded extracellular action potentials from the hippocampi of relatively freely moving rats while these animals were either learning or exercising instrumentally conditioned responses. The records showed that individual CA3 pyramidal cells often behave in a way simply analogous to that of the whole animal. Their task required a rat to freeze for one second upon hearing a tone (CS) and then push a food pedal or a water pedal (CR), depending on the tone frequency, to obtain the reward. On the average, the firing rate of a "food unit" in a hungry rat would immediately increase after the food tone sounded, hold steady at a high value for one second, and then return to baseline whether the animal satisfactorily performed the CR or not. The results were similar for a water unit. Thus, the CA3 sector was some-

how associated with the freezing act in eating and drinking situations.

6. Recent studies by McLardy[23,24] indicate that in all probability a reasonably intact hippocampal gyrus (instead of hippocampus, as popularly believed) is necessary for consolidation of complex memories. If true, this frees the hippocampus for more extensive motor control and evaluating activity than was heretofore plausible, and thus provides an indirect argument favoring concern with act decisions. It also suggests that CA1, into which CA3 feeds via the Schaffer collaterals, may be free to help govern the tempo of act decisions (referred to in Evidence 4c above), especially acts requiring intermediate memory span, as in threat-escape within relatively novel environments. Such a time domain involvement would appear compatible with our earlier postulate[25] that a main function of the postcommissural fornix, deriving mostly from CA1, is to serve as a thalamocortical relevance-weighter and attention-setter. Such involvement could be compatible with the type of time-binding implied by Walter's frontal Contingent Negative Variation (CNV) wave,[26] suggesting the presence of a strong frontal lobe influence over the hippocampus, and CA1 in particular, via the uncinate fasiculus and entorhinal cortex: our "Aim" inputs in Fig. 2 of McLardy and Kilmer.[25]

Model of How Sector CA3 Operates

The histology of the hippocampus is at least as well documented as that of most other cerebral structures. In addition, its anatomy appears more tightly organized and more highly stylized than that of any other part of the brain except, possibly, the cerebellum. It is thus relatively easy to construct a circuit model of the CA3 sector in which elements and lines in the model are easily identified as caricatures of corresponding cell groups and fiber systems in the brain.

Figure 5 shows some typical Ammon's horn (i.e., hippocampus) pyramids of the type indicated in Fig. 3, but in greater detail. Note especially how the axon collaterals from the CA3

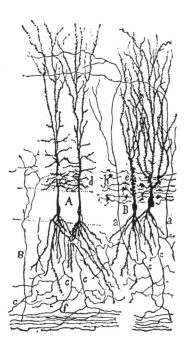

Fig. 5. Figure 475 from S. R. Cajal, *Histologie du système nerveux de l'homme et des vertébrés*, vol. II. (Paris: Maloine, 1911). Cajal's caption (translated): Pyramidal cells of the Ammonsohn; rabbit aged one month. This Golgi method A, small pyramidal cells are pyramids of region CA1; B, large pyramidal cells are pyramids of region CA3; a, thick acending collaterals; c, axis-cylinder; d, spinous process of the trunk of small pyramidal cells; e, excrescences on the trunk of large pyramidal cells; f, fine collateral going to the white matter; g, collateral issuing from alveus fibers; h, mossy fibers related to the large pyramidal cells.

type, "B," ramify so as to enable these cells to feed into both basal and apical dendrites of nearby pyramids. Figure 6 is a diagrammatic representation of the arrangement of afferent sites on CA3 and CA1 pyramids as well as on dentate granule cells. Note the remarkable degree of afferent segregation. Figure 7 shows the range of short-axoned neuron types in CA1. The corresponding picture for CA3 would be nearly identical to Fig. 7, but is not included here because nowhere in the literature is it compactly represented. The cells in Fig. 7 whose

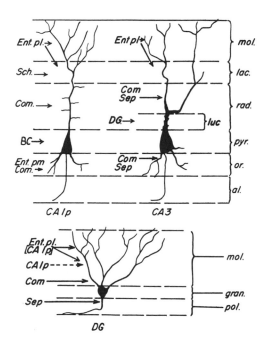

Fig. 6. Types of Cells with Short Axis Cylinder in Field CA1; Twelve-Day-Old Mouse, Golgi Method. (Reprinted, by permission, from Raisman, Cowan, and Powell, "The Extrinsic Afferent, Commissural and Association Fibres of the Hippocampus," *Brain*, Fig. 8, pp. 963-996, 1965.)

Note: A diagrammatic representation of two pyramidal cells from field CA1 posterior and field CA3, respectively, and a dentate gyrus granule cell to show the lamination of the afferents upon the dendrites. Abbreviations: al, alveus; BC, basket cells; Com, commissural fibres of the hippocampus; DG, dentate gyrus; Ent, entorhinal area; Sep, septum; gran, stratum granulosum; lac, stratum lacunosum; luc, stratum lucidum; mol, stratum moleculare; or stratum oriens; pol, stratum polymorphy; pyr, stratum pyramidale; rad, stratum radiatum.

axons for the most part terminate in many small bushlets in the pyramidal layer are called basket cells.

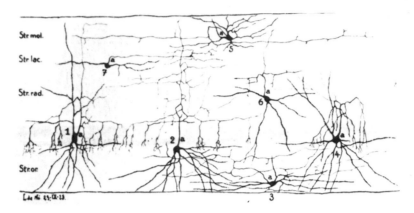

a. Basket Cells Shown in 1 and 2

b. Basket Cells Shown in 4 and 5

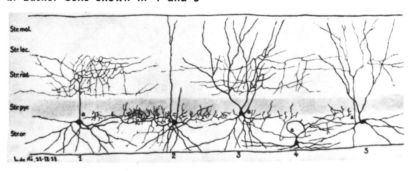

c. Basket Cells Shown in 2 and 4

Fig. 7.   Types of Cells with Short Axis Cylinder in Field CA1, twelve-day-old mouse, Golgi method. (Reprinted, by permission, from Lorente de Nó, "Studies on the Structure of the Cerebral Cortex, II: Continuation of the Study of the Ammonic System," *Journal of Psychol. Neurol. (Lpx)* vol. 46, p. 113, 1934.

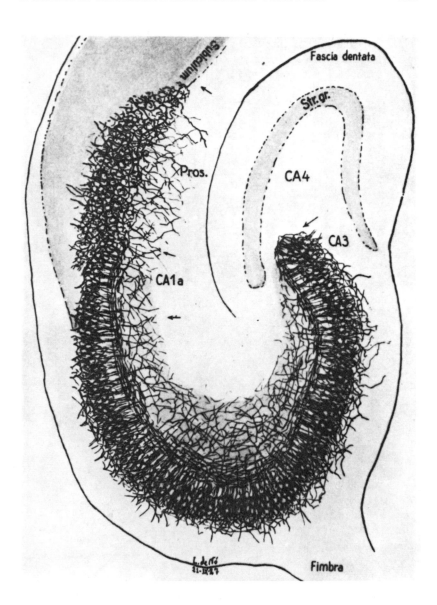

Fig. 8.   Outline of Basket Cell Axonal Plexus in a Typical Transverse Section of the Mouse Hippocampus; Twelve-day-old mouse, Golgi method. Reprinted, by permission, from Lorente de Nó, "Studies on the Structure of the Cerebral Cortex, II: Continuation of the Study on the Ammonic System," *Journal of Psychol. Neurol.* (Lpz) vol. 46, pp. 113–177, 1934.

Note: The plexus of endramifications of axons of basket cells in the Ammonshorn and Prosubiculum. In CA4 the plexus is absent. The granule cells of the Fascia dentate (str. gr.) are enveloped by a similar plexus. (See Figs. 23 and 23a, B.p.) Note that in CA1$_a$ and Prosubiculum the plexus exists only in the inner upper layers.

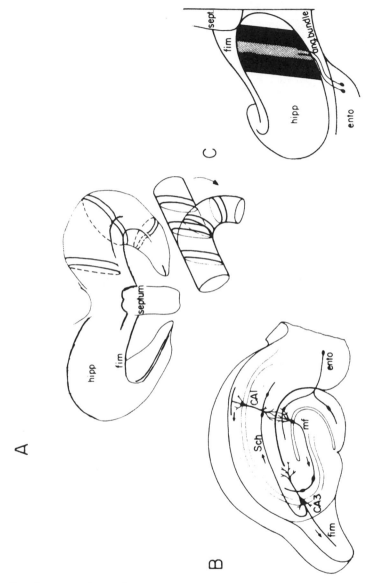

Fig. 9.   Response in a Transverse Hippocampal Section to a Focal En-
torhinal Excitation. (Reprinted, by permission, from Andersen and Lomo,
"Organization and Frequency Dependence of Hippocampal Inhibition," *Basic
Mechanisms of the Epilepsies*, Jasper *et al.*, Eds. [Boston: Little, Brown, and
Co., 1969], Fig. D21-1.)

Note: Schematic drawing of hippocampal formation in rabbit. (A) Hippocampal formation
viewed from above; heavy lines indicate slices (see text). Inset shows relative position of
slices in a curved and straight tissue cylinder. (B) Diagram of tissue sliced with four-
neuronal chain, arranged in the plane of the slice. (C) Diagram of hippocampal formation
viewed from above with an excited beam of cells (hatched), bordered on each side by a strip
of inhibited neurons (black).

Since almost all neurons of the hippocampus are pyramids or basket cells,* we will consider only those circuit relations that concern these kinds of cells. Figure 8 outlines the basket cell axonal plexus in a typical transverse section of the mouse hippocampus. There, Lorento de Nó emphasizes, the part of a basket cell axon which tends to run colinearly with the pyramidal layer usually occurs in the stratum radiatum (Fig. 6), although one might not infer this emphasis from Cajal.[27] Cajal and Lorente de Nó both show the typical basket cell axon distributing over a larger area in the transverse plane than the typical pyramid axon (apart from its main extrinsic efferent and, if the pyramid is in CA3, its Schaffer collateral).

There is good evidence, for example, from observations by Spencer and Kandel[28] and by Andersen *et al.*,[29] that hippocampal basket cells inhibit pyramids, and that pyramids excite both pyramids and basket cells. If this be true, Fig. 9c shows (1) an excited beam of hippocampal pyramids of width determined by the hippo-axial extents of the local excitatory pyramid-to-pyramid collaterals and (2) an inhibited beam of width determined by the hippo-axial extents of the inhibitory basket cell-to-pyramid axons stemming from basket cell bodies located in the excited beam. This inference assumes that the fibers drive the pyramids in the excited beam hard enough for the pyramids to prevail over their basket cell inhibition, and that, outside the excited beam, the prevailing inhibition is due to monosynaptic transmission of basket cell spikes originating within the excited beam. This explanation, together with the presumption that it would have been noted if hippo-axially sectioned Golgi pictures of basket cells and pyramids differed radically from transversely sectioned ones, leads us to suppose that basket cells usually distribute to much larger surrounds than do pyramids.

Returning now to Fig. 4, our CA3 model concentrates on the strikingly independent F_1-S loop. A caricature of its circuitry, as revealed in Figs. 3 and 5 through 9, is described in Figs. 10 through 12.

---

*To be documented in reports by Lomo and associates.

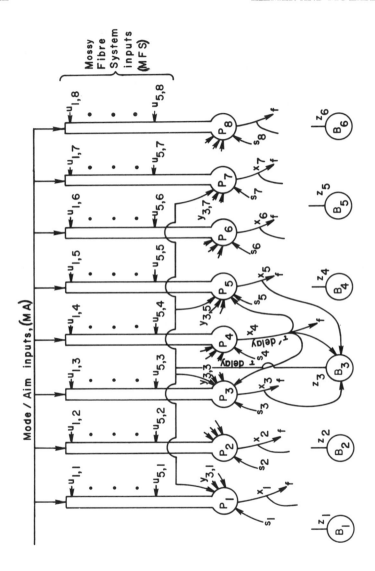

Fig. 10. Kilmer–McLardy Computer Simulation Model of the CA3 Basket Cell–Pyramidal Cell Circuitry of the Hippocampus.

The P_i are pyramidal cells with output firing rates x_i; the B_i are basket cells with output firing rates z_i. All firing rates are limited to between 0 and 100 pulses per second. Each B_i inhibits all P_i into which it fires; each P_i excites all P_i and B_j into which it fires. Each P_j computes the nonlinear function Ω_i of its $u_{i,j}$ that is indexed by MA, the gross behavioral mode input pathway. The s_i are septal reward/punishment reinforcement inputs to the P_i. The f outputs of the P_i are the precommissural fornix efferents from CA3. Mossy fiber system (MFS) inputs are organized as synapses-de-passage, and each MFS line is binary.

$$\frac{dx_i(t)}{dt} = \left[\underbrace{-a\,x_i(t) - \beta}_{\substack{\text{decay} \\ \text{term}}} \underbrace{\sum_m \frac{\sqrt{z_m(t\text{-}\tau)}\ f^2\left(z_m(t\text{-}\tau)\right)}{g^2\left(z_m(t\text{-}\tau),\ y_{mi}(t)\right)}}_{\substack{\text{inhibitory effect} \\ \text{from the basket cells.}}} \right. \tag{1}$$

$$\left. + \upsilon\underbrace{\sum_j h\left[x_j(t\text{-}\tau)\right]}_{\substack{\text{excitatory effect} \\ \text{from the pyramidal} \\ \text{collateral inputs to} \\ P_i.}} + \underbrace{\frac{d\,\Omega_i(t)}{dt}}_{\substack{\text{excitatory effect} \\ \text{from the mossy fiber} \\ \text{and MA inputs to } P_i.}} \right] K_1$$

$$y_{mi}(t) = w_{mi}(t) \Big/ \sum_j |w_{mj}(t)| \left.\right\} \begin{array}{l} \text{the } y_{mi} \text{ are just the } w_{mi}\text{``normalized''} \\ \text{so that } \sum_j |y_{mj}| = 1 \end{array} \tag{2}$$

and

$$\frac{dw_{mi}(t)}{dt} = \left[\underbrace{-\mu w_{mi}(t)}_{\substack{\text{decay} \\ \text{term}}} + \underbrace{K_2 s_i(t)\left[z_m(t\text{-}\tau) - \bar{z}_m\right]\left[x_i(t) - \bar{x}_i\right]}_{\substack{\text{cross-correlation} \\ \text{increment}}} \right], \tag{3}$$

where z_m is as specified below, $\bar{z}_m$ and $\bar{x}_i$ indicate the recent average z_m and the recent average x_i respectively, and $s_i(t)$ at any time is either -1 for positive reinforcement, -1 for negative reinforcement, or 0 for no reinforcement. The $h(x_j)$ curve in the excitatory term of (1) is a straight line running through $h(x_j) = 30$ when $x_j = 0$, $h(x_j) = x_j = 50$, and $h(x_j) = 70$ when $x_j = 100$. The solution to (3) is:

$$(4)$$

$$w_{mi}(t) = \underbrace{w_{im}(0)\, e^{-\mu t}}_{\substack{\text{residue at } t \\ \text{of initial } w_{mi}}} + \underbrace{\int_o^t K_2 s_i(v)\left[z_m\,(v\text{-}\tau) - z_m\right]\left[x_i\,(v) - \bar{x}_i\right]e^{-\mu(t\text{-}v)}\,dv}_{\substack{\text{residue at } t \text{ of the sum of all past cross-correlation} \\ \text{increments, each time-weighted for recentness.}}}$$

it is assumed that as far as each $w_{mi}(t)$ is concerned, time does not advance unless $s_i(t) = +1$ or -1.
The value of $z_m(t)$ for any B_m is given by

$$(5)$$

$$z_m(t) \;=\; \left.\begin{array}{c} p\sum\limits_{i=1}^{3} x_i\,(t\text{-}1) \\[6pt] \hline \epsilon + d\,(t) \end{array}\right\} \quad\begin{array}{l}\text{for overall average inhibitory effect}\\[6pt]\text{for learned selective inhibition}\end{array}$$

if x_1, x_2, and x_3 constitute B_m's input. The value of $d(t)$ is the Euclidean distance from the actual (x_1, x_2, x_3) point to the nearest "ideal" (x_1, x_2, x_3) point. Each "ideal" (x_1, x_2, x_3) point corresponds to a maximally informative x_1, x_2, x_3 input to B_m.
Ω_i in (1) is of the form

$$\sum_{j=1}^{5} a_{ij}\, v_{ji} \;+\; \sum_{j,k=1}^{5} a_{ijk}\, v_{ji}\, v_{ki} \quad,$$

where v_{ji} is the jth MFS input to P_i.
The a_{ij} and a_{ijk} are trainable independently of the y_{mi}.

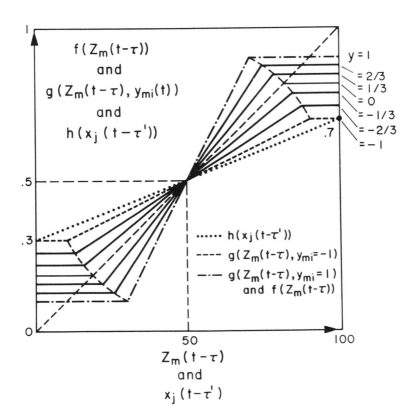

Fig. 11. Graph of the f and g Functions in the Second Term on the Right of Eq. (1), Page 143.

Note: The solid off-diagonal lines give six g curves, one for each $y = y_{mi}(t)$ value indicated. The f curve is identical to the g curve for $y = 1$.

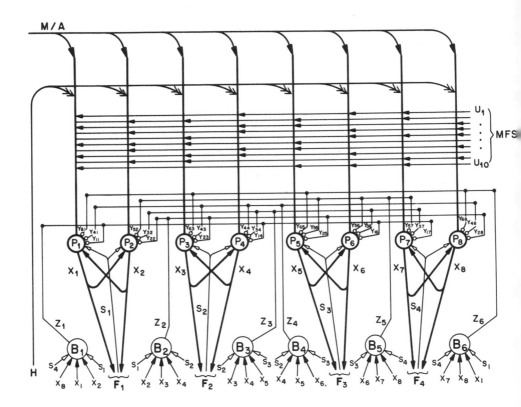

Fig. 12. Detailed Connection Diagram for the First Simulation Run of the Model Sketched in Fig. 10.

Note: The MA input is not shown since it has been held constant to this point. The task of the circuit is to decide on one of $2^4 = 16$ acts; therefore, four output bits are provided over F_1, F_2, F_3, F_4 according to the following code. If $(x_1 + x_2 (50 + 50) = 100$, the F_1 bit is 1, otherwise it is 0; similarly for the other $(x_{2j\text{-}1} + {}_2j)$ and F_j. If an incorrect output is given, $s_j = -1$ for only the F_j whose $(x_{2j\text{-}1} + x_{2j})$ is closest to 100; this insures that all trial and error learning is reasonable rational (the rule is "doctored" so that no F_j bit can keep reversing its value upon successive presentations of a corresponding MFS input). Each P_i undergoes periodic w_{ij} and w_{ijk} retraining, but only two widely space P_i are ever retrained at once. After each successive MFS, (F_1, F_2, F_3, F_4), (s_1, s_2, s_3, s_4) event occurs, each y_{ij} that is not connected to a P_i being retained receives a training increment.

The model in Figs. 10 and 12 has the smallest possible number of lines and elements consistent with our intuitive ideas about hippocampal operation. In the caption to Fig. 10, the pyramidal outputs, x_i, are described by only first-order differential-difference equations because the aim of the first model is to concentrate on determining correct relative directions of interactions over reasonably long time spans. The model has two types of memory. The first consists of weights associated with the nonlinear Ω_i functions computed by the pyramid, the second, of the y_{ij} elements between the basket cells and the pyramids. The equations governing the y_{ij} were inspired by some ideas of Grossberg.[30-32] The model's most significant memory provisions are the throughput memory inside the pyramids and the feedback memory around the basket cell pyramidal loops.

The circuit in Fig. 10 operates as follows. The pyramids, P_i, compute nonlinear functions, Ω_i, of their inputs over MFS as directed by MA. MA tells each pyramid, in a sense, what kind of input it should attend to at the moment. Each pyramid's output is also partly determined by effects circling around the pyramid-to-pyramid negative feedback loops. Moreover, the various amounts by which each basket cell inhibits the pyramids into which it fires are learned under control of the s_i reinforcement variables. The action sequence of the circuit is: (1) an MFS input is presented; (2) the circuit computes its response; (3) the response is evaluated; and (4) the pyramidal and y_{ij} memory elements are adjusted according to the evaluation. Then the next MFS input is presented. Andersen and Lømo's data[33] on the inhibitory, warm-up, and fatigue stages of hippocampal pyramidal cell activity in response to continued stimulation over afferent pathways provides some support for the validity of the model's action sequence.

Since Eq. (1) is only first order, x_i has no inertial component. The decay term of (1) is the simplest one that could force x_i toward zero in the absence of any net driving effect on P_i. The second and third terms on the right side of (1) add to give the momentary excitatory and inhibitory effects on P_i. Since P_i is immersed in a rich feedback field, the effect in (1) of changing dx_i/dt (instead of x_i) in accordance with the net drive on P_i properly reflects the regenerative nature of the field.

In order to explain our concept of the function of the model's (and, therefore, to some extent, of the hippocampal CA3's) lateral inhibitory basket cells, we refer to Fig. 12, where the general plan of Fig. 10 is specified in detail. Figure 12 assumes that each circuit output is defined by four F_i bits, so the model is limited to $2^4 = 16$ acts. Each act, once specified, is carried out by motor circuits located elsewhere. Every basket cell in Fig. 12 is excited by a set of pyramids such that some pyramidal excitation patterns raise that basket cell's output firing rate to much higher values than do other pyramidal patterns. This much at least is corroborated by neurophysiology. But further neurophysiological information on basket cell response characteristics is so scant that our modeling must proceed by speculation.

Suppose that, normally, when all of the x_i into a B_m are either quite high or quite low, the P_i that generate them have sufficient information to be quite sure of at least their own F_k bit values. The B_m into which such P_i feed then also receive relatively large amounts of information (that is, very little equivocation). Consequently, each such B_m might best respond with a high z_m in order to bring the P_i into which that B_m fires into better functional alignment with the P_i feeding that B_m. This would reduce the output uncertainties of the P_i into which that B_m feeds. Neurophysiologists have long regarded interneurons such as basket cells, in general, as sharpeners of circuit actions. But if the foregoing is correct, the basket cells might now be more precisely viewed as P_i aligners working from P_i groups with low output uncertainty toward P_i groups with light output uncertainty. The B_m axonal anatomy certainly suggests such an interpretation.

Each B_m in Fig. 12 is specified so that its output is high when and only when its pyramidal input pattern carries high information (or is "ideal," in the terminology of Fig. 10). The problem of evaluating the four y_{mi} connected to each B_m (Fig. 12) so that B_m properly performs its alignment function is easily solved. Each y_{mi} is slightly modified after each MFS input occurs in such a way as to enable it to approximate continuously the cross correlation between z_m and x_i, as modified by a septal reinforcement signal, s_i. The purpose of s_i is to tell, after each MFS input, whether or not the response bit to which x_i contributed should be rewarded or punished. If rewarded, a regular cross correlation increment is added to y_{mi}. This increment is given by the second term on the right of Eq. (3) in the caption to Fig. 10, which $s_i = +1$. If punished, a negative cross correlation increment is added to y_{mi}. This insures that y_{mi} learns a typically rewarded covariation between z_m and x_i instead of just a typically occurring covariation. As a result, B_m does its job through the y_{mi}, but under the ultimate control of septal reinforcement criteria. Neurophysiologically speaking, this arrangement is heterodox because it postulates a simple learning mechanism in basket cell axonal arbors. Such a mechanism has been promulgated by McLardy[34] for more than a decade, and Lettvin et al.[35] recently have postulated plastic axonal computers in the synaptic reticular spinal cord.

Another view of the function of the model's basket cells is that they suppress the individual pyramidal cell output excursions caused by reductions in pyramidal input information. This raises the problem of how incrementally to train the pyramids when, in order to sharpen pyramidal outputs toward relatively high and low values, the basket cells suppress all trained x_i increments that bring x_i closer to fifty, the no-information rate. This problem is noteworthy due to the importance of incremental learning. If too much one-shot learning were allowed, either in the model or in the brain, too many spurious responses might occur in the wake of circuit noise bursts.

One way to train pyramids incrementally without disposing of the inhibitory basket cells would be to simultaneously retrain only a small number of pyramids while their basket cell inhibition was removed and then reinstate the inhibition for a final phase of refined training that relied on different circuit mechanisms. That this type of operation may occur in the hippocampus is suggested by Olds's experiments, which were partly described under point 5 (page 134), toward our CA3 hypothesis. Olds noticed that, typically, CA3 units apparently acquire their learned responses in a few hours (during which time they continue to fire at high rates, as if no longer inhibited), whereas the whole animal takes days to acquire the corresponding conditioned behavior.* Olds suggested that periodic waves of inhibition removal and pyramid retraining, with periods of five to seven days in the rat, could also explain various other single unit effects.

The P_i-to-P_j connections in Fig. 12 have been specified so as to enhance intra-F_k cooperation and to facilitate the P_i training algorithm given in the Appendix.

To date, the model described in Figs. 10 through 12 has been tonically balanced, and the P_i training algorithm has been satisfactorily employed in simulation. The program for a complete simulation is now being debugged on the Michigan State University CDC 6500 computer.

Other Models of the Hippocampus

Olds[9] proposed a circuit model of the hippocampus in which the main elements were two completely retrainable random access memory grids, the first feeding into the second, and the second furnishing motor outputs. McLardy and Kilmer[25] have constructively criticized this model on anatomical and overall functional grounds. We believe that, despite its provocative value, it is too simplified to provide new insights into the normal operation of hippocampal circuitry.

Dichter and Spencer[28] simulated a simple circuit model of the hippocampus to check some notions they had about circuit interactions occurring in penicillin-induced interictal discharges in cat hippocampus. Their simulation was aimed at explaining intercellular PSP waves in hippocampal pyramids and must be judged as a strikingly successful attempt. It must be emphasized, however, that the purpose of their model was not to explain normal operation but to demonstrate possible circuit concomitants in various aspects of seizures.

---

*Personal communication.

Appendix

NOTES ON THE PYRAMIDAL CELL TRAINING ALGORITHM

The Ω_i term in Eq. (1) of Fig. 10 is of the form

$$\Omega_i = \sum_{j=1}^{5} a_{ij} v_{ji} + \sum_{j,k=1}^{5} a_{ijk} \, v_{ji} \, v_{ki}$$

where v_{ji} is the jth MFS input to P_i. This can also be expressed as

$$\Omega_i = \vec{W}_{i1} \cdot \vec{U}_i + \vec{W}_{i2} \cdot \vec{U}_i^2$$

where

$$\vec{U}_i^2 = df \sum_{j,k=1}^{5} u_{ji} \, u_{ki}$$

and $\vec{W}_{i2}$ is a 25-component vector.

Whenever $\vec{W}_{i1}$ and $\vec{W}_{i2}$ for a P_i are being retrained, that P_i is, in effect, partially disconnected from the rest of the circuit. This is to eliminate certain disruptive effects of feedback. Partial disconnection of P_i is performed in the following manner. Denote the other P_j in the same F_k as P_i by P_i^c, then replace the x_i input to P_i^c by P_i^c's output. Also fix at 50 the x_i input to each basket cell into which P_i fires. When the $\vec{W}_{i1}$, $\vec{W}_{i2}$ training of P_i is complete, reinstate the original P_i connections.* This will enable P_i to again excite P_i^c and a set of basket cells informatively. After P_i is reinstated, all further adjustments with respect to its circuit actions must occur among the y_{ij} memory elements throughout the circuit.

Only two widely spaced P_i^c are ever partially disconnected for training at the same time. This keeps the overall circuit operational at all times. P_i^c training occurs only in one P_j, P_{j+4} pair at once, $j = 1, 2, 3, 4$, and the training epoch for each P_j, P_{j+4} pair lasts for three successive presentations of a

---

*The period over which a P_1 is disconnected might correspond to the period of pyramidal cell buzzing and learning observed by J. Olds in hippocampal CA3 (see "Model of How Sector CA3 Operates").

MFS training sequence. This training sequence has sixteen inputs in all, and associated with each input is a correct F_1, F_2, F_3, F_4 response. The reinforcement signals with respect to $\overrightarrow{W}_{i1}$, $\overrightarrow{W}_{i2}$ for P_j, P_j+_4, as well as the s_1, s_2, s_3, s_4 reinforcement signals for the y_{ij}, are determined by a comparison between the actual and the correct F_1, F_2, F_3, F_4 responses.

Note the large fan-out which arises from each P_i feeding a set of B_j and each B_j feeding a set of P_k. Denote the direct effects on x_i of the sequence of $\overrightarrow{W}_{i1}$, $\overrightarrow{W}_{i2}$ adjustments occurring over a P_i training epoch by Δx_i. Then, because of the large fan-out, Δx_i should normally be much greater than the $\Delta x_i \longrightarrow z_j \longrightarrow x_i$ effects fed back, which appear when P_i is reconnected into the circuit at the end of a training epoch. If this were not so, our model would suffer from all of the problems that normally make trainable closed loop circuits impractical. Thus, after a P_i is reconnected, the effects of subsequent y_{ij} adjustments are normally smaller than those of P_i's previous $\overrightarrow{W}_{i1}$, $\overrightarrow{W}_{i2}$ adjustments.

The rules for adjusting $\overrightarrow{W}_{i1}$ and $\overrightarrow{W}_{i2}$ when a P_i is partially disconnected will now be given. Let the $\overrightarrow{W}_{i1}$, $\overrightarrow{W}_{i2}$ reinforcement signal for P_i be s_k, that is, the reinforcement signal for all of the y_{ji} associated with the F_k that contain P_i. Let all of the y_{ji} into P_i be held constant during P_i's $\overrightarrow{W}_{i1}$, $\overrightarrow{W}_{i2}$ training epoch, but let them be released for further adjustment after P_i's training epoch is complete. Let F_1, F_2, $_3$, F_4 be denoted by $\overrightarrow{F}$. Then there are six cases to consider for each MFS input:

Case 1. $\overrightarrow{F}$ is correct and the F_k that contains P_i is 1. Form $G_a(\Omega_i) = (90 - \Omega_i)/10$ and then add $G_a(\Omega_i) \overrightarrow{U}_i$ to $\overrightarrow{W}_{i1}$ and $G_a(\Omega_i) \overrightarrow{U}_{i}^{\%}$ to $\overrightarrow{W}_{i2}$.

Case 2. $\overrightarrow{F}$ is correct and the F_k that contains P_i is 0. Form $G_s(\Omega_i) = (\Omega_i - 10)/10$ and then subtract $G_s(\Omega_i) \overrightarrow{U}_i$ from $\overrightarrow{W}_{i1}$ and $G_s(\Omega_i) U_i^{\%}$ from $\overrightarrow{W}_{i2}$.

If $\overrightarrow{F}$ is incorrect, $s_i = -1$ for only the F_k whose x_j sum is closest to $50 + 50 = 100$. All other $s_i = + 1$. This is to insure that the model's trial and error learning, which occurs whenever the model gives an incorrect $\overrightarrow{F}$ response, is somewhat rational. In order to prevent any F_k bit from simply reversing its value upon successive presentations of some MFS training input under the foregoing rule, P_i remembers whether its s_k was -1 both prior to and since the most recent F_k bit change for the MFS input in question. If for some MFS input it was, s_k cannot be -1 again until some other F_j has undergone a trial-and-error bit reversal for that input. With this in mind, the rules for the remaining cases are as follows.

Case 3. $\vec{F}$ is incorrect, the F_k that contains P_i is 1, and the associated s_k is -1. Proceed as in Case 2.

Case 4. $\vec{F}$ is incorrect, the F_k that contains P_i is 0, and the associated s_k is -1. Proceed as in Case 1.

Case 5. $\vec{F}$ is incorrect, the F_k that contains P_i is 1, and the associated s_k is $+1$. Proceed as in Case 1.

Case 6. $\vec{F}$ is incorrect, the F_k that contains P_i is 0, and the associated s_k is $+1$. Proceed as in Case 2.

The reason for training $\overrightarrow{W}_{i1}$ several times faster than $\overrightarrow{W}_{i2}$ is that, roughly, this enables a five-weight linear approximation to the best Ω_i to be obtained first and a twenty-five-weight non-linear correction term to be added on last. This is probably not far from optimal as a strategy for rapid training.

The $\overrightarrow{W}_{i1}$ and $\overrightarrow{W}_{i2}$ vectors for each P_i are retrained according to a periodic schedule, and after every MFS, $\vec{F}$, (s_1, s_2, s_3, s_4) event, every y_{ij} that is not connected to a partially disconnected P_i is given a unit training increment. The fading rate of the y_{ij} is low, as indicated by $e^{-16\mu} = 9/10$, but the $\overrightarrow{W}_{i1}$, $\overrightarrow{W}_{i2}$ vectors of a P_i can change greatly over one MFS training sequence. Thus, the y_{ij} adjustments represent a much slower form of learning than the $\overrightarrow{W}_{i1}$, $\overrightarrow{W}_{i2}$ adjustments. The former might be analogous to the memory consolidation that we tentatively postulate occurs during REM sleep, and the latter to whatever memory consolidation occurs within a few hours after an attended percept.

REFERENCES

1. W. Kilmer; W. S. McCulloch; and J. Blum. "A model of the vertebrate central command system." *Int. Jnl. Man-Machine Studies* 1 (1969): 279–309.
2. T. McLardy. "Hippocampal formation as detector-coder of temporal patterns." *Perspec. Biol. Med.* 2 (1959): 443–452.
3. P. D. and M. D. MacLean. "The limbic system with respect to self-preservation and the preservation of the species." *Jnl. of Nervous and Mental Disease* 127, no. 1 (1958): 1–11.
4. J. D. Green. "Hippocampus." *Physiol. Rev.* 44 (1964): 56–60.
5. G. Raisman; W. M. Cowan; and T. P. S. Powell. "The extrinstic afferent, commissural, and association fibers of the hippocampus." *Brain* 88 (1965): 963–997.
6. ———. "An experimental analysis of the efferent projection of the hippocampus." *Brain* 89 (1966): 83–108.
7. S. E. Glickman; and B. Schiff. "A biological theory of reinforcement." *Psychological Review* 74, no. 2 (1967): 8–109.
8. G. Raisman. "The connexions of the septum." *Brain* 89 (1966): 317–348.
9. J. Olds. "The central nervous system and the reinforcement of behavior." *American Psychologist* 24 (1969): 114–132.
10. P. L. Parmeggiani. "On the functional significance of the hippocampal theta-rhythm." In *Progress in Brain Research, 27: Structure and Function of the Limbic System*, edited by W. R. Adey and T. Tokizane. Amsterdam: Elsevier Publishing Co., 1967.
11. T. L. Bennett. "Evidence against the theory that hippocampal theta is a correlate of voluntary movement." In *Communications in Behavioral Biology.* In Press.
12. ———. "Hippocampal EEG correlates of behavior." *Electroencephalography and Clinical Neurophysiology* 28 (1970): 17–23.
13. R. J. Douglas. "The hippocampus and behavior." *Psychological Bulletin* 67, no. 6 (1967): 416–442.
14. D. P. Kimble. "Possible inhibitory functions of the hippocampus." *Neuropsychologia* 7 (1969): 235–244.
15. H. Noda; S. Manohar; and W. R. Adey. "Spontaneous activity of cat hippocampal neurons in sleep and wakefulness." *Experimental Neurology* 24 (1969): 217–231.
16. ———. "Correlated firing of hippocampal neuron pairs in sleep and wakefulness." *Experimental Neurology* 24 (1969): 232–247.
17. W. W. Meissner. "Hippocampal functions in learning." *Jnl. Psychiat. Research* 4 (1966): 235–304.
18. T. McLardy. "Insight deficit after neonatal fornicotomy or laterodorsalis thalamatomy in rats." *Brain Research* 16 (1969): 285–287.
19. R. L. Isaacson; A. J. Nonneman; and L. W. Schmaltz. "Behavioral and anatomical sequelae of the infant limbic system." In *The Neuropsychology of Development*, edited by Robert L. Isaacson. New York: John Wiley & Sons, Inc., 1968.

20. E. Glickman. "Ethological aspects in the study of reward mechanisms." In *Proceedings of Third Annual Winter Conference on Brain Research*, Snowmass-at-Aspen, Colorado, January 1970.
21. T. E. Cadell. "The effect of fornix section on learned and social behaviors in rhesus monkeys." Ph.D. thesis, University of Wisconsin, 1963.
22. J. Olds; and T. Hirano. "Conditioned responses of hippocampal and other neurons." *Electroenceph. and Clinical Neurophysiol.* 26 (1969): 159–166.
23. T. McLardy. "Memory function in adult hippocampal gyri, but not in hippocampus." *Intnl. J. Neurosci.*, in press.
24. ———. "Memory Consolidation in Rats with Sulfide-Loaded Hippocampal Zinc-Rich Synapses." In *Exper. Neurology.* In press.
25. ———; and Kilmer, W. L. "Hippocampal Circuitry." *American Psychologist* 25 (1970): 563–566.
26. W. G. Walter. "Electric signs of expectancy and decision in the human brain." In *Cybernetic Problems in Bionics*, edited by H. L. Oestreicher and D. R. Moore. New York: Gordon and Breach Science Publishers, 1968.
27. Ramon y, S. Cajal. *Histologie du système nerveux de l'Homme et des vertébrés*, vol. 2. Paris: Maloine, 1911.
28. W. A. Spencer; and E. R. Kandel. "Synaptic inhibition in seizures." In *Basic Mechanisms of the Epilepsies*, edited by H. H. Jasper, A. A. Ward, and P. Pope. Boston: Little, Brown & Co., 1969.
29. P. Andersen; J. C. Eccles; and Y. Loyning. "Pathway of post-synaptic inhibition in the hippocampus." *Jnl. Neurophys.* 27 (1964): 592–607.
30. S. Grossberg. "Nonlinear difference-differential equations in prediction and learning theory." *Proc. National Acad. Sci.* 58 (1967): 1329-1334.
31. ———. "Global ratio limit theorems for some nonlinear functional-differential equations." *Bull. Amer. Math. Sci.* 74 (1968): Part I, pp. 95–99; Part II, pp. 100–105.
32. ———. "A prediction theory for some nonlinear functional differential equations." *Jnl. Math. Anal. Appl.* (1968): Part I, 21, pp. 643–694; Part II, 22, pp. 490–522.
33. P. Andersen; and T. Lomo. "Organization and frequency dependence of hippocampal inhibition." In *Basic Mechanisms of the Epilepsies*, edited by H. H. Jasper, A. A. Ward, and P. Pope, pp. 604–609. Boston: Little, Brown & Co., 1969.
34. T. McLardy. "Conference on Cerebral Systems and Computer Logic." Unedited Abstracts. Pasadena: Cal. Tech., 1960, pp. 51–52.
35. J. Lettvin, et al. "Multiple Meaning in Single Vienal Units," Paper presented at AAAS Meeting, Boston, December 1969.

ADDITIONAL READINGS

Adey, W. R. "EEG Studies of Hippocampal System in the Learning Process." *Physiologie de l'Hippocampe*, Colloques Internationaux Du Centre National De La Recherche Scientifique 107 (1962):203–224.

Altman, J. and Gopal, D. D. "Autoradiographic and Histological Evidence of Postnatal Hippocampal Neurogenesis in Rats." *J. Comp. Neur.* 124,3 (June 1965):319–336.

Andersen, P. and Lomo, T. "Control of Hippocampal Output by Afferent Volley Frequency." In *Progress in Brain Research, 27: Structure and Function of the Limbic System.* Edited by W. R. Adey and T. Tokizane, pp. 400–412. Amsterdam: Elsevier, 1967.

Blackstad, T. W. et al. "Distribution of Hippocampal Mossy Fibers in the Rat. An Experimental Study with Silver Impregnation Methods." *J. Comp. Neur.* 138 (1970):433–450.

Cragg, B. G. "Autonomic Functions of the Hippocampus." *Nature* 182 (1958):675.

Cragg, B. G. "Olfactory and Other Afferent Connections of the Hippocampus in the Rabbit, Rat, and Cat." *Exp. Neurol.* 3 (1961):588–600.

Cragg, B. G. and Hamlyn, L. H. "Some Commissural and Septal Connexions of the Hippocampus in the Rabbit. A Combined Histological and Electrical Study." *J. Physiol.* 135 (1957):460–485.

DeJong, R. N.; Itabashi, H. H.; and Olson, J. R. "Memory Loss Due to Hippocampal Lesions." *Arch. Neurol.* 20 (1969):339–448.

Dichter, M. and Spencer, W. A. "Penicillin-induced Interictal Discharges from the Cat Hippocampus. I: Characteristics and Topographical Features." *J. of Neurophysiology* 32, 5 (1969):649–662.

Dichter, M. and Spencer, W. A. "Penicillin-induced Interictal Discharges from the Cat Hippocampus. II: Mechanisms Underlying Origin and Restriction." *J. of Neurophysiology* 32, 5 (1969):663–687.

Douglas, R. J. "The Hippocampus and Behavior." *Psychol. Bull.* 67 (1967):416–422.

Ellen, P. and Powell, E. W. "Differential Conditioning of Septum and Hippocampus." *Exp. Nerol.* 16 (1962):162–171.

Ford, J. G.; Bremmer, F. J.; and Richie, W. R. "The Effect of Hours of Food Deprivation on Hippocampal Theta Rhythm." *Neuropsychologia* 8 (1970):65–73.

Gloor, P.; Vera, C. L.; and Sperti, L. "Electrophysiological Studies of Hippocampal Neurons. I: Configuration and Laminar Analysis of the 'Resting' Potential Gradient of the Main Transient Responses to Perforant Path, Fimbrical, Mossy Fiber Voltage, and Spontaneous Activity." *Electroenceph. Clin. Neurophysiol.* 15 (1963):353–378.

Gloor, P.; Vera, C. L.; and Sperti, L. "Electrophysiological Studies of Hippocampal Neurons. II. Secondary Post-synaptic Events in Single Cell Units." *Electroenceph. Clin. Neurophysiol..* 15 (1963):379–402.

Gloor, P.; Vera, C. L.; and Sperti, L. "Electrophysiological Studies of Hippocampal Neurons. III: Responses of Hippocampal Neurons to Repetitive Perforant Path Volleys." *Electroenceph. Clin. Neurophysiol.* 17 (1964):353–369.

Gogolak, G. et al. "Septal Cell Activity in Rabbit under Reticular Activity." *Brain Res.* 5 (1967):508–510.

Grossberg, S. "Neural Pattern Discrimination." *J. Theor. Biol.* 27 (May 1970): 291–337.

Hailman, J. P. "How an Instinct Is Learned." *Scientific American* 221, 6 (December 1969):98–106.

Kandel, E. R.; Spencer, W. A.; and Brinley, F. J. "Electrophysiology of Hippocampal Neurons. I: Sequential Invasion and Synaptic Organization. II: After-potentials and Repetitive Firing." *J. Neurophysiol.* 24 (1961):225–285.

Kilmer, W. L. and McLardy, T. "A Model of Hippocampal CA3 Circuitry." *International J. Neuroscience* 1 (1970):107–112.

McLardy, T. "Intravital Non-toxic Sulfide Loading of Synaptic Zinc in Hippocampus." *Exper. Neurol.* 28 (1970):416–419.

Lorente dé No, R. "Studies on the Structure of the Cerebral Cortex. II: Continuation of the Study of the Ammonic System." *J. Psychol. Neurol.* 46 (1934):113–177.

McLardy, T. "Neglected Key to Hippocampal Function." *Electroenceph. Clin. Neurophysiol.* 14 (1962):296.

McLardy, T. "Neurosynicitial Aspects of the Hippocampal Mossy Fibre System." *Confinia Neurologica* 20 (1960):1–17.

McLardy, T. "Second Hippocampal Zinc-rich Synaptic System." *Nature* 201, 4914 (1964):92–93.

McLardy, T. "Zinc Enzymes and the Hippocampal Mossy Fibre System." *Nature* 194, 4829 (1962):300–302.

McLardy, T. "Some Cell and Fibre Peculiarities of Uncal Hippocampus." In *Progress in Brain Research* 3. Edited by W. Bargmann and J. P. Schade. pp. 71–88. Amsterdam: Elsevier, 1963.

Nauta, W. J. H. "Hippocampal Projections and Related Neural Pathways to the Mid-brain in the Cat." *Brain* 81 (1958):319–340.

Orbach, J.; Milner, B.; and Rasmussen, T. "Learning and Retention in Monkeys after Amygdala-hippocampus Resection." *Arch. Neurol.* 3 (1960):230–251.

Oswald, I. "Human Brain Protein, Drugs, and Dreams." *Nature* 223 (1969):893–897.

Pestche, H. and Stumpf, C. H. "Hippocampal Arousal and Seizure Activity in Rabbits; Toposcopical and Microelectrode Aspects." *Physiologie de l'Hippocampe* No. 107. Paris: Center for Scientific Research, 1962:121–134.

Porter, R.; Adey, W. R.; and Brown, T. S. "Effects of Small Hippocampal Lesions on Locally Recorded Potentials and on Behavior Performance in the Cat." *Exp. Neurol.* 10 (1964):216–235.

Powell, T. P. S.; Guillery, R. W.; and Cowan, W. M. "A Quantitative Study of the Fornix-mamillo-thalmic System." *J. Anat.* 91 (1957): 419–435.

Radulovacki, M. and Adey, W. R. "The Hippocampus and the Orienting Reflex." *Exp. Neurol.* 12 (1965):68–83.

Raisman, G. "A Comparison of the Mode of Termination of the Hippocampal and Hypothalmic Afferents to the Septal Nuclei as Revealed by Electron Microscopy of Degeneration." *Exp Brain Res.* 7 (1969): 317–343.

Smythies, J. R. *The Neurological Foundations of Psychiatry.* New York: Academic Press, 1966.

Spencer, W. A. and Kandel, E. R. "Hippocampel Neuron Responses to Selective Activation of Recurrent Collaterals of Hippocampofugal Axons." *Exp. Neurol.* 4 (1961):149.

Spencer, W. A. and Kandel, E. R. "Electrophysiology of Hippocampal Neurons. III: Firing Level and Time Constant." IV: Fast Prepotentials." *J. Neurophysiol.* 24 (1961):225–285.

Valenstein, E. S. "Steroid Hormones and the Neuropsychology of Development." In *The Neuropsychology of Development.* Edited by Robert L. Isaacson. New York: John Wiley & Sons Inc., 1968.

Valenstein, E. S. and Nauta, W. J. H. "A Comparison of the Distribution of the Fornix System in the Rat, Guinea Pig, Cat, and Monkey." *J. of Comp. Neurology* 113, 3 (1959):337–363.

Valenstein, E. S. and Valenstein, T. "Interaction of Positive and Negative Reinforcing Neural Systems." *Science* 145 (1964):1456–1458. Also in *Brain and Behavior 4: Adaption.* Edited by K. H. Pribram. New York: Penguin Books, 1969.

Walter, W. G. "Slow Potential Changes in the Human Brain Associated with Expectancy, Decision, and Intention." *Electroenceph. and Clin. Neurophysiol.* 26 (1967):123–129.

Walter, W. G. et al. "Contingent Negative Variation: an Electric Sign of Sensory-motor Association and Expectancy in the Human Brain." *Nature* 203 (1964):380–384.

Ward, Alan J. "Early Infantile Autism: Diagnosis, Etiology, and Treatment." *Psychological Bulletin* 73, 5 (1970):350–362.

Neuromime Nets as the Basis for the Predictive Component of Robot Brains*

ANTHONY N. MUCCIARDI, Ph.D.

Adaptronics, Inc.
McLean, Virginia

Introduction

A universal desire among cyberneticians is to gain an understanding of the operations of the brain so that that knowledge may be applied to the design of artificial brains, as in robots. While this goal still eludes us, there is a sufficient body of knowledge available to guide the design of robotic brains. Living nervous systems, viewed as computing devices, have the following broad properties:

1. reliable computation with unreliable components;
2. ability to process many variables simultaneously;
3. ability to choose relevant variables from a large group of variables;

*The support and aid of the entire Adaptronics staff is gratefully acknowledged. My special thanks to Elsie C. Orr, who created the programs for both of the example problems presented in Section 4. I am indebted to my colleagues, Roger L. Barron and Lewey O. Gilstrap, for many of the ideas presented in this paper. Most of the original concepts of this class of neuromime nets are the work of Lewey O. Gilstrap. Certain portions of this work were supported by Pratt & Whitney Aircraft Division, United Aircraft Corporation.

4. ability to solve problems on the basis of examples, or by trial and error;

5. adaptability to changing conditions.

All of these properties except the first can be duplicated in robotic brains by using two widely known techniques: *surface approximation* and *surface searching*. The first property, reliable computation with unreliable components, can also be duplicated by using a combination of two other techniques: modular construction and *stochastic computation* (encoding analog, or sign and magnitude, information in pulse density signals and computing with these pulse density signals).

A general approach to computation called *adaptive computation* has evolved during the past two decades. Since hardware versions of adaptive computation devices are "programmmed" by input data rather than being restructured on the basis of an assumed model of the problem that gave rise to the data, the approach is also referred to as *self-programming, or self-organizing*. Strictly speaking no system can be truly self-programming," for the existence of a self-programming system would imply behavior independent of external inputs. A more accurate description for adaptive computers would be "environmentally programmed."

This paper deals with an adaptive computation device, a neuromime network, which is modularly constructed of two-input, nonlinear building block elements connected in a series-parallel fashion. Each element in the net generates a nonlinear transformation of its sensed inputs. It is shown that a multinomial description of the environment which accounts for nonlinear interactions of the sensed inputs is not only practical but highly desirable. Modeling is accomplished by fitting a hypersurface (the network's input-output function) to the input data or by fitting hypersurfaces to the boundaries separating classes of data in a multidimensional sensor space.

A guided accelerated random search (GARS) is shown to be an effective and efficient network training procedure. GARS is superior to a steepest ascents search because it can avoid becoming trapped on local extrema and because its computation time increases approximately linearly with dimension. Two key parameters of the GARS algorithm—the step size probability distribution and the fraction of terms undergoing change—are discussed.

The performance assessment function, which is the criterion used to guide the search algorithm, is a critical factor in network training. A number of candidate performance assessment functions are presented and their merits outlined. The main conclusion is that the performance function must provide analog information, be sensitive to trends in the data, and be independent of the number of samples in the training set.

Some of the properties of neuromime nets constructed of the two-input nonlinear modular elements have been described by Gilstrap.[9-13] A historical review of neuron modeling and neuromime net studies is presented in Ref. 9. Brooks[7,8] was among the first to propose random methods for seeking maxima and to show their great advantage over steepest ascent techniques, particularly for large-dimensional problems. Important contributions in random search techniques also were made by Gurin,[14] Matyas,[16] Rastrigin,[17] and Yudin.[18] Barron[1,3] has incorporated a GARS algorithm into a self-organizing control scheme. Reference 4 contains a survey of parameter search methods.

Modeling and Prediction

Introduction

Stafford Beer has stated that cybernetics begins where the possibility of mathematical description of the controlled plant terminates.[6] Ivakhnenko[15] has further stated that "the recognition systems and devices constructed with them as the basis (self-learning sensors, predicting filters, self-organizing quantizers, etc.) will without doubt be the primary apparatus of cybernetic control, which really begins where the possibility of mathematical description of the plant and the disturbances acting on it ends."

These statements reflect the fact that the really interesting physical processes are usually those for which the explicit governing equations are either unknown or computationally unfeasible to solve. The neuromime nets presented below are ideally suited for this class of problems, since no *a priori* knowledge of the interactions among the inputs is required. Indeed, the net's task is to find the main interactions and their relative strengths (as reflected in the magnitude of the assigned weight) by training.

The two tools required for solving modeling and prediction problems are the techniques of *hypersurface approximation* and *hypersurface searching*. The former is the algebraic model of the system parameterized by a set of (network) coefficients, and the latter is the technique for finding the best values of these coefficients. A neuromime net has a hypersurface approximation, or curve-fitting capability; therefore, all problems that are reducible to fitting a curve or interrogating the fit to obtain outputs for given inputs can be handled by the class of neuromime nets presented below.

Figure 1 shows a generalized block diagram of a modeling-prediction network. The net output, δ, is a function of the N-dimensional input vector, X, and the D-dimensional internal net coefficient vector, W. (In general, $N < D$.) The $(D + 1)$-dimensional hypersurface, $\delta = \delta(X,W)$, is the network model of the physical process which generated the data X. $\delta_j = \delta(X_j,W)$ is the predicted outcome for the jth input vector. The net in Fig. 1 nonlinearly transforms the N-dimensional

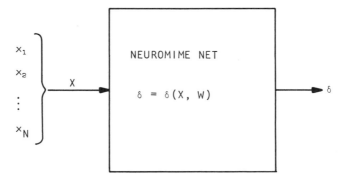

Fig. 1.   Generalized Block Diagram of a Modeling-Prediction Neuromime Network.

input space into a 1-dimensional space. If more than one output is desired, the structure shown in Fig. 2 is used. In this case, one net is used for each of the K desired outputs. Each net in Fig. 2 is trained to extract the information from the input vector which is necessary to yield the best estimate of its particular parameter.

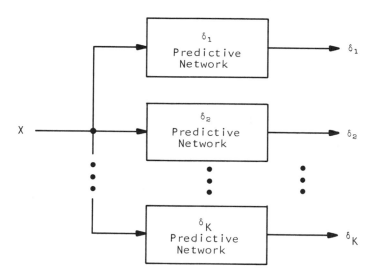

Fig. 2.   Neuromime Nets Structured to Generate Multiple Outputs.

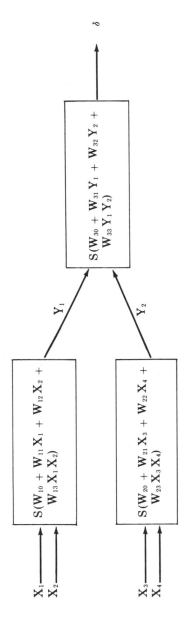

$$Y_1 = S(W_{10} + W_{11}X_1 + W_{12}X_2 + W_{13}X_1X_2)$$
$$Y_2 = S(W_{20} + W_{21}X_3 + W_{22}X_4 + W_{23}X_3X_4)$$
$$\delta = S(W_{30} + W_{31}Y_1 + W_{32}Y_2 + W_{33}Y_1Y_2)$$
$$= S[W_{30} + W_{31} S(W_{10} + W_{11}X_1 + W_{12}X_2 + W_{13}X_1X_2)$$
$$+ W_{32} S(W_{20} + W_{21}X_3 + W_{22}X_4 + W_{23}X_3X_4)$$
$$+ W_{33} S^2(W_{10} + W_{11}X_1 + W_{12}X_2 + W_{13}X_1X_2)$$
$$(W_{20} + W_{21}X_3 + W_{22}X_4 + W_{23}X_3X_4)]$$

$$= V_0 + V_1X_1 + V_2X_2 + V_3X_3 + V_4X_4 + V_5X_1X_2 + V_6X_1X_3$$
$$+ V_7X_1X_4 + V_8X_2X_3 + V_9X_2X_4 + V_{10}X_3X_4$$
$$+ V_{11}X_1X_2X_3 + V_{12}X_1X_2X_4 + V_{13}X_1X_3X_4$$
$$+ V_{14}X_2X_3X_4 + V_{15}X_1X_2X_3X_4$$

Fig. 3.   A Two-Layered Net which Implements a Complete Multilinear Multinomial of Its Four Inputs.

where:

$$V_0 = S^2W_{30} + S^2W_{31}W_{10} + S^2W_{32}W_{20} + S^3W_{33}W_{10}W_{20}$$
$$V_1 = S^2W_{31}W_{11} + S^3W_{33}W_{11}W_{20}$$
$$V_2 = S^2W_{31}W_{12} + S^3W_{33}W_{12}W_{20}$$
$$V_3 = S^2W_{32}W_{21} + S^3W_{33}W_{10}W_{21}$$
$$V_4 = S^2W_{32}W_{22} + S^3W_{33}W_{10}W_{22}$$
$$V_5 = S^2W_{31}W_{13} + S^3W_{33}W_{13}W_{20}$$
$$V_6 = S^3W_{33}W_{11}W_{21}$$
$$V_7 = S^3W_{33}W_{11}W_{21}$$
$$V_8 = S^3W_{33}W_{12}W_{21}$$
$$V_9 = S^3W_{33}W_{12}W_{22}$$
$$V_{10} = S^2W_{32}W_{33} + S^3W_{33}W_{10}W_{23}$$
$$V_{11} = S^3W_{33}W_{13}W_{21}$$
$$V_{12} = S^3W_{33}W_{13}W_{12}$$
$$V_{13} = S^3W_{33}W_{11}W_{23}$$
$$V_{14} = S^3W_{33}W_{12}W_{23}$$
$$V_{15} = S^3W_{33}W_{13}W_{23}$$

Multinomial Description of Physical Processes

The network models a physical process by the representation

$$\delta = \delta(X,W). \tag{1}$$

Due to the connectivity of the nonlinear modular elements, Eq. (1) is a multinominal in the inputs x_i. The two-layered net shown in Fig. 3, for example, implements a complete multilinear multinomial in its four inputs (s is a scaling factor). As shown in the figure, this is a function in which all possible cross products of the inputs appear, and no input appears to a power greater than one. The derivative of δ with respect to x_i would, in this case, be a constant and hence independent of x_i. Note that the 2^4 terms of a four-variable multilinear multinomial would be written as shown in Fig. 3, with the v's denoting the coefficients. The net implements this algebraic expression, but the net uses 12 coefficients rather than 16. However, the 16 v's are nonlinearly dependent on the 12 net w's, as shown in the figure. The net in Fig. 4 implements a multinomial in which each x_i appears to all powers up to three, but not all possible cross products appear. Therefore, the complexity of the function implemented, the hypersurface, is controlled both by the net connectivity pattern and by the depth (number of layers) of the net. Other techniques which are used to fit hypersurfaces are examined below.

Multiple Linear Regression

A simple method used to model a process is to fit a linear hypersurface to the data points

$$\delta_j = \sum_{i=1}^{N} w_i x_{ji} + w_0 \tag{2}$$

where δ_j is the predicted outcome for given x_j. The weights are chosen to satisfy the criterion

$$\min P = \sum_{j=1}^{T} (z_j - \delta_j)^2 \tag{3}$$

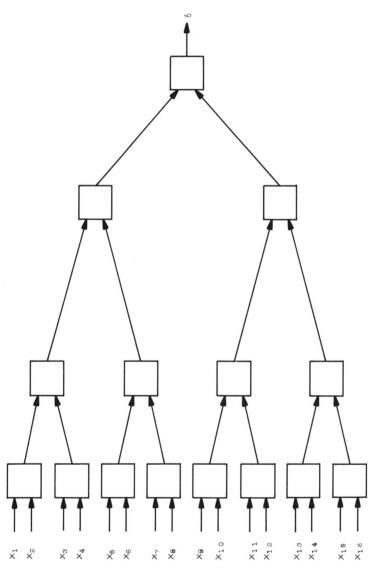

Fig. 4.   Four-Layered Triangular Net.

where z_j is the (known) true outcome for X_j, δ_j is the predicted outcome obtained from Eq. (2), and T is the number of data points. A matrix inversion technique is used to find the w's.

Multiple linear regression can be used whenever the system equation is linear in the unknown *coefficients*. Even though Eq. (4) is nonlinear in the x_i for $p_i=1$

$$\delta_j = \sum_{i=1}^{T} w_i x_{ji}{}^{p_i} + w_0 \tag{4}$$

it is the equation of a hyperplane in the $(N+1)$-dimensional W-space and is thus solvable by the same procedure used to solve Eq. (2).

Nonlinear Regression

No general deterministic approach exists for finding the weights when they appear nonlinearly in the model equation. An example is the function implemented by the net shown in Fig. 3. The element in the second layer creates cross products of the weights (coefficients) in the resultant input-output equation. A search algorithm has to be employed to find the set of weights satisfying Eq. (3).

Advantage of Neuromime Net Modeling Over Classical Fitting Techniques

The two major problems in constructing a nonlinear algebraic function with a large number of independent variables are: (1) the unfeasibility of writing out a multinomial of high degree in more than a few variables, and (2) the unfeasibility of finding the coefficient values of such a multinomial by conventional matrix-inversion methods. The solution to these two problems as provided by the neuromime net is to approximate the multinomial using a modular computing element and to find the coefficients by a stochastic approximation to the desired values using a guided random search (training) algorithm.

Because of its series-parallel connection of modular elements, a net is an economical method of implementing the general nonlinear multinomial function. The net shown in Fig. 3 implements a complete multilinear multinomial of its four inputs, yet it requires 12 rather than $2^4 = 16$ coefficients. Similarly, the triangular net shown in Fig. 4 implements a complete multilinear multinomial of its 16 inputs and requires $4 \times 15 = 60$ coefficients rather than $2^{16} = 65,536$ coefficients. The number of terms in a multinomial of degree p in N variables is $(p + N)! / p! N!$. If a 24-variable problem were to be fitted with a 5th-degree expression, $(24 + 5)!/24!5! = 118,755$ terms would be required. A modular rectangular network of 12 rows and 6 layers giving 72 elements will implement a 5th-degree expression. However, only $4 \times 72 = 288$ coefficients are required.

When comparing the ratios 12/16, 60/65,536, and 288/118,755 of terms in the two multilinear and the 5th-degree multinomials, respectively, it must be noted that while the net implements the proper algebraic expression, the resultant function has fewer degrees of freedom than would be the case if the same function were written out giving each term a unique weight (as shown in Fig. 3). The above ratios in fact are the ratios of the degrees of freedom between the network-implemented functions and the same function written with unique weights. Thus, the coefficients of the terms in the multinomial will be functions of the much smaller set of network coefficients: the 12, 60, and 288, respectively. However, the net provides many degrees of freedom, and almost any desired set of coefficients of the terms in the multinomial can be obtained. It is possible therefore to approximate a highly nonlinear function of many input variables in a very economical fashion using neuromime net modeling.

Properties of a Multinomial Description
of a Physical Process

The two theoretical questions that are traditionally asked about solutions, existence and uniqueness, are largely irrelevant in the network approach to modeling. Since a set of coefficients will always be produced by the search (training) procedure, the question of existence is replaced by the practical question of quality of the solution. If the obtained coefficients are not unique, i.e., if two or more different sets of coefficients give about the same error rates, the solution with fewer variables is probably more physically meaningful, although either solution could be used for prediction.

Adaptive Neuromime Network Characteristics

Network Structure

Basic Components

The type of network studied in this paper is shown in Fig. 5. The basic component of the neuromime network is the two-input, one-output element with the transfer function

$$y = s(w_0 + w_1x_1 + w_2x_2 + w_3x_1x_2) \qquad (5)$$

where x_1, x_2 are the two inputs, y is the output, w_1 are the adjustable coefficients, and s is a scaling factor. All the variables are continuous and, for convenience, are scaled to the $[-1, +1]$ range. (The output is scaled by the s term.) Uniform connectivity patterns are used between layers, and layer ℓ receives inputs from layer $\ell - 1$.

An element with the transfer function given in Eq. (5) can synthesize Boolean functions as well as continuous functions of its inputs. If x_1 and x_2 are binary, any Boolean function of x_1, x_2 can be obtained by thresholding y:

$$(6)$$

$$z = \begin{cases} 1, & \text{if } y \geq 0 \\ 0, & \text{if } y < 0 \end{cases}$$

where the coefficients, w_1, take on any continuous value. By suitable choices of the w_1, any of the $2^{2^2} = 16$ Boolean func-

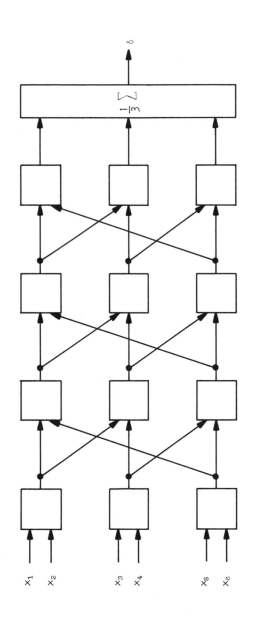

Fig. 5. Uniform Spiral Twelve-Element Network.

tions of x_1, x_2 can be obtained. In the multivariate case, arbitrary logical functions of the N variables can be obtained by thresholding the ouput of the nonlinear multinomial. While each element in the net can synthesize all 2^{2^2} Boolean functions of its two inputs, it is not generally possible for the net to synthesize all 2^{2^N} Boolean functions of its N inputs. It would require $2^N/4 = 2^{N-2}$ modular elements, properly interconnected for the net to generate the 2^N necessary coefficients. However, the approximation to multivariate logic functions obtained with a net of smaller size can be sufficiently close for many physical problems.

Connectivity: Cross-coupling and degree of function implemented

The network connectivity patterns studied to date have all employed a feed-forward technique, so that layer ℓ receives its inputs from layer $\ell-1$. Gilstrap[9,10] has found that the performance of feed forward nets is relatively unaffected by its connectivity pattern as long as the condition he terms "*sufficiently rich*" is fulfilled. A network connectivity is sufficiently rich if each element in the input layer has at least one path to each element in the output layer. For example, the net in Fig. 4 is a uniform spiral with a pitch of 1: elements from a given layer are fed into the same row in the next layer and to an element one row lower. Elements in the last row wrap around to connect with elements in the first row. At the third column, each of the six input variables is cross-multiplied with all others, including itself. The fourth layer, in this case, provides additional cross-coupling of the inputs as well as raising each of the x_i to one additional power. With a sufficiently rich connectivity pattern, an L-layered net implements an $(L-1)-$ degree hypersurface in the N input variables.

Transformation properties of layered nets

The outputs of the first layer are components of an $(N/2)-$

dimensional vector which is the nonlinear transformation of the N—dimensional input vector implemented by layer $\ell 1$. For a given set of weights, the first layer maps the set of input vectors into the (N/2)—dimensional space $\mathcal{L}^{(1)}$, the second layer maps the points in $\mathcal{L}^{(1)}$ into $\mathcal{L}^{(2)}$, for a given set of weights, and so on. The last layer maps $\mathcal{L}^{(L)}$ into the K— dimensional output space. The purpose of the first $\ell -1$ layers is to transform the original input space into a space $\mathcal{L}^{(\ell-1)}$ in which the points associated with a particular decision are more tightly clustered (i.e., their intraclass distances are smaller) than they were in the original N—dimensional sensor space.

Network Training Algorithm

Unguided and guided searches

Neuromime nets have not been more widely used for modeling physical processes because of the lack of an efficient training algorithm. Barron[3,5] has argued that a guided accelerated random search is an effective and efficient training algorithm for globally training a network. The following general description is from Ref. 5.

> The two fundamental types of parameter search algorithm are the *unguided* searches, both systematic and purely random, and the *guided* searches, which use performance trend information to quicken their convergence. The most familiar of the guided searches is the classical steepest descent method. With this method, the gradient of the system performance surface is computed from systematic explorations about the existing operating point and the next step is conducted in this gradient direction. The past decade has seen increasing attention given to *guided random* searches. Here, information acquired during the search is used to control the probability distribution of future steps. Two versions of the guided random method are employed. The simpler of these uses constant step magnitudes, the directions of the steps being statistically governed by performance trend data. This method is applicable to self-organizing (short-term memory) systems. In some cases, the step magnitudes are varied as a deterministic function of error levels.
> The other, more general, version of the guided random search is a stochastic process in which the parameter vector, W, at time t is taken in the form

$$W(t) = W^* + C(t)\ \xi(t) \tag{7}$$

where W^* represents the mean of W, usually the "best-to-date" value from prior experiments in the search, i.e., W^* is the current estimate of the best W; C is a transformation matrix that is usually modified as information is gained and system performance changes; and ξ is a normal random vector, often defined for convenience as having a unit covariance matrix. The algorithm characterized generally by Eq. (7), with W^* and C being continually adjusted so as to guide further explorations, is a powerful tool in multidimensional, multimodal surface search problems.

Numerous investigators have examined one or more characteristics of the guided random search, making comparisons with the gradient search, and Barron has summarized these as follows.

1. The guided random search converges faster for spaces of high dimensionality.
2. It is an effective search for multimodal surfaces (the gradient search is basically suited only for unimodal surfaces).
3. It is an effective search for time-varying surfaces.
4. It is more effective in the presence of sensor noise.
5. It searches simultaneously on all parameters.
6. The guided random search can be mechanized simply and in software versions takes less storage and less computation time.

Appendix A in Ref. 5 presents a survey of parameter space search algorithms, with particular emphasis on methods of guided random search. Because the principal factor governing the convergence time of a guided random search is the amount of resolution required in the terminal part of the search, no special insight is required in selecting the starting parameter values.

Several forms of guided random search offering great speed and flexibility are described in Ref. 5. The most powerful of these searches, known as the *guided accelerated random search* (GARS), adjusts its own first and second statistical moments so as to speed search convergence. The first statistical moment is the mean of the experimental step, while the second moment determines the variance of this step about its mean. The ratio of the number of steps required, on the average, for convergence of the accelerated random search to the number of steps required by a representative gradient search (on a unimodal surface) is approximately $\dfrac{\log_2 D}{2D}$ where D, the dimensionality of the search process, is the sum of the number of all the independent parameters plus dependent (criteria) variables. The above ratio, which is an estimate first offered by L. O. Gilstrap, Jr., applies whenever the number of independent parameters is more than three.

Elements of an accelerated guided random search

The following description of the accelerated random search is excerpted from Ref. 11.

> Let $W = (W_0, W_1, \ldots, W_{D-1})$ be a point in the D = dimensional parameter space being searched. Associated with each point in this space is a performance assessment score, $P(W)$, which is a measure of the value or utility of that point. Typically, the objective of any search is to find the point, W^*, which yields the maximum (or minimum) value of P. Frequently, there are constraints on the permissible choices for W; among the simplest of these constraints is an upper and lower bound on each of the variables being searched. One consequence of a constraint of this type is that the maximum or minimum found within a permissible region may not correspond to the theoretically optimum point, since that point might lie outside the permissible region. Also, there is, in general, no guarantee that the point W^* in a bounded space is unique, but uniqueness is not always an essential characteristic of a solution to a search problem.
>
> The rule for halting the search process, called the *stop rule*, may depend on such practical matters as having a fixed time in which to perform the search or may be determined from the score function itself. For example, if a minimum value of the score function is sought and if that minimum value is zero, then the search can be halted if a randomly selected set of coefficients produces a score that is arbitrarily close to zero.
>
> In an unguided (or parallel) search, the sequence of trial points, $(W1), W(2), \ldots, W(k)$, is selected according to a fixed formula or algorithm which does not take into account the results of each trial point. In a guided search, the score from one trial point is used to guide the selection of the next trial point [as shown in Eq. (7)] and the search becomes an iterative procedure.

Most of the guided random searches are modifications to the basic, unguided random search. In the unguided random search, points are selected at random from the total space being searched; scores are noted for all of the points and, after k trials, the best estimate for W^* is simply the point corresponding to the maximum score obtained during the k trials. Brooks[7] has shown that the probability, $p(f)$, that W^* lies in a certain fraction, f, of the total space after k trials is

$$p(f) = 1 - (1 - f)^k \qquad (8)$$

which approaches unity as k increases indefinitely. The expected number of trials to achieve a given level of confidence that the maximum lies in a fraction, f, of the total space can be obtained from Eq. (8).

$$k = \frac{\log [1 - p(f)]}{\log (1 - f)} \qquad (9)$$

In the basic, unguided random search, the sampling of points is obtained from a rectangular distribution, and no use is made of information gained on prior trials.

Although the unguided random search is slow compared to all guided searches, it is independent of the modality of P, i.e., it can be used to find the global maximum of P and is not subject to "trapping" by local maxima. Because of this desirable feature of the unguided random search, several modifications to the algorithm have been devised to improve the rate at which it converges. The simplest of these modifications is the change from sampling from a rectangular distribution for each variable to sampling from a normal distribution centered about the point corresponding to the maximum score obtained from the beginning of the search to the current trial. This search is guided, but it makes minimal use of prior information. Additional modifications to this algorithm include reversal, hill climbing, acceleration, and smoothing of the terminal search. These modifications assume continuity of P but are so designed that the search reverts to an unguided search if continuity does not hold and no correlations can be found in the accumulated information.

Reversal is based upon the principle that the opposite of downhill is usually uphill. Hence, if a given step, $\Delta W(k)$, produces a worsening of the score, $\Delta W(k+1)$ is set to $-\Delta W(k)$. If this step also produces no improvement in score, then the step $\Delta W(k + 2)$ is taken at random.

Once a direction is found that produces an improvement in score, either by a random trial or by reversal, the continuation of trials in the same direction is called simply *hill climbing*. Although an uphill direction selected at random will not, in general, coincide with the direction of the maximum slope, improvement in performance may be noted for several steps in any uphill direction. Since the expected number of experiments required to find an uphill direction (not necessarily the maximum slope) is about one-half, then hill climbing is seen to be a means for exploiting this limited information acquired by random trials.

The information as to whether a given direction is uphill or downhill is of limited value, and it should be exploited as quickly and efficiently as possible. This can be done by lengthening the average step size as long as performance continues to improve. Both arithmetic and geometric progressions of step sizes have been used in random searches during the hill-climbing phase. This increase in step size at each step is called *acceleration* of the earth. In a geometric acceleration, e.g., doubling the step size each step, large overshoots can occur and Matyas[16] has employed a deceleration to come as close as possible to the highest point in the given random direction. However, it would appear that deceleration falls in the category of effort that produces diminishing returns. Since the highest point along a randomly selected uphill direction will not, in general, coincide with W^*, the highest attainable point, a new direction would have to be established after deceleration in any event, and the number of steps needed for deceleration can usually produce as much improvement in a new random direction starting from the point just prior to overshooting. Matyas also employed a bound on the largest possible step size to prevent large overshoots, but this also appears to be an unnecessary refinement if deceleration is not employed. However, bounds may be employed to avoid large changes in the experimentation, which can be desirable for some types of physical process control.

Although bounding the maximum possible step size does not apparently speed up the random search, control of the average step does appear to provide some improvement in the terminal search. Scaling of the average step size as a function of the score provides smoothing of the search in the region near the maximum as well as improving the speed of the search. In searching for minima using, for example, least squares score functions, average step size can be set proportional to the best-to-date score to provide automatic and continuous scaling of step size. The constant of proportionality can be adjusted for each problem. In searching for maxima, scaling can be inversely proportional to the score or can be any convenient, monotonically decreasing function of score.

In use, the accelerated random search which employs reversal, hill climbing and acceleration have been found to be fast and effective means for searching multi-dimensional spaces. Barron[1] has reported that reasonably close convergence has been attained in searching spaces of 400 dimensions in about 250 trials using only reversal and hill climbing.

Properties of the guided random search: step size and activity factor control

As shown in Eq. (7), the next trial point is some step from the best point to date

$$W(k+1) = W^* + \Delta W(k+1) \qquad (10)$$

where the step $C(k+1)\,\xi\,(k+1)$ is written as $\Delta W(k+1)$.
$\Delta W(k+1)$ is chosen from a probability distribution centered
at zero and whose variance is a function of either the iteration
number or the performance deficit, $\Delta P = P_{max} - P^*$, where
P^* is the value obtained using W^* and is the best score to date.
The step size distribution is obtained by normalizing the sum
of R uniformly distributed random numbers, r_i, and by scaling
the result to the $[-1, +1]$ range

$$p(\Delta W) = 2\left(\frac{1}{R}\sum_{i=1}^{R} r_i\right) - 1. \qquad (11)$$

The distribution $\dfrac{1}{R}\displaystyle\sum_{i=1}^{R} r_i$ is rectangular for $R = 1$, triangular

for $R = 2$, and resembles a normal distribution for larger
values of R. It tends to normality as R increases as predicted
by the Central Limit Theorem. Since the variance of the above
distribution is inversely proportional to R, the magnitude of
the step size is controlled by controlling R, and hence the
variance of the distribution.

If the score associated with $W(k)$, P_k, exceeds the best-to-
date, P^*, W^* is set equal to the newly found best point and the
search is accelerated in this direction:

$$W^* = W(k) \qquad (12a)$$

and

$$\Delta W(k+j) = 2^j \cdot \Delta W(k) \qquad (12b)$$

for $j \le Q$, where Q is a constant. When $j > Q$, the step increments are computed by

$$\Delta W(k+j) = 2^Q \cdot \Delta W(k) \qquad (13)$$

as long as $P_{k+j} > P^*$, P^* is reset to P_{k+j}, and the accelerated
climbing phase continues. At the first occurrence of $P_{k+j} < P^*$,
the search reverts back to random explorations about the new
W^* point.

The concept of a "reflecting barrier" is used to keep each

parameter within its preset boundaries during the search. Every time $W(t)$ is computed from Eq. (10) each $w_i(t)$ is compared to its preset boundaries, $w_{i\,max}$ and $w_{i\,min}$. If the computed $w_i(t)$ is outside these limits by some amount, it is reflected back inside the region by the same amount. For example, if $w_i^* = 0.7$ and $\Delta w_i(t + 1) = 0.4$, from Eq. (10), $w_i(t + 1) = 1.1$. If the range of w_i is $[-1, +1]$, the computed value exceeds the region by 0.1, so it is reflected back by this amount. Thus, the actual value used is $w_i = 1 - 0.1 = 0.9$. This is rigorously stated as

$$w_i(t+1) = \begin{cases} w_i(t+1), \\ \qquad \text{if } w_{i\,min} \leq w_i(t+1) \leq w_{i\,max} \\ w_{i\,min} + \text{mod}(w_{i\,min} - w_i(t+1), B), \\ \qquad \text{if } w_i(t+1) < w_{i\,min} \\ w_{i\,max} - \text{mod}(w_i(t+1) - w_{i\,max}, B), \\ \qquad \text{if } w_i(t+1) > w_{i\,max} \end{cases} \qquad (14)$$

where $B = w_{i\,max} - w_{i\,min}$, and $\text{mod}(a,b) = a - [a/b]\, b$, where $[X]$ denotes the integer whose magnitude does not exceed the magnitude of x and whose sign is the same as x.

An activity factor, α, has been incorporated into the GARS algorithm to enable the system to examine subspaces for the optimum value throughout the search. α is the fraction of the D variables which is adjusted during the random explorations. The identity of the specific αD variables is a random quantity. Analogously to the step size variance, α can be a function of either time (iteration number) or the performance deficit, ΔP. The search process is fairly sensitive to α. Good results have been obtained by using values of α between 0.1 and 0.5.

The multimodal capability of the GARS algorithm can be compromised by decreasing the step size variance too quickly. Intuitively, it seems desirable to decrease the variance as the performance function approaches its maximum value; however, if the variance is permitted to become too small too quickly, GARS may become trapped on a local mode. This may be avoided in one of two ways: (1) by making the variance a function of iteration number rather than a function of ΔP or (2) by selecting ΔW by alternately sampling from a distribution whose variance decreases with trial number and a fixed distribution which allows for larger steps. In the latter case, the random exploratory phase consists of both "coarse tuning" (large explorations about the best-to-date point) and "fine tuning" (small steps about the best-to-date point).

Performance Assessment Criteria

The performance assessment, or score, function is used to guide network training. The performance assessment function should provide analog information about the quality of W and should be independent of the number of training points employed. This insures that the change in performance score due to a single error, $\partial P/\partial\ e_j$, is independent of the number of training points, and, therefore, that the net is sensitive to trends in the data for large training sets. The choice of a performance function must also take into account whether or not the errors involved are time dependent.

For the case of time-independent variables, the device must learn the input-output function over a range of values of the input variables. If $\delta_j = \delta(X_j, W(k))$ is the net output for the jth input vector at some time k in the search procedure, and z_j is the known true output, the score for the kth trial state is obtained by the following candidate functions. A quadratic function of the error follows.

$$\max P_k(X, W(k)) = P_k = -\sum_{j=1}^{T} (z_j - \delta_j)^2 = -\sum_{j=1} e_j^2 \quad (15)$$

A sum of errors to any even power is

$$\max P_k = -\sum_{j=1}^{T} e^{2p}. \quad (16)$$

A weighted summation of the absolute errors is

$$\max P_k = -\sum_{j=1}^{T} (a + b|e_j|). \quad (17)$$

A summation of the inverse absolute errors is

$$\max P_k = \sum_{j=1}^{T} \frac{a}{|e_j| + b}. \quad (18)$$

Because the z_j may change with time in the case where the variables are time-dependent, the above performance function forms do not necessarily apply. P_k evaluated using $W(k)$ and P_{k+j} evaluated some time later using the same $W(k)$ will differ. This is to say that the hypersurface being searched and its optimum point vary with time. In a nonstationary environment, therefore, the training algorithm must be (1) sufficiently sensitive to detect the time shifts of the performance hypersurface and (2) able to track the extremum of the hypersurface. The *search loss*, which is the time (number of iterations) required to locate and track the extremum, has to be held to a small number. These requirements may be expressed as

$$\max P = \frac{1}{k} \sum_{\text{all } k} P_k. \tag{19}$$

Network Training Considerations

Design of a training set: overfitting

The training set is used to determine the coefficients of the hypersurface implemented by the net. It is important to select a training set that is representative of all the data to be ultimately processed. The size of the training set must be selected to avoid the problem of overfitting. Overfitting means that the hypersurface has more degrees of freedom than there are points to be fitted, so that an infinite number of solutions (fits) is possible. Any training algorithm terminates with the first solution found, so there is no guarantee that predictions based on this fit of the hypersurface will be more accurate (on the testing set) than predictions based on a hypersurface at some other location. Overfitting is avoided by using at least as many training points as there are degrees of freedom.

Testing sets and generalization capability

The network generalization capability is best exploited by

(1) controlling the overfitting problem discussed above, (2) insuring that the training set is representative of future data to be processed by the network, and (3) monitoring the performance score on an independent testing set during the training exercise. Whenever a new best-to-date point, W^*, is obtained, the score for the testing set, $P^*_{test}(X_{test}, W^*)$, should be computed. The W^* which produced the largest P^*_{test} is the set of coefficients which will yield the best generalization results.

Adaptive updating of the training set

An important feature of on-line operation of a predictive neuromime network is periodic updating of the training set and subsequent retraining of the network. Consider the case of a net trained to dichotomize the input (sensor) space into regions A and B. Assume the net has been trained to give zero Type I (false alarm: A called B) and zero Type II (false dismissal: B called A) error rates. The hypersurface decision boundary implemented by the net accurately separates the data in the training sets. This hypersurface is the best estimate of the true location of the decision boundary based on the set of training data. A Type II error made during subsequent on-line operation is commonly caused by incorrect location of the decision boundary due to an incomplete (i.e., unrepresentative) initial training set. This type of error implies that the point in question was closer to the true decision boundary than the adjacent members in the B training set. This point is therefore made a member of the B training set, and the net is retrained using the augmented training set. A new location of the decision boundary is found which is the best-to-date estimate of the true decision boundary. This replacement/retraining procedure is repeated whenever there is a Type II error or at predetermined intervals. In this manner the net adaptively updates its information regarding the location of the decision boundary.

Illustrative Examples

Example 1: Location of a Decision Boundary

The objective of this problem was to dichotomize a 6-dimensional sensor space into regions A and B, where A is the set of points whose desired output is positive (i.e., the set of points on the positive side of the decision hypersurface, $\delta > 0$) and B is the set of points whose desired output is negative (i.e., the set of points on the negative side, $\delta < 0$). The data were generated from a simulation of a physical fluid flow process described by the following equations.

$$x_1{}^2 = K_1 x_4 f(x_1, x_2) \tag{20}$$

$$x_5 = \frac{[K_2 + K_3 x_6{}^2 f(x_1, x_2)]^{K_4} + K_5}{K_3 x_6{}^2 g(x_1, x_2)} \tag{21}$$

where x_2, x_4, x_6 are the independent variables and the K's are constants. $f(x_1, x_2)$ and $g(x_1, x_2)$ are nonlinear functions which were generated in tabular form in obtaining the data base. $f(x_1, x_2)$ was one of the net inputs and labeled x_3. The 4-layered net shown in Fig. 4, with 48 adjustable coefficients, was used. This net implements a third-degree hypersurface in the 6-dimensional input space. The function implemented is an incomplete cubic: each input variable appears to the first, second, and third power, with the remaining terms made up of cross products of the input variables. The use of a cubic multinomial is arbitrary; the best test of its sufficiency is the ability of this network to dichotomize the A and B sets accurately. The inputs (x_i), the net coefficients (w_i), and the net output (δ) are continuous and are scaled to the $[-1, +1]$ range.

Generation of the training and testing sets

A representative training set of 96 A and 96 B vectors was generated as follows. The allowable ranges of x_2, x_4, and x_6 were uniformly divided. Two sets of values for x_1, x_3, x_5 were obtained for each set of values of x_2, x_4, and x_6: one set of x_1, x_3, x_5 values in the A region and the other set in the B region. The two values of x_1 were the roots to the quadratic Eq. (20).

The range of x_4 was selected so that both of the x_1 roots would be real and unequal. One value of x_3 was obtained for each value of x_1, and similarly, an x_5 was determined for each value of x_1 and x_3. The larger of the two roots was known from physical considerations to be in the A region and the smaller root in the B region.

The testing set was generated in the same manner, except that x_2, x_4, x_6 were randomly chosen in their $[-1, +1]$ ranges rather than uniformly selected as they had been for the training set.

Training set cluster analysis.

The type of hypersurface used to separate the two regions, the decision boundary, depends on the distribution of the points from both classes in the 6-dimensional input space. If the two classes are linearly separable, a hyperplane is adequate, but if the two classes overlap, a nonlinear hypersurface is required. In this problem the classes were shown to overlap. An estimate of the amount of overlap between the A and B distributions was obtained as follows. The mean vector of the ninety-six points of each class, $\overline{X}_A$ and $\overline{X}_B$, was computed. A line was constructed passing through the two mean points:

$$Y = \overline{X}_A + a(\overline{X}_B - \overline{X}_A) \qquad (22)$$

where Y is the vector comprising the coordinates of any point on the line. Each point from the two classes was perpendicularly projected onto this line, and the coordinates of each point on the line were found:

$$\qquad (23)$$

$$Y = \overline{X}_A + \frac{(X - \overline{X}_A) \cdot (\overline{X}_B - \overline{X}_A)}{(\overline{X}_B - \overline{X}_A)^2} \cdot (\overline{X}_B - \overline{X}_A).$$

A marker point Y' on the line was arbitrarily selected to be to the "left" of $\overline{X}_A$ [i.e., $a < 0$ in Eq. (22)]. The distance from Y' to each Y was computed. If the distributions were linearly separable, the distance from Y' to the furthest A point would have been smaller than the distance to the closest B point. A hyperplane positioned to minimize the overall error rate would misclassify 24 A and six B points in the training set, giving 24.9 percent Type I (false alarm) and 6.3 percent Type II (false dismissal) error rates. The overall error rate using a hyperplane would be 15.6 percent.

Network training

The guided accelerated random search (GARS) algorithm described on pages 172 ff. was used to determine the forty-eight network coefficients in the prediction network. Each of the forty-eight coefficients was initially set equal to zero, and the goal was to find a set of coefficients which maximized the performance function

$$\max P = -\left\{ K_6 \left[\frac{1}{T_A} \sum_{i=1}^{T_A} (-S\delta_{A_i})^2 + \frac{1}{T_B} \sum_{j=1}^{T_B} (-S-\delta_{B_j})^2 \right] + K_7 f_a + K_8 f_d \right\} \tag{24}$$

where K_6, K_7, K_8 are weighting constants; T_A and T_B denote the number of A and B training points, respectively; δ_{A_i} and δ_{B_j} are the net (analog) outpts resulting from the ith A point and j^{th} B point, respectively; f_a and f_d are the false alarm and dismissal rates; and S is a constant. A value of P was computed for each set of forty-eight coefficients determined by GARS, and training was scheduled to continue until (1) the maximal of P $(= 0)$ was achieved or (2) a predetermined number of iterations had been completed.

The performance function given in Eq. (24) can best be viewed by considering each of the three weighted terms. If $K_7 = K_8 = 0$, maximizing P is equivalent to solving two least-squares problems simultaneously, since

$$\frac{1}{T_A} \sum_{i=1}^{T_A} (S-\delta_{A_i})^2 = \begin{array}{l} \text{means square distance of the A} \\ \text{points to some positive point,} \\ + S \end{array} \tag{25}$$

$$\frac{1}{T_B} \sum_{j=1}^{T_B} (-S - \delta_{Bj})^2 = \begin{array}{l}\text{mean square distance of the B points} \\ \text{to some negative point, } -S.\end{array} \quad (26)$$

The hypersurface which maximizes P will dichotomize the space, so that the A points are on the positive side of the hypersurface ($\delta > 0$), and the B points are on the negative side of the hypersurface ($\delta < 0$).

If $K_6 = 0$, the performance measure of Eq. (24) minimizes the average risk associated with erroneous decisions and is therefore a Bayes decision rule. A Bayes decision rule is

$$\min P = \sum_{j=1}^{M} b_j \, p(X|j) \, p(j) \quad (27)$$

where M is the number of classes, b_j is the penalty for errroneously deciding in favor of class j, $p(X|j)$ is the conditional probability density function of class j at point X, and $p(j)$ is the *a priori* probability of class j. Minimizing P is equivalent to maximizing $-P$, so that Eq. (27) becomes

$$\max(-P) = b_A \, p(X \epsilon B|A) \, p(A) + b_B \, p(X \epsilon A|B) \, p(B) \quad (28)$$
$$= b_A \, f_a \, p(A) + b_B \, f_d \, p(B)$$

using f_a and f_d as estimates of the conditional probability density functions. Matching the corresponding terms in (24) and (28) (with $K_6 = 0$) gives:

$$K_7 = b_A \cdot p(A)$$
$$K_8 = b_B \cdot p(B)$$

which establishes (24) as a Bayes decision rule for the case of $K_6 = 0$.

One of the key requirements of a two-class prediction problem is to decrease the risk of false dismissal (f_d) calls, since this is usually the more serious of the two types of error. The net f_d error rate can be reduced in one of two ways. K_8 can be assigned a greater value than K_7, thereby alloting a greater penalty to f_d's in the training phase. The other method is to set more stringent criteria for an A prediction by the net. The net output, δ, is a function of the distance of a vector point from the decision boundary. An offset, ϵ, can be assigned to the net output such that A calls are issued only if the quantity ($\delta - \epsilon$)

is greater than zero. ϵ can be considered a trainable parameter, and its value can be determined along with the net coefficients during the training phase.

The magnitude of the step sizes during training were chosen from a distribution obtained by summing R uniformly distributed random numbers (r_i) and scaling the result to the $[-1, +1]$ range, as shown in Eq. (11). The expected value of ΔW is zero, and its variance is inversely proportional to R. The variance was decreased automatically during training at approximately each decade change in the performance deficit ($\Delta P = P_{max} - P^*$), as shown in Table 1.

Table 1
Training Step Size Distribution

ΔP	R
> 0.1	1
0.1 − 0.01	2
0.01 − 0.001	4
0.001 − 0.0005	16
0.0005 − 0	32

Training and testing set error rates

After completion of training, the decision-making ability of a classificatory system can be summarized in a "confusion matrix," which follows.

$$
\begin{array}{cc}
 & \text{System's Classification} \\
 & \begin{array}{cc} j & k \end{array} \\
\begin{array}{c} \text{True} \\ \text{Classification} \end{array} \begin{array}{c} j \\ k \end{array} & \begin{pmatrix} c_{jj} & c_{jk} \\ c_{kj} & c_{kk} \end{pmatrix}
\end{array}
$$

c_{jj} = number of samples from class j that were correctly assigned by the system to class j

c_{jk} = number of samples from class j that were erroneously assigned by the system to class k

Some of the confusion matrices obtained during training are listed in Table 2. It can be seen that the net was trained to zero error. The testing set confusion matrix is shown below.

Net's
Classification

$$
\text{True Classification} \quad
\begin{array}{c}
\\
A \\
\\
B
\end{array}
\left(
\begin{array}{cc}
A & B \\
374 & 0 \\
\\
0 & 71
\end{array}
\right)
$$

The net also yielded an overall zero error rate on this set.

Table 2
Network Training Error Rates

Fraction of Search Time	"Confusion Matrix"		False Alarm Error Rate f_a	False Dismissal Error Rate, f_d	Overall Error Rate	Performance P*
0.	A B	A B 0 96 0 96	1.0000	0.0	0.500	−0.0005000
.07		8 88 0 96	0.9166	0.0	0.4583	−0.0004583
.08		16 80 0 96	0.8333	0.0	0.4167	−0.0004169
.09		82 14 41 55	0.1458	0.4270	0.2865	−0.0002865
.14		89 7 45 51	0.0729	0.4687	0.2510	−0.0002674
.17		86 10 5 91	0.1041	0.0521	0.0781	−0.0000786
.26		84 12 3 93	0.1250	0.0313	0.0781	−0.0000785
.36		87 9 0 96	0.0939	0.0	0.0469	−0.0000504
.52		94 2 4 92	0.0208	0.0417	0.0313	−0.0000315
.89		93 3 0 96	0.0313	0.0	0.0156	†
1.		96 0 0 96	0.0	0.0	0.0	†

†Values not available.

Example 2: Prediction

The objective of this problem was to predict the number of cooling zones required to cool a hot, moving slab. The heat transfer process was modeled by fitting a hypersurface to a set of training data in a 12-dimensional sensor space. The data was obtained from the actual physical process and consisted of 722 sets of observations. Each observation was composed of ten measurements, $m_1, \ldots, m_{10}$. The problem was to predict the number of cooling zones, Z, required to cool the moving slab from temperature m_1 to temperature m_2. The temperature of the cooling fluid is m_3, the flow rate of the fluid is proportional to m_4 and m_5, the slab is traveling at velocity m_7, and m_6, m_8, m_9, m_{10} are physical parameters of the slab.

Twelve variables were input to the net; their relationship to the measured variables was as follows.

$$(29)$$

$$
\begin{aligned}
x_1 &= m_1 \\
x_2 &= m_2 \\
x_3 &= (m_1 - m_3) \\
x_4 &= 1/(m_2 - m_3) \\
x_5 &= \sqrt{m_4} \\
x_6 &= 1/\sqrt{m_5} \\
x_7 &= m_6 \\
x_8 &= m_7 \\
x_9 &= (m_1 - m_2) \\
x_{10} &= 1/(m_2 - m_8) \\
x_{11} &= m_9 \\
x_{12} &= m_{10}
\end{aligned}
$$

Predictive Network

The two-layered net shown in Fig. 5, with fifty-six adjustable coefficients, was used. The elements in this net are different from the 2-input elements previously discussed in this paper. The three elements in the first layer each implement all $2^4 = 16$ terms of a multilinear multinomial of their four inputs. The element in the second layer implements all $2^3 = 8$ terms of a multilinear multinomial of its three inputs. The respective multinomials are:

(30)

$$y_n = w_{no} + \sum_{i=1}^{4} w_{ni} x_i + \sum_{i=1}^{3} \sum_{j=i+1}^{4} w_{nij} x_i x_j +$$

$$\sum_{i=1}^{2} \sum_{j=i=1}^{3} \sum_{k=j+1}^{4} w_{nijk} x_i x_j x_k + w_{n1234} x_1 x_2 x_3 x_4$$

for $n = 1, 2, 3$ and

(31)

$$\delta = w_{40} + \sum_{i=1}^{3} w_{4i} y_i + \sum_{i=1}^{2} \sum_{j=i+1}^{3} w_{4ij} y_i y_j +$$

$$w_4, 123\ y_1 y_2 y_3.$$

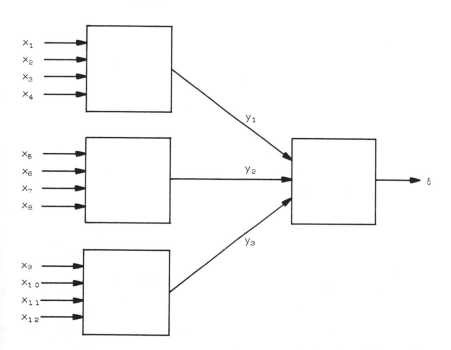

Fig. 6. Neuromime Net Which Implements Complete Multilinear Multinomial of Its Twelve Inputs.

Each element in the first layer in Fig. 5 provides up to 4-way interactions of its four inputs, and the complete net provides up to 12-way interactions of the twelve input variables. It can be seen from Eq. (29) that the first element in layer one implements a quadratic in m_1 (the incoming temperature of the slab) via the x_1x_3 term. m_1 is raised to the third power when the x_1x_3 term of y_1 is multiplied by the x_9 term of y_2 in the second layer (and the associated weight is nonzero). Thus, the net implements a cubic in the key variable, m_1.

A network of 2-layered elements, algebraically equivalent to the net in Fig. 5 could have ben used. However, since GARS' ability to train neuromime networks is independent of the element employed in the net, the structure of the network in Fig. 5 demonstrates the robustness of the GARS training algorithm.

Network training

The 722 12-dimensional data points were divided into training and testing sets of 76 and 646 points, respectively. Each of the 56 network coefficients was initially set equal to zero, and the goal was to find a set of coefficients which maximized the performance function

$$\text{max } p = \sum_{i=1}^{T} \frac{100}{|e_i| + 1} \qquad (32)$$

where T is the number of training points, and e_i is the error between the (known) true Z for the ith training point and the predicted Z, $\hat{Z}$, for the same point: $e_i = Z_i - \hat{Z}_i$. Training was scheduled to continue until (1) the maximal value of P $(= 100T)$ was achieved and (2) a predetermined number of iterations had been completed.

The magnitude of the step sizes during training was chosen according to Eq. (11). The variance was a function of iteration number rather than of the performance deficit ΔP, as in

Example 1. The step-size distribution, which was chosen arbitrarily, is listed in Table 3.

Table 3
Training Step Size Distribution

Iteration	R
1-100	2
101-200	4
201-300	8
301-400	16
> 400	32

Training and testing set error rates

Approximately 950 iterations were required to train the net. From Table 3 it can be seen that small steps were taken during the last half of the training exercise. The training and testing set error rates are presented in Table 4. An acceptable error for this physical process is a predicition within two cooling zones of the true value. It can be seen that (1) the fraction of errors made in each zone is very similar for both the training and testing sets, and (2) only 3 out of 722 predictions are outside of the acceptable range.

Table 4
Training and Testing Set Error Rates

Data Set	Number of Points	Zero Error	1 Zone Error	2 Zone Error	3 Zone Error	> 3 Zone Error
Training	76	54	18	3	1	0
Testing	646	365	244	35	2	0

Summary and Conclusions

A neuromime network composed of two-input nonlinear elements is proposed as the basis for the predictive components of intelligent devices. Each element in the net implements the transfer function, $y = w_0 + w_1x_1 + w_2x_2 + w_3x_1x_2$, where the inputs ($x_i$), weighting coefficients (w_i), and output

(y) are continuous variables. The elements in the layered network are connected in a feed-forward arrangement so that elements in layer ℓ receive their inputs from elements in layer $\ell - 1$. L-layered networks of uniform connectivity patterns which implement L -1 degree hypersurfaces are examined.

An accelerated guided random search algorithm was shown to be an effective and efficient network training algorithm. The network was globally trained using this algorithm. The guided random search produces faster convergence despite high dimensionality, multimodality, and time-varying surfaces.

The objective of network training is to find a set of coefficients which maximizes the system assessment function. Some candidate performance assessment functions were given for stationary and nonstationary signal-generating processes.

Two physical examples were presented to illustrate the utility of the neuromime net. The objectives of the two problems were, respectively, to learn the location of the decision boundary in a 6-dimensional sensor space and to model a heat transfer process by fitting a hypersurface to a set of training data in a 12-dimensional sensor space. Error rates of the trained nets used in each problem were well within the acceptable.

It has been demonstrated that a neuromime network modularly constructed of the two-input nonlinear elements is a powerful modeling device for use in cybernetic systems. Adaptive neuromime networks offer considerable insight into the structural and behavioral characteristics of intelligent devices.

REFERENCES

1. R. L. Barron et al. *Advanced Computer Concepts for Intercept Prediction, vol. 1: Conditioning of Parallel Networks for High-Speed Prediction of Re-entry Trajectories; vol. 2: Adaptive Inferential Measurement Processes and Their Applications*, Adaptronics, Inc. Summary Technical Report under Contract DA-36-034-AMC-0099Z, Nike-X Project Office, U.S. Army Matériel Command, Redstone Arsenal, Alabama, November 1964.
2. R. L. Barron. "Parameter Space Search Techniques for Learning Automata," *Proc. 1966 Bionics Symp.*, Dayton, Ohio, May 1966.
3. R. L. Barron. "Self-organizing and Learning Control Systems," in *Cybernetic Problems in Bionics*, 1966 Bionics Symposium, May

2–5, 1966, Dayton, Ohio, AD #811249. (New York: Gordon and Breach 1968), pp. 147–203.

4. R. L. Barron. "Inference of Vehicle and Atmospheric Parameters from Free Flight Motions," in *AIAA Guidance, Control and Flight Dynamics Conference*, AIAA preprint #67–600, August 1967.

5. R. L. Barron. "Adaptive Flight Control Systems," in *NATO AGARD Bionics Symposium*, Brussels, Belgium, September 18–20, 1968.

6. S. Beer. *Decision and Control*, (New York: John Wiley & Sons, Inc. 1966).

7. S. H. Brooks. "A Discussion of Random Methods for Seeking Maxima," *Operations Research*, 6 (1958), pp. 244–51.

8. S. H. Brooks. "A Comparison of Maximum-seeking Methods," *Operations Research*, 7, (1959), pp. 430–57.

9. L. O. Gilstrap, Jr. et al. *Study of Large Neuromime Networks*, Adaptronics, Inc. Final Technical Report under Contract AF 33(615)-5125, AFAL-TR-67-316, AF Avionics Laboratory, AD #824470, December 1967.

10. L. O. Gilstrap, Jr. and A. V. M. Ferris-Prabhu. *Neuromime Networks for Multiprocessors*, Adaptronics, Inc. Final Technical Report under Contract F33615-C-1791, AF Avionics Laboratory, October 1968.

11. L. O. Gilstrap, Jr. "An Adaptive Approach to Smoothing, Filtering, and Prediction," 1969 *NAECON Proceedings*, pp. 275–80.

12. L. O. Gilstrap, Jr. *Large Neurotron Networks*, Adaptronics, Inc. Final Technical Report under Contract F33615-C-68-1395, AF Aerospace Medical Research Laboratory, July 1969.

13. L. O. Gilstrap, Jr. *Large Network Study*, Adaptronics, Inc. Final Technical Report under Contract F33615-69-C-1331, AF Aerospace Medical Research Laboratory, April 1970.

14. L. S. Gurin. "Random Search in the Presence of Noise," trans. from *Teknicheskaya Kibernetica* no. 3, (1966), pp. 252–60.

15. A. G. Ivakhnenko. *Kiberneticheskiye Sistemy S Kombinirovannym Upravleniyem* [Cybernetic Systems with Combined Control], (Izdatel'stvo Tekhnika, 1967).

16. J. Matyas. "Random Optimization," trans. from *Avtomatika i Telemekhanika*, vol. 26, (1965), pp. 246–53.

17. L. A. Rastrigin. "The Convergence of the Random Search Method in the Extremal Control of a Many-parameter System," trans. from *Avtomatika i Telemekhanika*, vol. 24, (1963), pp. 1467–73.

18. D. B. Yudin. "Quantitative Analysis of Complex Systems, II (Random Search)," trans. from *Teknicheskaya Kibernetika* no. 1, (1966), pp. 1–13.

Simultaneous Performance of Twenty-Five Different Tests Per Minute in a Centralized Cybernetic Clinical Laboratory*

ARTHUR E. RAPPOPORT, M.D.
JAMES A. HILL, M.D.
WILLIAM D. GENNARO, M.T. (ASCP)

Youngstown Hospital Association
Youngstown, Ohio

The steadily increasing demand for clinical laboratory tests led to the development of many unique, automated chemistry and hematology instruments. These, in turn, further fueled the desire for even more tests. As a result, in the past fifteen years, we have witnessed the invention throughout the world of such mechanized chemical devices as the Technicon single and multiple channel Auto-analyzers and various SMA instruments; the Hycel Mark X, the Vickers Multichannel 300, the Perkin-Elmer C-4, the Autochemist, the Dupont ACA, Braun Syste-Matik, Philips Unicam, and many others. Similarly, hematology laboratories experienced the introduction of the various Coulter counters, the Technicon SMA/4A and 7A, the Fisher Hema-lyzer, and other devices.

*This investigation was supported by PHS Grant HS 00060-03 from the National Center for Health Services Research and Development.

Although such instruments were extremely effective in permitting large-scale testing, they proved to be a mixed blessing. Their striking advantages in test performance were matched by a distressing inability to handle much of the paper work associated with their use. It became necessary, therefore, to expand these mechanized measuring systems to include instruments which could automatically process the large amounts of data being generated. As a result, attempts were initiated during the early 1960s to combine electronic data processing (EDP) techniques with automatic analytic technology.

We began to study this problem in 1963 while acting as consultants to the IBM Advanced Systems Development Division. In 1964, we succeeded in developing a prototype of the first completely integrated, cybernetic clinical laboratory system, as defined above. Its formal debut occurred later that year when routine hemoglobin determinations were performed for most pathologists attending the Joint Annual Meeting of the College of American Pathologists and American Society of Clinical Pathologists, held in the Americana Hotel, in Miami.

At that time, we demonstrated a continuously mechanized test performance and documentation process; it was initiated with automatic specimen identification by a machine readable, prenumbered and prepunched stub-card attached to the test tube containing a mixture of blood and cyanmethemoglobin. The specimen was transported automatically by conveyor belt through the analytic device. Through a mechanical tilting of the test tube at a certain station, the solution was poured into a flow-cell cuvette of a colorimeter which automatically measured the percentage T. The electronic signals from both the specimen identification unit and the colorimeter were inputted into an IBM 1440 computer, where the concentration of hemoglobin was calculated automatically from primary standards already stored in the computer's memory. These test result data were merged automatically with the previously entered demographic data of the pathologist from whom the specimen was obtained. Within fifteen minutes after onset of the test process, each pathologist received a punch card on which was printed his name, the name of his hotel, his room number, and his hemoglobin value. The clinical accuracy of the data was subsequently checked by personal communication with most of the participants, two of whom confirmed the existence of polycythemia in the face of markedly elevated hemoglobin values.

In 1965, the year after the success of this initial venture, a full-scale Data Acquisition System (DAS) was introduced— the IBM 1080. This could be coupled to all automated, semiautomated, and manually operated laboratory electronic instruments. The DAS possessed peak-picking, peak-holding, multi-plexing and analog-to-digital (A/D) conversion capabilities. The output of the DAS was punched on cards; these were processed by a computer which prepared a print-out of all results according to the patients tested. The DAS was subsequently expanded to include the ability to input into the computer results of manually performed subjective tests such as urinalysis, microscopy, and microbiology to produce a total Laboratory Information System (LIS). This basic concept has continued to grow without interruption since 1965.

Without wishing to describe the progressive, step-by-step developments we have made since inception of the system, we present the following description of the current state of the art of the DAS and LIS in the Youngstown Hospital Association Department of Laboratories.

The 1000-bed Youngstown Hospital Association comprises two hospital units located four-and-a-half miles apart. The South Side Unit contains approximately 400 beds and possesses active outpatient and emergency departments and an extremely active traumatic surgery service. The North Side Unit contains approximately 600 beds, and houses the major clinical facilities for elective and special surgery (intensive care and open-heart surgery and neurosurgery), most of the internal medicine services (CCU, cardiovascular laboratories), the obstetrics service, and a large pediatric division. Although both units possess laboratories, the major installation is located at the North Side Unit.

The computer center, containing an IBM 360/40 (128K), is based in the North Unit. It is connected to the South Side Unit by means of high-speed communications terminals.

Blood and other samples are transported at frequent intervals by shuttle service from the South Side Unit to the North Side Laboratory. They are merged with North Side samples and processed in large batches on the automated devices in the Centralized Cybernetic Clinical Laboratory (CCCL). We have succeeded in centralizing at the North Side Unit all of the pathologic anatomy (surgical pathology, exfoliative cytology, autopsy, and histology); most of the chemistry; about three-fourths of hematology; all virology, and about one-half of microbiology, in addition to all medical secretarial and clerical functions. All blood-banking collection, processing, and immunohematologic testing activities as well as all serologic procedures for syphilis have been concentrated at the South Side Unit. If blood is needed for transfusion at the North Side Unit, it is furnished from the South Side Blood center.

Figure 1 demonstrates the structural and operational organization of the CCCL in the North Side Unit.

Note the wide variety of Technicon automated instruments:

a. one SMA 6/60 capable of performing sequential tests for glucose, urea, chloride, CO_2, sodium, and potassium. To this instrument, we have attached two additional AA channels for simultaneous testing of uric acid and creatinine on the same sample, thus permitting performance of 8 tests per minute per sample;

b. nine single and dual AA channels bound together by stream splitters and capable of performing simultaneous determinations of acid phosphatase, alkaline phosphatase, total bilirubin, direct bilirubin, SGOT, LDH, CPK, calcium, and phosphorus on a single specimen, nine tests per minute per sample;

c. one SMA/4A Hematology Autoanalyzer available for RBC, WBC, hemoglobin, and hematocrit measurements on each sample: four tests per minute per sample.

d. All of these instruments are interfaced to the DAS through

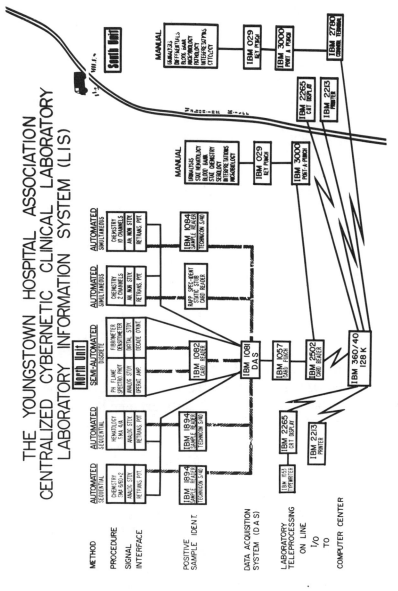

Fig. 1. Organization Chart of Cybernetic Laboratory.

appropriate retransmitting potentiometers attached to the shafts of the strip chart recorders by which the analog signals are transmitted to the multiplexer.

In addition to these automated devices, we have developed technology for automatic documentation of the electronic output of conventional, stand-alone, semiautomated instruments. Thus, also connected to the DAS are two Coleman Spectrophotometers; one B-D Fibrometer, one IL Flame Photometer; one Beckman pH meter and one Beckman Analytrol. The connections are achieved by locally designed operational amplifiers or digital devices, which were specifically built for the instruments being interfaced.

Figure 1 also demonstrates the various kinds of automatic specimen identification units which operate in tandem with all these analytic instruments. We consider the automatic machine-readable identification of test tubes and specimens of such importance in a cybernetic laboratory that the development of this technology has received our continuous, intensive attention. Four methods are currently operational in our laboratory, as will be described below.

Before automatic specimen and patient identification can be discussed, it is necessary to outline briefly our present method for initiating laboratory test requests. Six different, two-part, carbon interleaved, tab-card test requisitions are stored on all nursing stations. These list all the automated and semiautomated, chemical and hematology tests arranged according to certain groups, as well as all other manual procedures (urinalysis, serology, microbiology, etc.). We shall describe only the requisition and methods used for automated and semiautomated tests. (See Fig. 2.)

The top card lists all the tests in columns and possesses a preprinted and prepunched specimen number. The bottom card is essentially similar in appearance except that it comprises four detachable stubs, corresponding to the listed tests, each possessing the same preprinted and prepunched number. The patient's identification is imprinted simultaneously on both cards by means of an addressograph plate. The desired tests

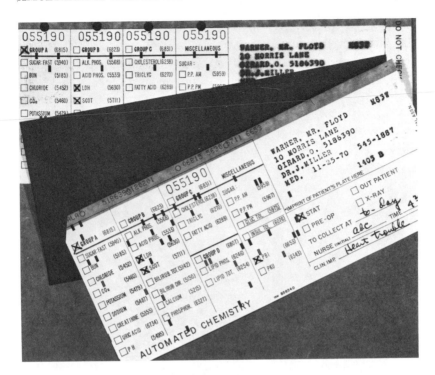

Fig. 2a. Carbon Interleaved, Prenumbered and Prepunched, Requisition Form for Automated Chemistry.

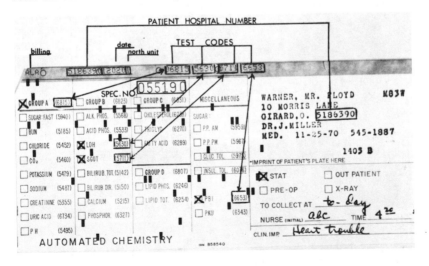

Fig. 2b. Top Card Showing in Detail the Various Keypunched Data.

are checked in the appropriate box. The requisition is sent to
the laboratory, where the two cards are separated. The top
card is keypunched with the patient's hospital number, the
date, and the code numbers of the ordered tests. Thus, an
identifying link is created between the patient's hospital number and the preprinted and prepunched specimen number.
This card is inputted into the computer and stored in the
patient's master record, which is already on file on random
access discs.

The bottom card is used by the phlebotomist who procures

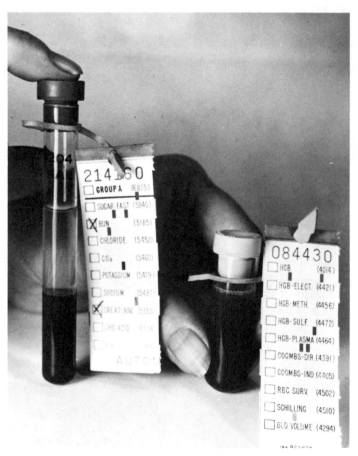

**Fig. 3. Blood Specimens with Attached Identifying Stub Cards; the Left
Tube for Chemistry Examinations Has Been Centrifuged.**

the blood sample from the patient for the tests requested by the physician. We employ 10 ml. Heparin Vacutainers for most of the chemistry tests and 3.5 ml. EDTA Vacutainers for hematology tests.

After venipuncture, the appropriate stubs are detached from the bottom card and attached to the test tube utilizing a specially designed rubber strap. (See Fig. 3.) The test tube now is identified by the specimen number, which has been merged with the patient's hospital number in the computer.

In the chemistry laboratory, the tubes and the attached stub-cards are placed in a specially designed tube holder and centrifuged. Specimens for hematology are not centrifuged.

Two specially designed specimen identification turntables were designed to input the machine-readable, stub-card identifying numbers into the DAS. (See Fig. 4.) One type (IBM 1084) is used with the single, dual, and multiple simultaneous Autoanalyzers: the other (IBM 1894), with the various SMA

Fig. 4. Special Turntable to Aspirate Plasma Specimens from the Tubes for Analysis and to Read the Punched Numbers on the Stub Cards.

systems. While both are similar in appearance, their methods of operation are quite different. They replace the conventional Technicon Turntables. The electronic and mechanical differences between these two types need not be discussed at this juncture.

For chemistry tests, the original Vacutainer tube is placed at random in the Sampler holder after centrifugation. Loading lists are not necessary, since the tube "speaks for itself" through the identifying stub-card.

The tube is placed on the outer bracket of the tube holder, while the stub-card is fitted into a slot on the inner side of the tube holder. As the turntable indexes counterclockwise, one position per minute, a mechanical card-reader in the turntable "reads" the specimen number on the stub-card and enters it into the DAS, after which the plasma is aspirated from the tube and pumped into the Technicon instrument for analysis.

Thus, at the beginning of the test cycle just prior to aspiration the system receives the sample's specimen identification number. Approximately eight to nine minutes later, the analog value of the peak is transmitted by the potentiometer to the DAS multiplexing unit, and A/D conversion is carried out. All identification numbers and digitized analog signals are punched on punch cards in sequence.

In hematology, essentially the same identification system is used except that whole blood is aspirated, since we are interested in counting red and white blood cells and determining the packed cell volume in addition to performing a chemical test for hemoglobin.

A third device for specimen identification is the IBM 1082 card reader. (See Fig. 5.) This is employed with such semi-automated, interfaced instruments as the pH meter, spectrophotometer, or Flamephotometer. The sample is identified by number similarly with the stub-card attached at the bedside. In order to identify the specimen in the DAS, a test card is prepared that is duplicated from the top copy and bears the keypunched patient hospital number, specimen number, test identification number, and date.

Fig. 5. A Card Reader to Identify the Specimen; Note the Small Operational Amplifier to Interface the Spectrophotometer to the Computer.

The test is performed in the conventional fashion, using the interfaced instruments and adding reagents manually.

When the test instrument has come to equilibrium and displays a definite analog or digital value, the test card is inserted into the 1082 card reader. This elicits a command from the DAS to obtain the electronic value of the measurement from the operational amplifier interface and to merge that value with the specimen number. This method permits automatic specimen identification and employment of any electronic device which has been properly interfaced to the DAS.

A fourth device is the recently developed Rapp-SpecIdent device. (See Fig. 6.) This is a static stub-card reader which can read the number punched into the stub-card attached to the tube. This method is in lieu of utilizing the large test card in the 1082 card reader, as described above. Another recently developed application of the Rapp-SpecIdent stub-card reader is in connection with conventional single or dual Auto-analyzer technology when loading the Sampler plate.

In our present application, it is used during the simultaneous determination of serum cholesterol and triglyceride. In these tests, alcohol-treated plasma or serum must be prepared prior to testing. The pretreated plasma is transferred to a conven-

Fig. 6. Static Stub-Card Reader for Specimen Identification.

tional Auto-analyzer plastic cup and placed in the sample
tray. When that has been done, the stub-card, still attached to
the original tube, is inserted into the stub-card reader, which
accesses the specimen number into the system. Since both
steps are done in serial fashion, the sequence of the identification data will conform with the sequence of the tray loading
and test performance in the DAS, and the test result will be
merged in the DAS with the specimen identification of the
patient. The introduction of such a simple step to the DAS
demonstrates graphically how easily the need for writing loading lists, work lists, and manual calculations can be eliminated.

All punched cards produced by the DAS are loaded into
a Card Reader (see Fig. 7); this is attached on-line to the
computer, where the outputs of the automated and semiauto-

Fig. 7.   Teleprocessing Unit; Note Card Reader on the Right.

mated instruments are processed. The first step is an immediate feedback of calibration standard values.

The results are shown on the laboratory Cathode Ray Tube (CRT) display (Fig. 8), and printed on the attached printer. This instantaneous, on-line I/O, data-processing and tele-processing information loop furnishes information vital to the establishment, by laboratory personnel, of the accuracy, precision, and reliability of the operating analytical system. If all displayed values obtained from the calibration standards, pooled serums, drift controls, and commercial quality control specimens (Monitrol) meet specified control limits, the total system is allowed to continue to test patient samples. It must be emphasized that continuous visual confirmation of the efficient operation of the system also is achieved by personally monitoring the strip charts of the test instruments.

In AA technology, it is customary to include pooled serum,

Fig. 8.   Closeup of CRT and Printer.

drift, and commercial control samples at regular intervals. The specimen ID numbers and raw data values are transmitted continuously to the computer, which calculates the results and determines the precision and accuracy of each batch of each automated run. Subsequently, patients' and quality control values are presented periodically on the CRT for personal, critical evaluation by the medical technologists and clinical pathologists; they make the decision whether or not to accept the results and whether to enter them in the patient's master medical record. This constant control procedure insures absolute reliability. Total technical and documentation backup are available in the event of Teleprocessing or computer failure, since raw data and ID cards are always available for reprocessing.

Using the full gamut of electronic automated instruments previously described, we can perform and document on the average twenty-five different tests per minute. By means of computer-controlled test performance and teleprocessing, we exercise constant critical supervision of all aspects of the various test systems.

It must be emphasized that during the same period that the

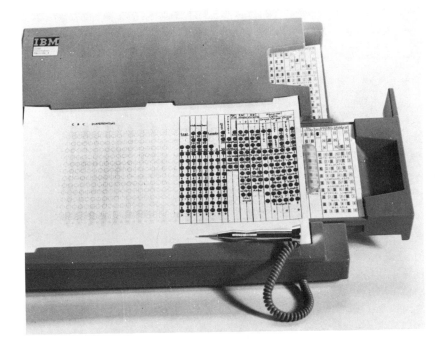

Fig. 9.   Information Recorder and Overlay for Manual Punching Port-A Punch Cards with Results of Manual Examinations (Differential Count).

DAS is operating, all manual tests such as urinalysis, blood smear differential counts, and serology, microbiology, pathologic anatomy, virology, and cytology tests are also being performed and recorded at both hospital units.

The technologist enters the results of these examinations either on Port-A-Punch cards, using the IBM 3000 Information Recorder (Fig. 9), or by writing the results on test cards, which are subsequently keypunched. These cards are also loaded into the Card Readers of the teleprocessing system in the North and South unit laboratories, and the results are merged in the patient master record in the computer with the automated results which have already been accessed.

At approximately 1:00 p.m. daily, ward reports (Fig. 10) are printed simultaneously, in duplicate, on high-speed printers at both North and South units. The ward report presents the name, ward, room and bed number and the results of all automated, semiautomated, and manual tests, for each patient, per-

```
                    THE YOUNGSTOWN HOSPITAL ASSOCIATION

    WARD 1 NORTH                        NORTH WARD REPORT    06/07/71 01 HR 15 MIN

      0183-A            DOROTHY L        5290562      KISKADDON R M MD
        CULTURE FECES                    TAKEN          06/06/71

      0184-A          AGNES              5291097      GREEN L N MD
        RBC                  MILL/CMM    5.20
        WBC                   TH/CMM     10.4        *
        HGB              12-16 G%        11.0        *
        PCV              37-48%          33.0        *
        PCV              37-48%          36.2        *
        CORP CONST-MCV   82-92 CMU       69.6        *
                MCH      27-31 MCGM      21.2        *
                MCHC     32-36%          30.4        *
        BUN            10-20 MGM%        16.7
        GLUCOSE FASTING 70-110 MGM%      89.5

      0185-B          MYRON J            5291739      SHENSA L S MD
        RBC                  MILL/CMM    5.65
        WBC                   TH/CMM     12.8        *
        HGB              12-16 G%        16.5        *
        PCV              37-48%          49.0        *
        CORP CONST-MCV   82-92 CMU       86.7
                MCH      27-31 MCGM      29.2
                MCHC     32-36%          33.7
        DIFFERENTIAL-SEGS         %      48
                STABS             %      8
                ECS               %      2
                LYMPHS            %      39
                MONOS             %      3
                PLATELETS                OK
        URINE-COLOR/APPEAR               YELL HAZY
                SPECFIC GRAVITY          1.035
                PH                       6.0
                PROTEIN                  TRACE
                SUGAR                    NEG
                WBC             #/HPF     1-4
                CASTS           #/HPF    FEW/MUCUS
                TYPE                     VOIDED
        BILIRUBIN TOT   0.1-1.5 MGM%     .7
        BILIRUBIN DIRECT 0-0.4 MGM%      .3
        ALK PHOS       3-13 K/A UNITS    10.4
        BUN            10-20 MGM%        16.4
        CREATININE     0.9-2.0 MGM%      1
        URIC ACID      2.8-7.5 MGM       5.8
        CALCIUM          9-11 MGM%       10.8
        PHOSPHORUS     2.7-4.0 MGM%      2.3         *
        NA PLASMA      136-145 MEQ/L     142
        K PLASMA       3.5-5.0 MEQ/L     3.9
        CL PLASMA      96-105 MEQ/L      105.6       *
        CO2 CONT PLASMA 25-32 MEQ/L      27.4
        PH PLASMA VENOUS 7.32-7.45       7.34
        GLUCOSE FASTING 70-110 MGM%      100.8
        ACID PHOS      0-6.5 K/A UNITS   3.9
        SGOT            5-40 K UNITS     16.1
        LDH            30-130 WAC UNITS  90.4
        CREAT PHOS KIN   0-40 UNITS      19.9
```

Fig. 10. Copy of Ward Report.

formed that day up to that hour. The ward reports are first checked by the pathologists and, after approval, the originals are distributed to the wards. Corrections, additions, or deletions are entered into the computer through the CRT keyboard. These reports give the physicians and ward personnel the results of the tests that were performed that morning.

During the afternoon, laboratory testing continues. The re-

CHARLES K DR 42 NORTH UNIT PATIENT SUMMARY HOSP-NO 5181917 11/28/70 PAGE NO 1
BROCKER R J MD PROV.DIAG- ANEMIA ADM.DATE 11/17/70
WARD 2 NORTH WEST
TIME OF REPORT 06/35 PM

		SUNDAY 11/22/70	MONDAY 11/23/70	TUESDAY 11/24/70	WEDNESDAY 11/25/70	THURSDAY 11/26/70	FRIDAY 11/27/70	SATURDAY 11/28/70
HEMATOLOGY								
RBC	MILL/CMM						2.48	
WBC	TH/CMM		3PM 13.6	9.5	7.9	8.5 9AM	9.9	8.3
HGB	12-16 G%	11.8					7.7	
PCV	37-48%	26.0	3PM 24.5	26.0	25.0	26.5	24.0	22.5
CORP CONST-PCV	82-92 CMU						96.8	
MCH	27-31 MCGM						31.0	
MCHC	32-36%						32.1	
DIFFERENTIAL-SEGS							88	
LYMPHS							10	
MONOS							2	
PLATELETS							OK	
RBC SIZE							SLT-MACRO	
RBC SHAPE							SLT-TARGET	
RBC CHROMIA							SLT-HYPO	
PLATELETS	150-350 TH/CMM	177	177	211.0	193.0	213	174	172.0
RETICULOCYTES	0.5-1.5%						0.4	
CHEMISTRY								
BUN	10-20 MGM%	45	51	54		51	51	54
CREATININE	0.9-2.0 MGM%	3.9	3.9	3.9		3.3	3.3	3.6
CREATININE UR	1.5-2 G/24 HR	1.8 SAT						
URIC ACID	2-6 MGM%	8.4	8.4	7.8		6.0	6.0	6.3
CALCIUM	9-11 MGM%	19.2	19.2	18.3	17.6	16.9	13.9	10.9
NA PLASMA	136-145 MEQ/L	135	135	134		137	134	137
K PLASMA	3.5-5.0 MEQ/L	4.4	4.6	4.1		3.9	3.8	3.7
CL PLASMA	96-105 MEQ/L	89	89	93		99	98	96
CO2 PLASMA	25-32 MEQ/L	27	36.0	33		28.5	23	27
PH PLASMA VENOUS	7.32-7.45	7.36	7.35	7.44		7.40	7.44	7.46
GLUCOSE FASTING	70-110 MGM%	141	159	174		123	126	138
BENCE JONES PROTEIN	NEG			SEE BELOW				
IMMUNO-DIFFUSION				BELOW				
ELECTROPHORESIS URINE								
ALBUMIN	G%		12%					
BETA	G%		73%					
GAMMA	G%		15%					

PATHOLOGIST CONSULTATION	11/21	IMMUNODIFFUSION STUDIES MORE SUGGESTIVE OF MACROGLOBULINEMIA RAPP	
HEMATOLOGY INTERPRETATION	11/25	BONE MARROW PLASMA CYTOID INFILTRATION DIAGNOSTIC MULTIPLE MYELOMA LP	
URINALYSIS INTERPRETATION	11/23	ELECTROPHORESIS BENCE JONES PROTEIN STRONG POSITIVE BETA PEAK ON	
URINALYSIS INTERPRETATION	11/24	IMMUNO-ELECTROPHORESIS OF BENCE JONES PROTEIN DEMONSTRATES L CHAIN LAMBDA TYPE	
URINALYSIS INTERPRETATION	11/27	IMMUNODIFFUSION NEGATIVE FOR IGG AND IGA-POSITIVE AND ELEVATED FOR IGM-432% AVERAGE DN	
CHEMISTRY INTERPRETATION	11/19	SERUM PROTEIN ELECTROPHORESIS SHOWS AN M PEAK SUGGESTIVE OF MYELOMA OR MACROGLOBULINEMIA-IMMUNOGLOBULINS TO FOLLOW JRH	
CHEMISTRY INTERPRETATION	11/20	IMMUNODIFFUSION-MGM%	G A M

IMMUNODIFFUSION-MGM%
HYLAND 280 24 980 1-40IL
DADE 200 10 UNSAT
PFIZER 190

CHEMISTRY INTERPRETATION	11/22	RESULTS MAY BE AFFECTED-SPECIMEN DRAWN DURING IV INFUSION
BACTERIOLOGY INTERPRETATION	11/16	URINE COLONY COUNT,****STREP FAECALIS,STAPH ALBUS, ***UNDER 10 THOU ORG/ML,TETRACYCLINES,NOVOBIACIN,VIBRAMYCIN,KAFOCIN,

Fig. 11. Copy of Patient Summary Report.

sults are handled in a similar fashion and are entered into the patient's master file.

At the end of the day's laboratory activity (5:00 p.m.), patient summary reports (Fig. 11) are printed. These contain all of that day's test data for all patients. This report is inserted daily into the patient's medical chart. If tests are performed on subsequent days, new reports are printed each day and placed within the chart, while the previous day's report is discarded. Thus, the patient summary report represents a cumulative, updated report containing the results of all tests performed for an entire week from Sunday through Saturday.

In the patient summary report, one can follow on a horizontal print line the chronological, sequential, day by day values obtained for each procedure. Clinically relevant procedures—or those which test for the same type of substance or are performed by essentially similar techniques—are clustered in vertical listing. This arrangement permits logical and efficient analysis of the test data by the attending physicians. Hematology, chemistry, and serology results are listed together under major categories. Within these classifications, all tests relating to specific diseases are subdivided into groups, i.e., liver, kidney, or other disease profiles. Similarly listed are tests relating to specific metabolic substances, such as glucose, protein, or lipid.

Free, narrative text reports such as pathology tissue diagnoses, microbiological reports, and pathologist consultations and interpretations are inputted into the computer either by means of a key punch or by the typewriter keyboard console of the CRT. These dated entries appear on the bottom of the patient summary report.

One may inquire of the computer about the result of any test performed on any patient during his current period of hospitalization in either the North or South unit. Such inquiry is carried out in the laboratory by using the keyboard console to enter the patient's number, test number, and date. The test result is immediately shown on the CRT screen or may be printed on the printer.

Conclusion

There are substantial tangible and intangible advantages to this system. We believe that the most important factor which justifies installation of the described devices is the assurance of quality control of the test results that is afforded by the watchful eye of the computer and its programs. We are impressed by the marked improvement in accuracy and precision of test results which can be attained by automated devices. It is possible, with the computer, to include such vital systematic control activities as correcting for contamination or carry-over from one sample to another or adjusting instrument base line drift—such contamination, carry-over, and drift being among the acknowledged drawbacks of the continuous flow technique of the Autoanalyzer. It would be relatively impossible to effect such beneficial adjustments without a substantial, general purpose computer.

Of prime importance is the ability to create cumulative, updated medical reports which portray concisely the daily and total laboratory status of each patient and which permit one to compare these data with other, previously performed tests. Thus, trends in the medical progress of the case can be recognized easily. Doctors are less likely to overlook vital results, and they can attain a panoramic view of the laboratory aspects of the medical problem more rapidly and efficiently.

We have no doubt that patient care has been improved significantly. The ability rapidly to render necessary laboratory information works to shorten the hospital stay. This effect is being studied.

Through computer-coupled automation, there has been an enormous enhancement of technologist productivity. Since personnel cost is the largest single expense in the clinical laboratory, improvement in technologist utilization exerts an immediate, gratifying reduction of total laboratory expense. Studies are under way in our laboratory to measure the impact of the described system upon the number and type of technologists required. It should be self-evident, however, that if twenty-five tests per minute can be performed by only a handful of technologists operating the various analytic systems, significant economies can be achieved. We have compared the direct expense incurred by manual test performance and conventional documentation with the cost of automated test performance and computerized documentation of all paperwork. The results of these operational research studies are being prepared for publication, but it can be stated categorically at this time that the direct cost per test has been reduced to about one quarter of the former cost through computer coupled automation.

Space utilization is improved substantially because of the significant reduction in the staff in relation to the volume and variety of tests performed. In addition, the automated devices require relatively little space.

The key to the economic success of such a venture lies in the capability to perform routine automatic testing of large batches of specimens at one time and to present the results to the attending physicians within four to six hours. Sufficiently large batches can be secured only in exceedingly large institutions or by centralizing the workload of numerous small institutions. In the latter situation, it is necessary that adequate specimen transportation systems be created to ship samples to the centralized laboratory rapidly, safely, and on time. An adequate communication network is required to transmit the results of tests back to the originating laboratory and to furnish "hard" copy for inclusion into the patient records. (Figure 1 demonstrates how these problems have been solved in Youngstown.)

To select the optimal data-processing equipment configuration, one must first be cautious and aware of the numerous important cost factors which are involved. On-line systems may appear to be more elegant, but the cost of the hardware is significantly greater than in off-line systems, and software represents an extremely expensive item. In addition, it is necessary to plan intensively for backup and fail-safe devices in the event of instrument failure. This technology also is necessary on evenings and weekends, when large, on-line systems are usually not operational or economically feasible.

There are those who recommend dedicated laboratory systems. We believe that the cost of such systems to the institution is excessive, that the alleged advantages are apparent and not real, and that using these systems means forgoing the many advantages of the shared system.

We believe that a shared, off-line system is most advantageous from the economic and operational standpoints. Shared systems require close and harmonious cooperation between laboratory and computer center personnel. These groups must understand each other's problems and requirements and be willing to resolve them in a mutually satisfactory fashion. In our system, we can utilize much of the data already filed in a patient's master record without duplicating its input and filing.

All test results are filed in the laboratory. Since the computer prepares a cumulative report, it is only necessary to file the print-out prepared on Saturday, which contains the weekly record. This is prepared in duplicate. The original is mailed to the attending physician's office, so that he can have there a complete record of all hospital laboratory data. The second copy is retained in the laboratory, pursuant to legal requirements and the regulations of the Joint Commission on Accreditation of Hospitals.

After the patient is discharged, the data stored on random access disc files are transferred to magnetic tape and thus are available for use in subsequent admissions. Analysis of these stored laboratory data, correlating age and sex with results, is being performed with the goal of establishing normal values for the Youngstown population.

Resolution of many of the problems facing pathology and medicine may be achieved by harnessing successfully, the "Four Horsemen" of laboratory technology—Centralization, Automation, Computerization, and Teleprocessing.

ADDITIONAL READINGS

Rappoport, A. E. *Administrative and Professional Applications of Data Processing in the Laboratory.* Transactions, 16th Annual Meeting, College of American Pathologists. Chicago, Illinois, September 1962.

Rappoport, A. E. "Introduction to a Computer-Assisted Clinical Laboratory." *Symposium Coll. Am. Path.* (1964):4.

Rappoport, A. E. A Comprehensive Medical Data Profile System Symposium on Recent Developments in Research Methods and Instrumentation, October 4–7, 1965.

Rappoport, A. E. *Criteria for Automation,* vol. XLVI. Albany: New York State Assn. of Public Health Laboratories, May 19–20, 1966.

Rappoport, A. E. *Realities of Machine Interaction—Real Life with Real Time.* Clinical Lab Information Systems and Automation Seminar, Univ. of California, Ext., Los Angeles, April 6–7, 1968.

Rappoport, A. E. "Punch Card Technique Saves Technologist Time." *Modern Hospital* 111 (1968):86–87.

Rappoport, A. E.; Gennaro, W. D.; and Constandse, W. J. "Computer-Laboratory Link is Base of Hospital Information System." *Modern Hospital* 110, 94 (1968):101–2.

Rappoport, A. E.; Gennaro, W. D.; and Constandse, W. J. "A Clinical Laboratory System Achieved Through Computer-Coupled Automation." *Biomedical Science Instrumentation* 5 (1968):47–62.

Rappoport, A. E. "Automation and Data Processing in Pathology, Acquisition and Processing by Computer of Chemical Laboratory Data." *College of Pathologists,* edited by T. P. Whitehead, London, February, 1969. *J. Clin. Path.* Suppl.

Rappoport, A. E. and Gennaro, W. D. "A Cybernetic Hematology Laboratory Utilizing the Technicon SMA 4A Coupled to an IBM 1080 Data Acquisition System." In *Advances in Automated Analysis,* vol. 1, Technicon International Congress, June 4–6, 1969, Chicago: Mediad Publishing.

Rappoport, A. E.; Gennaro, W. D.; and Constandse, W. J. "Should the Laboratory Have Its Own Computer?" *Hospital Progress* 50 (1969): 114–24.

Rappoport, A. E. and Gennaro, W. D. "You Get the Blood, Computer Does CBC." *Modern Hospital* 113 (1969):103.

Rappoport, A. E. and Rappoport, Emily. "Laboratory Automation." *Hospitals, JAHA* 44 (1970):114–21.

Rappoport, A. E. and Gennaro, W. D. "Computer-Coupled Automation in a Regionalized Hospital Clinical Laboratory." *23rd ACEMB,* Washington, D.C., November 15–19, 1970.

On the Use of Examples in Adaptive Systems*

W. R. SPILLERS

Columbia University
New York, New York

Introduction

A remarkable scientific occurrence is taking place today. Despite increased specialization within fields of study, groups with widely disparate backgrounds are joining their efforts around nuclei provided by related applications or common technology. There are, for example, many areas which share an interest in problems dealing with the manner by which points are connected by lines and which are formally united through graph theory.[1] It is to the question of the representation and manipulation of "examples" which can be described by graphs that this paper is devoted.

Central to this paper is the question of complete automation, which is presumed to require adaptive capabilities. While effective, sophisticated, adaptive man-made systems do not yet exist, the strong dependence upon examples in human learning and teaching[2] encourages the study of their possible usage in automation. This is particularly true in the design of structures (buildings, bridges, aerospace vehicles, etc.), where a student is taught very simple examples upon which he later

*This work has been supported by the National Science Foundation.

generalizes. The motivation for this work, then, is the desire
to be able to generalize automatically upon existing designs
for structures; being unable to treat such a complex problem
directly, this paper considers the problem of generalizations
upon the topology of a structure or its *graph* and provides a
mechanism for part of the more difficult problem.

The term "example" here is synonymous with the term
"graph," and the question is how to "generalize" upon a given
example automatically. To be able to generalize upon an example implies the ability to manipulate examples, and it is
to this more restricted end that this paper is specifically devoted. Notation is discussed, followed by remarks on the use
of nilpotent matrices as learning operators; finally, applications
are considered.

Representation of Graphs

In spite of its considerable literature, there is in graph theory
no uniformly accepted algebraic treatment of graphs. In fact
the representation used by Polya,[3] who was concerned with
enumeration, is quite different from the hypercubes of Roth[4]
and Wang algebra,[5] which are useful in circuit design. More
recently, Grenander[6] has attempted to subsume graphs into
the very general framework of pattern recognition. It is an
extension of his notation which is used here.

Graph theory is concerned with points (nodes) and lines
(branches) connecting these nodes. A graph which is a collection of nodes and branches can be described[6] by a triangular
array I of the form

$$I = x_{12} \, x_{13} \, x_{14} \ldots x_{1n}$$
$$x_{23} \, x_{24} \ldots x_{2n}$$
$$x_{34} \ldots x_{3n}$$
$$\cdots$$
$$x_{n-1,n}.$$

The implication here is that the graph which I represents contains n nodes which have been numbered; the elements x_{ij} of
the array I are defined

$$x_{ij} = \begin{cases} 1 \text{ if nodes i and j are connected by a branch} \\ 0 \text{ if nodes i and j are not connected by a branch.} \end{cases}$$

It is a simple matter to obtain a binary vector (matrix) representation of this graph by mapping the array I into a linear array such as follows.

$$\alpha = \begin{bmatrix} x_{12} \\ x_{13} \\ \cdot \\ x_{1n} \\ x_{23} \\ x_{24} \\ \cdot \\ x_{2n} \\ x_{34} \\ \cdot \\ x_{n-1,n} \end{bmatrix}$$

In order to make the machinery of vector spaces[7] available, it is convenient to define multiplication and addition modulo 2, for example

y \ x	0	1
0	0	1
1	1	0

$$\underline{x+y}$$

y \ x	0	1
0	0	0
1	0	1

$$\underline{xy.}$$

Using these definitions of addition and multiplication, binary matrices can be manipulated in an otherwise ordinary manner.

Nilpotent Matrices

Continuing in a formal vein for a moment, in linear algebra an n x n matrix T is nilpotent if $T^n = 0$ while $T^{n-1} \neq 0$. A nilpotent matrix has the interesting property that for any n x 1 column matrix α such that $T^{n-1} \alpha \neq 0$, the matrices

$$\alpha, T_\alpha, T_\alpha^2, \ldots, T^{n-1}\alpha$$

are linearly independent and therefore form a basis. It is then possible to express any other vector β in terms of this basis as

$$\beta = \sum_{i=1}^{n} a_i \, T^{i-1} \alpha \qquad (1)$$

in which the a_i 's are coefficients to be determined recursively, as follows.

$$T^{n-1} \beta = a_1 \, T^{n-1} \, \alpha + a_2 \, T^{n-1} \, \alpha$$
$$T^{n-2} \beta = a_1 \, T^{n-2} \, \alpha + a_2 \, T^{n-2} \, \alpha$$
$$T^{n-3} \beta = a_1 \, T^{n-3} \, \alpha + a_3 \, T^{n-3} \, \alpha$$

.

.

.

This is perhaps a good place to consider a simple application of this notation. Figure 1 indicates a decomposition of graph β into two components. In terms of the above notation

$$\alpha = \begin{bmatrix} 1 \\ 0 \\ 0 \\ 1 \\ 0 \\ 0 \end{bmatrix} \qquad \beta = \begin{bmatrix} 1 \\ 0 \\ 0 \\ 1 \\ 1 \\ 1 \end{bmatrix} \qquad T = \begin{bmatrix} 0 & 0 & 0 & 0 & 0 & 0 \\ 0 & 0 & 1 & 0 & 0 & 0 \\ 0 & 0 & 0 & 1 & 0 & 0 \\ 1 & 0 & 0 & 0 & 0 & 0 \\ 0 & 1 & 0 & 0 & 0 & 0 \\ 0 & 0 & 0 & 0 & 1 & 0 \end{bmatrix}$$

from which the decomposition, $\beta = \alpha + T^4\alpha$, indicated in the figure, follows directly.

Applications in Adaptive Systems

The notation just described for the algebraic treatment of graphs by no means constitutes an adaptive system, since at the very least an adaptive system would include a learning

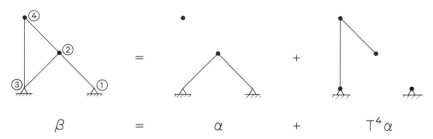

Fig. 1.   Decomposition of Graph β into Two Compents.

algorithm and a merit function with which it would be possible to rate solutions as they are generated. In spite of these missing elements, it is still possible to identify two types of "generalization" which are possible within the present context. (Generalization is taken to mean the construction of an improved solution using a given example or set of examples.)

One approach, usually impractical, to the design of an adaptive system is exhaustive search; i.e., at each step all possibilities are investigated. Exhaustive search is reminiscent of a situation which occurs in the analysis of physical systems in which, for example, from all possible solutions to a partial differential equation it is desired to select the one which satisfies the boundary conditions of interest. A common procedure is to construct a complete set of functions in terms of which *any* solution, including the one of interest, can be represented. This complete set being given, solving the problem requires only the determination of coefficients in a series expansion. Presumably this is more efficient than enumerating at some point all possible solutions. The algebraic treatment of graphs described in this paper makes the same procedure available to topological problems. It is therefore possible for the case of a graph with 4 node which can be represented [see Eq. (1)]

$$\beta = a_1\,\alpha + a_2\,T\alpha + a_3 T^2\alpha + a_4 T^3\alpha + a_5 T^4\alpha + a_6 T^5\alpha \qquad (2)$$

to study the behavior of a merit function with respect to the six a_i's rather than investigate the 2^6 possible graphs.

In practical problems, the series representative of a solution is usually truncated, and an improved solution (in a least squares sense) can be achieved by including additional terms. This is a kind of generalization which can be performed on graphs: starting with an example and then generating a complete set makes possible the automatic improvement of solutions by adding terms to an existing approximation—the example.

The second type of generalization to be discussed involves the selection of the nilpotent matrix T. If the matrix α in Eq. (1) or (2) is regarded as an example, the matrix T has some of the characteristics of a "learning operator," since it is used to generate other graphs from α. In the same vein, a "learning algorithm" would simply produce modifications of the matrix T. Selecting T is again reminiscent of using a complete set of functions in solving a physical system. There are cases, for example, when Legendre polynomials or Bessel series are used rather than Fourier series simply because they may converge more rapidly in a given application. It seems probable in applications that the matrix T will be similarly situation dependent.

With regard to the immediate implementation of the technique described in this paper, the primary difficulty lies in the selection and modification of the matrix T; about this a few general remarks may be made. The nilpotent matrix most commonly cited in the literature is

$$T = \begin{bmatrix} 0 & 1 & 0 & 0 & . & . & . \\ & 0 & 1 & 0 & . & . & . \\ & & 0 & 1 & . & . & . \\ & & & 0 & . & . & . \\ & & & & . & 1 \\ & & & & & 0 \end{bmatrix}$$

or

$$T_{ij} = \begin{cases} 1 \text{ if } j = i + 1 \\ 0 \text{ otherwise} \end{cases}.$$

With regard to other possibilities, if T is nilpotent $\tilde{T}$ is also nilpotent since

$$(\tilde{T})^n = (\tilde{T^n}).$$

In a more general vein, an orthogonal transformation on the matrix T generates the matrix T', which is defined to be

$$T' = \tilde{R} \, T \, R$$

where R is any matrix with the property $\tilde{R}R = I$. If T is nilpotent so is T', since

$$(T')^n = \tilde{R}T^nR.$$

It may be noted that orthogonal transformations on the commonly used nilpotent matrix form a nontrivial class of nilpotent matrices, since permutation matrices are orthogonal. In fact, the matrix T used in Fig. 1 was obtained by taking the transpose of the commonly used nilpotent matrix after subjecting it to an orthogonal transformation which corresponds to a permutation of elements 2 and 4.

Concluding Remarks

This paper must be regarded as conjectural. While the mathematics used is straightforward, the indicated applications are essentially untried. The automation of structural design needs an algebraic representation of graphs, and that is not conjecture. But whether the material described in this paper fulfills that need and related needs in other fields remains to be seen.

REFERENCES

1. Oystein Ore. *Theory of Graph*, Amer. Math. Society Colloquium Publications, vol. 38, (Providence: American Mathematical Society, 1962).
2. H. A. Simon and P. A. Simon. "Trial and Error Search in Solving Difficult Problems: Evidence from the Game of Chess," *Behavioral Science* 7, (October 1962), pp. 425–29.
3. G. Polya. "Kombinatorische Anzahlbestimmungen Fur Gruppen, Graphe, und Chemische Verbindungen," *Acta Math.* 68, (1937), pp. 145–254.
4. J. P. Roth. "Algebraic Topological Methods in Synthesis," in Proc. Int. Symposium on the Theory of Switching, *The annals of the Computation Laboratory of Harvard University* 24, (1959), pp. 57–73.
5. R. J. Duffin. "An Analysis of Wang Algebra of Networks," *Trans. Amer. Math. Soc.* 93, 1 (October 1959), pp. 114–31.
6. Ulf Grenander. "Foundations of Pattern Analysis," *Quart. Appl. Math.* 27, 1 (April 1969), pp. 1–55.
7. Garret Birkhoff and Saunders McLane. *A Survey of Modern Algebra*, (New York: Macmillan, 1965).

First Steps Toward a Model of the Vertebrate Central Nervous System*

LOUIS L. SUTRO

Massachusetts Institute of Technology
Cambridge, Massachusetts

Introduction

Let us first try to answer the question: Why attempt to model the central nervous systems of vertebrate animals? There are two answers. First, because it appears likely that modeling will increase our knowledge of the operation of these systems; second, because it appears that such models have useful applications. Among them is that of taking the place of men in remote and hostile environments—on the planets and under the sea.

Methods of modeling vary from the detailed cell models described by Harmon,[1] through the simulation models of Kilmer, [2,3] Fukushima,[4,5] and Lerman (described here), to the system models known as robots and artificial intelligence. In this paper we will not consider the first of these forms of modeling, because the number of cells to be modeled is too large to permit modeling them all, one by one. We will confine our

---

attention to simulation models, in which a module functions like a group of cells in the vertebrate central nervous system, and to "robots" and artificial intelligence. The latter two may or may not be intended to model vertebrate nervous systems, but they usually do so, at least in spirit. The reason seems to be that the designers of "robots" and artificial intelligence, being animals, cannot help modeling themselves.

The "robot" at Stanford Research Institute, which feels its way among obstacles, has some of the spirit of an animal.[6] So does the arm at Stanford University's Department of Computer Science which picks up blocks at the command of someone talking to its computer.[7] So does the TV camera and computer at Project MAC, MIT, which can look at a pile of blocks and estimate the shape not only of the blocks on top, but of those partly obscured.[8]

Given these beginnings, how can we proceed in an orderly way to model usefully the central nervous systems first of lower vertebrate animals, then of man?

Warren McCulloch proposed an approach which we describe later. First, however, let us explain how our efforts began; then we will describe how we are carrying out, or plan to carry out, what McCulloch proposed.

The opportunity to design a model of vertebrate vision arose in answer to the need for equipment to be sent to Mars to reduce the amount of information required to communicate the appearance of a scene there.* At that time (1964), it was expected that it would be possible to transmit no more than a few TV pictures from the equipment first landed on Mars. If the information could be reduced, however, more pictures could be sent. Warren McCulloch pointed out that such reduction of information is performed by the retinas of animal eyes and other "computers," as he called them, farther back in their visual systems. He recommended that we begin by modeling the frog's eye, whose retina recognizes an insect and reports this information to the frog's brain.

---

*Contract NSR 22-009-138 with the Bioscience Programs, Office of Space Science and Applications, NASA.

Employing the experimental results of Lettvin, Maturana, Pitts, and McCulloch,[9] we devised first a simulation of some of their findings. Then, concentrating on the operation of one type of ganglion cell, Roberto Moreno-Diaz devised an analytical model of it.[10,11] This cell, known as the "bug detector," is the most complex in the frog's retina. Now that it was analyzed and capable of being simulated, we were ready for the next step.

McCulloch advised us that "there is nothing interesting between the vision of the frog and that of man." He also advised: "Sensations are only analytical aspects of perceptions. One does not begin with sensations. One ends with sensations when one analyzes perception. People have it backwards."[12]

Making it possible to approach a model of perception as more than models of senses was a second research and development program, begun in 1966, which we took as an opportunity to begin a model of the core of the central nervous system. This is described below in the section entitled "Steps Toward a Model of the Core of the Central Nervous System."

The McCulloch Approach

In the history of science, the earliest models of the human nervous system were graphical and verbal. In modern times, the media of drawing and words have been augmented by mathematics. Now computers augment these media, making it possible to code graphical, verbal, and mathematical concepts in a computer program and thus make the model dynamic. McCulloch had in mind a step beyond this.

McCulloch had the designer's view of a computer, namely, that it can be designed for the operation it is to model. This view is contrary to the popularly held view that a computer has to be of the kind offered by large manufacturers. Such a computer can be programmed for a wide variety of tasks, but for the single task to which McCulloch might have assigned it, it is likely to be slow and clumsy. Accordingly each computer in his block diagram is assumed to be a special computer.

McCulloch was well aware of the misunderstanding that could grow out of localizing functions of the nervous system and of embodying mental functions in physical devices. However, in order to give us a crude provisional plan of operation, he oversimplified the human brain. In the future we expect to back away from this oversimplification by adding more detail.

He identified five principal computers in the human nervous system. (See Fig. 1.) At the left, representing the senses, is the retina of the eye, which consists of three layers, two of which are engaged in computation. At the upper left is the cerebrum, which McCulloch called "the great computer." Here, computation is carried out in many layers, each of which, if unfolded, would be about the size of a large newspaper.

The computer that controls all of the others is shown at the center right. It is the reticular core of the central nervous system, extending all the way from the base of the brain through the spinal cord. It makes the major decisions, or, rather, shifts the focus of attention so as to decide what you will do from moment to moment. It weights which command function takes over. By weighting the system to select the task you will do, it controls all of the other computers and, through them, the whole organism.

The basal ganglia shown at the lower left are a computer made of clusters of nerve cells at the base of the cerebrum. They program all innate or learned movements, such as feeding yourself, walking, and throwing a ball. They can acquire programs by growing connections to the motor control nerve cells shown along the bottom of the illustration.

The fifth computer is the cerebellum, shown at the top, which programs the completion of a movement, such as your reaching to touch an object. It requires inputs from your vestibular system to detect the tilt and acceleration of your head and from sense cells in your skin and muscles to tell you what you are touching and what is your posture. It is a correlator, a smoother, and an end-decider.

Between the computers are switching structures such as the thalamus and cerebellum anteroom. The colliculus in lower

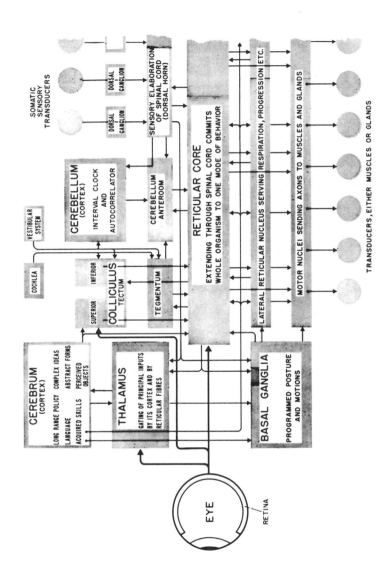

Fig. 1.   Block Diagram of Generalized Vertebrate Nervous System.

animals (fish, amphibians, birds) perceives form and movement. In higher animals, the superior colliculus controls the direction of gaze under the general direction of cortex. The inferior colliculus is probably concerned with auditory, vestibular inputs and the somatic body image. "Tectum" is another name for the colliculus. The base around it is the tegmentum.

Around the reticular core are specialized structures that could also be called computers, such as the nucleus of nerve cells that control respiration and other routine bodily functions and the dorsal horn of the spinal cord, through which pass the inputs from sense cells. Note that the reticular core acts on all the other computers, and they report to it.

The reticular core reaches decisions with the aid of raw data from the sensory transducers in the body (somatic), the retina, and the cochlea and computed data coming from the other four computers. Whether data from the retina is considered raw or computed is relative to one's frame of reference. It is the principal source of data to the primate brain, providing two of its three million inputs.

The computers of Fig. 1 are shown as they are arranged in animals where the spine is horizontal. Monkeys and man have the same computers in approximately the same relation, but the arrangement is tilted up, and the cerebrum, which is now very much larger, caps the stack.

All of these computers have a common ancestry. All developed in the course of evolution from the central computer, the reticular core, which has the complexity for their common tasks. As each particularized computer evolved from the "retic," some of its interconnections disappeared, while other interconnections became more plentiful.

From Control to Self-Command

As machines began to demonstrate the properties of animals, the demand rose, in the 1940's, for a language common to both the life sciences and invention. Many thought they had found this common language in the "science of communication and control in the animal and machine," which Norbert Wiener reported to the world as Cybernetics in 1948.[13] McCulloch, who was one of the founders of this school of thought, believed that something important was missing from Wiener's formulation.

The animal, McCulloch pointed out, is controlled, yes, but by what? A former student of McCulloch's, Dr. Arnold Scheibel, and his wife, Dr. Mila Scheibel, experimenting at the U.C.L.A. Medical School, concluded that the structure of the nervous system responsible for attention is the core of the reticular formation whose flat dendritic fields (Fig. 11) lie athwart the channels of information flow in the spinal column, sampling these channels and deciding among themselves to what the animal should attend.

The Scheibels' discovery was part of the answer to McCulloch's question. Another part of the answer was to show how the core of the reticular formation performed the operations claimed for it. Applying himself to this question, Dr. William Kilmer devised a programmed model in which modules, representing groups of reticular core cells, interact in the manner that the Scheibels describe and are capable of conditioning. This model was begun as an investigation into how a roving vehicle on Mars, operating under its own command but carrying general instructions as to what it should look for and what it should avoid, could decide from moment to moment what class of thing it would do: advance, retreat, stop to look, repair itself, etc. The model was thus begun under NASA support.* It was completed under Air Force Support.**

Watching this model operate, McCulloch was impressed by its similarity to the commander in military command and control systems. Thus was born "command and control in animals and machines" as a redefinition of cybernetics. The words "communication" and "computation," which Wiener used, are to be inferred. Dr. Roy Hermann has suggested that McCulloch's redefinition be further revised to "self-command and control

---

*Contract NGR-22-009-140 through the former Electronic Research Center, NASA.
**Contract AF 33(615)3885 through System Engineering Group, Wright-Patterson Air Force Base.

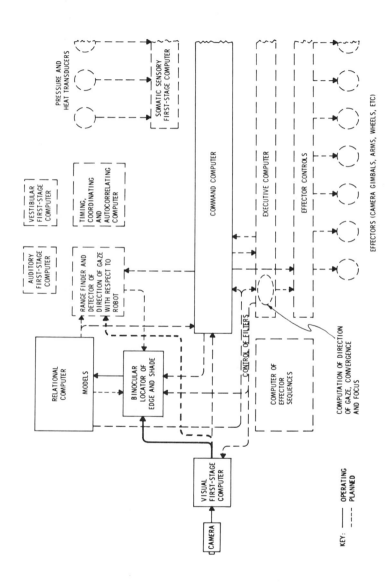

Fig. 2. Engineering Analog of Generalized Vertebrate Nervous System.

in animals and machines," so as not to suggest that the command is that of others.[31]

To devise the models we describe in this report, we needed to make preliminary engineering designs also of other blocks in the diagram of Fig. 1. The names we applied to the blocks and the interconnections we planned are shown in Fig. 2. Note the first-stage computers in four sensory subsystems and the controls exercised on their filters by the executive computer.

There is one error in this drawing which we will correct later. We have replaced the thalamus of Fig. 1 by a box representing only one of its functions.

Robots, Agents and Automata

Norbert Wiener persuaded the scientific world that the words "control," "servomechanism," "computation," etc., are applicable to both animals and machines, but he made no recommendation as to what to call the whole system of which those mechanisms are parts. McCulloch had suggestions here:

"We use the world 'robot' in two ways. The first, and less important, is as a machine that performs isolated functions of a human being. The second, and more important, is as a description of life, applicable to either living things or machines. Such a description is indifferent to whether the system is man-made or grown, whether it is built of hardware or living cells. This is a central theme of cybernetics: to use the same logic and mathematics to describe men and machines. Norbert Wiener looked at control this way. We are looking at both command and control. Thus, in the more important sense, a robot is a prescription for a system that until recently could be achieved only by the growth of living cells but is becoming something we can manufacture."[14]

McCulloch further defined a robot as a "stupid servant." Asked what we might call a robot that can think, McCulloch replied: "Artificial agent." He explained that the word "agent" comes from Latin and means "doer." We asked him if he meant to draw a parallel with artificial intelligence. "No," he said.

" 'Artificial intelligence' is a poor choice of words. Intelligence is never artificial. What is artificial is the agent that carries the intelligence." MacKay added that an agent is "one who acts in the light of data and in view of ends, as distinct from a mere generator of activity, such as a clock." He referred us to *The Self as Agent* by John MacMurray.[15]

"A robot has minimum spontaneous agency," McCulloch continued. Nevertheless, it requires "two sensory modalities for a sense of reality." MacKay added: "If I am hallucinating that salt cellar and reach out, it won't be there."

This discussion is not intended to disparage the research performed under the heading of Artificial Intelligence, but only to point out that "A.I.," as it is briefly called, has not made the modeling of animals a primary goal.

We foresee an evolving sequence of models, starting with a McCulloch robot, continuing through a McCulloch artificial agent, and extending to a McCulloch automaton. We put McCulloch's name with each of the terms to emphasize the duality implied by McCulloch's definitions, that is, that each of these models will be both a model of animals and a potentially useful device.

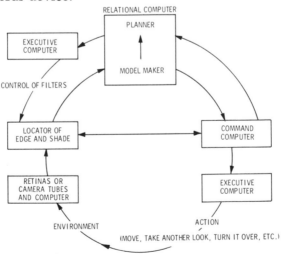

Fig. 3.   Flow of Information in a Robot or Agent.

---

[*]This conversation took place on the McCulloch farm at Old Lyme, Conn., 14 and 15 August, 1969.

Flow of Information Through a Robot*

McCulloch described the operation of a robot as "multiple loops of information flow, some closing through the robot, with computation in every loop." Figure 3 pictures, in its outer loop, the flow of information from the environment up into a McCulloch robot, through it, and down into the environment in the form of action. Two inner loops are shown: The one in the upper left corner is concerned with vision; that in the upper right provides the "particulars" needed for command computation. That the command computer receives information from all other computers and they receive information from it is indicated by the two-headed horizontal arrow in the center of the illustration.

While only one "outer loop" is shown in Fig. 3, two are needed for a sense of reality, and a third is needed if the robot is to move through its environment. For the robot planned for a Mars landing, outer loops were to be provided through senses of vision, touch, acceleration and relative position of the parts.

"An inner loop," such as that shown at the upper left of Fig. 3, "is everything that builds up within you the image of the outside world that enables you to move within it. It is all the matching responses. If you see something from one angle you have to calculate where it will be in your field of view when you view it from another angle." For each outer loop, there will be a corresponding inner loop of this kind.

Note that we have used the word "computer" in describing Figs. 1 and 2. We could as well have used the words "information processor."

Internal Organization of a Robot

If we accept the argument that there must be flows of information into, within, and out of a robot, then the question arises: What happens to the information as it flows through?

---

*Much of this concept came to McCulloch from Lewey Gilstrap, who attributes it to Sommerhoff.[30]

A colleague of McCulloch's, Jose da Fonseca, offered this answer: "Perception. In the language of psychology, perception implies many possible acts, each of which is a transform of sensory inputs. Neurophysiology shows that this transform takes place at different levels of the nervous system, the overriding level being that of the core of the reticular formation, which commits the whole organism to one mode of behavior or another. Thus, to perceive is to get set to act."[16]

The research of another colleague of McCulloch's, Donald MacKay, "suggests that perception is the activity of keeping up to date the internal organizing system that represents the external world by an internal matching response to the current impact of the world upon the receptive system. In a sense, the internal organizing system is continually making fast-time predictions on what is going on out there and what is likely to happen out there, and it takes anticipatory action accordingly.[17]

A model of the core of the reticular formation is described below the section entitled "Steps Toward a Model of the Core of the Central Nervous System."

Note the change in the definition of perception from the traditional view that it is a passive mechanical process in which the organism is delivered a stimulus and then executes a response, as though there were two sequential processes involved. MacKay develops this new view.[18]

Means of Keeping Up to Date the Internal Organizing System

If we were constrained to model only structures in the vertebrate nervous system whose function and operation has been clearly identified, we ought to stop here. Fortunately, the overall functioning of the brain is described with increasing clarity in the manner of McCulloch and MacKay in the previous section. Following McCulloch's lead, we design a computer to perform each function he or his successors define. Then we simulate this design on an existing computer. This permits us

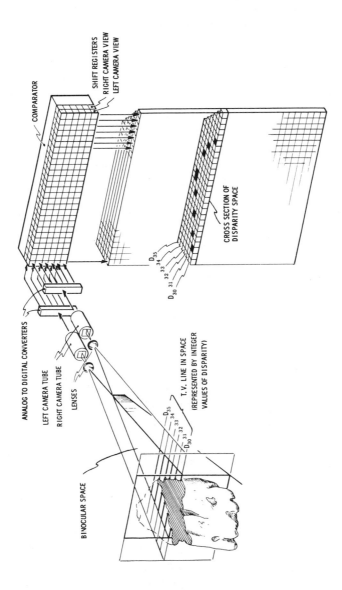

Fig. 4. Sequence of Operations Performed on a Single Scan Line of Left and Right TV Cameras.

to guess the details of a biological system and to discover by guess and test what these details probably are.

We have developed computer programs that operate on TV images, in the manner of the cells identified by Hubel, Wiesel, and others. We have developed another program that can compare a binocular pair of images to each other to form a three-dimensional model of a scene.[19] Bela Julesz had shown[20] that depth can be detected in noise-free scenes by shifting the left image past the right image, one picture element at a time, and comparing regions of the two images at each shift. Jerome Lerman has now shown how to detect depth in the images of scenes that are noisy and that contain ambiguities.[19]

Lerman's structure of a model of the environment is presented at the lower right of Fig. 4. This "disparity space," as presently simulated in our computer, is actually 36 planes (0 to 35) deep, but to keep the drawing simple we have shown only the planes near the camera, D_{30} to D_{35}.

Figure 4 shows, approximately, how the section is formed that crosses this disparity space; that is, it explains how the black squares got there. All the information in that cross section came from the TV lines on the face of the left and right camera tubes. Note that when the left TV line is projected out through its lens, it sweeps a V-shaped field, and that the right TV line sweeps another V-shaped field. Where the two V-shaped fields overlap is the binocular field of the camera tubes.

As the electron beam in the left camera tube sweeps a line of the left image, it forms a signal which goes to an analog-to-digital converter that converts it to a succession of "words" shown 6 bits high. Each word represents the luminance of one point in the line swept. One such word at a time enters the shift register called "left camera view" and then is shifted to make room for the next word, until that register is full.

The right camera tube sweeps its line later than the left camera tube sweeps its line so that when the digitized left view fills its register, the digitized right view lags behind it. Then, as the digitized right view catches up, the two images are compared point by point at 36 different amounts of overlap or

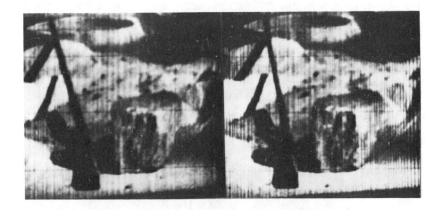

Fig. 5.   Images Acquired by TV Camera.

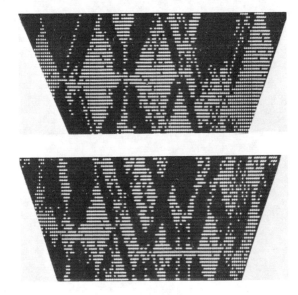

**Fig. 6.   Two Cross Sections of the Disparity Space Formed from the Stereo
Pair of Fig. 5; Each Cross Section Represents One TV Line.**

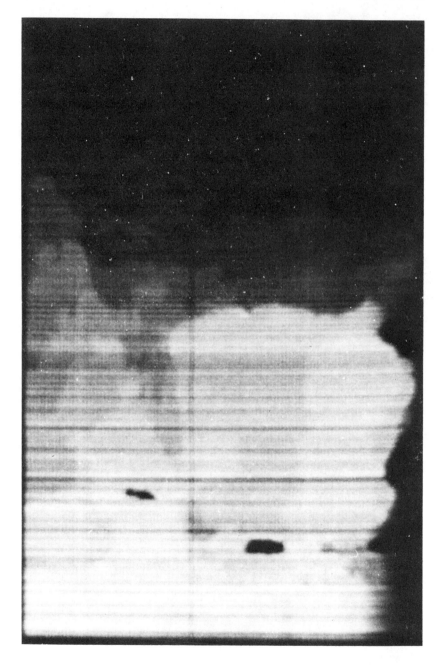

Fig. 7.   Range Map Formed from the Disparity Space Partially Illustrated
by Fig. 4; Nearness is Represented by Lightness of Gray.

disparity. If the difference in the luminance in each comparison exceeds a predetermined threshold, a 1 is placed in the cross section of disparity space representing the line just swept. In the illustration, a 1 is represented by a black square. Note that the line of 1's approximates the front surface of the rock.

Figure 5 shows left and right view of a Marslike scene, taken by the camera tubes of Fig. 4 and digitized.* Figure 6 shows two cross sections of disparity space that resulted from comparison of left and right lines at two levels in the images. White dots here have the same meaning as the black dots in Fig. 4. A diamond is formed in a cross section as an area of uniform luminance in the left view is moved past the corresponding area of luminance in the right view. The near point of the diamond is formed when the overlap or disparity is 1; the waist of the diamond when the overlap is complete; the far point when the overlap is down to 1 again.

An algorithm devised by Lerman reduces each diamond to a line and each stack of diamonds to a plane. Figure 7 plots such planes by making the nearest a light shade of gray, the most distant, black. Note how the stick and its shadows get

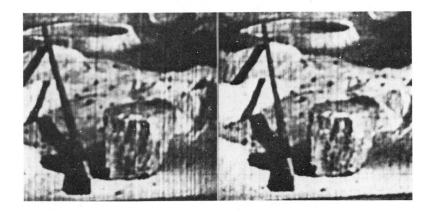

Fig. 8.   Images of Fig. 5 Contrast-Enhanced Once.

---

*A stereoscope suitable for viewing the stereo pairs in this paper is the PS-2, obtainable from Air Photo Supply, Yonkers, N. Y. Set the lenses 63mm apart unless your eyes are closer or farther apart.

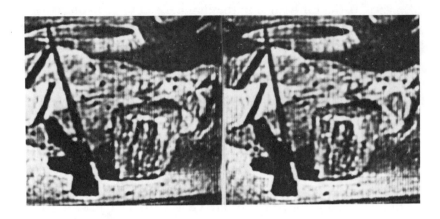

Fig. 9. Images of Fig. 5 Contrast-Enhanced Twice.

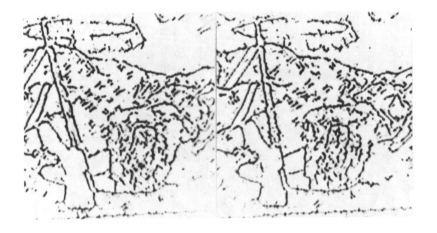

Fig. 10. Line Drawing Formed from Images of Fig. 5.

successively darker as they recede into the distance at the left.

Disparity space is not only a model of the binocular space at the left of Fig. 4, but also a space in which the extent to which one object blocks another (occlusion) can be determined, and errors, such as the black patches below the rock in Fig. 7, can be eliminated. Disparity space is thus a space where a robot can think about the pictures picked up by its camera-tube eyes. For example, it can decide how to get around the rock that blocks its path.

So far we have talked only of comparing the luminances of the left view with those of the right. It appears that economy can be achieved by first enhancing the contrast of each image (Figs. 8 and 9), then forming a line drawing (Fig. 10), and finally noting the gradation of tone across the line (light-to-dark or dark-to-light).[21] The robot will then have less to remember. Perhaps this is why Hubel-Wiesel cells evolved.

The strategy devised by Hatfield and Lerman, employed in

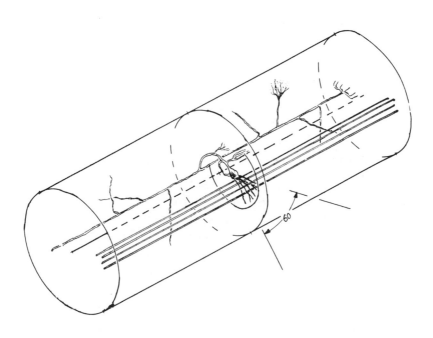

Fig. 11. Reticular Core Cell as Drawn by McCulloch.

the steps pictured in Figs. 8 to 10, models the layered disposition of neurons in the vertebrate nervous system, "where every neuron in a layer has much the same operation as its neighbor, but over a slightly different population of inputs. This disposition seems crucial. In a sense every such element in a layer performs an integral transform (but nonlinear) over a broad area of its input, and that input overlaps that of the neighbors. The operation of such a layer is almost holographic to its input, since a change of one point at the input is seen by many neurons, and each neuron sees a large fraction of the total input."[22] The use of this strategy is described by Sutro and Kilmer.[23]

Into this layered structure can be read the anticipated details of the appearance of the environment, for comparison with incoming details; meanwhile, the anticipated structure of the environment can be read into disparity space for comparison with its observed structure. The function of both the layered structure and the disparity space can then be "matching" in the sense that MacKay uses this word above, in the section entitled "Internal Organization of a Robot."

Steps Toward a Model of the Core of the Central Nervous System

Assembling all the known information about the central core of the nervous system in vertebrates, McCulloch and Kilmer gradually formed a concept of how it probably works.[3] Figure 11 is McCulloch's diagram of one of the million or more cells that form what is called the "reticular core" or "core of the reticular formation." Because the dendrites of each cell spread in a plane (approximately 60° as shown in Fig. 11), the anatomists, the Scheibels, say the cells remind them of a stack of poker chips.[24] Following this suggestion, Kilmer devised chiplike modules, each of which models many reticular cells. The modules interact, as the cells apparently do, to determine the mode of behavior or self-command of the robot. Moreover, each module stores the conditions under which it made previous decisions.

Figure 12 shows the stack of modules simulated by Jay

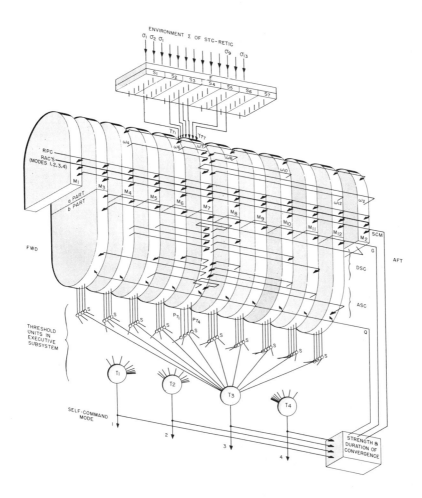

Fig. 12. Block Diagram of STC-RETIC and External Threshold Units; Connections Are Shown Only to M₇ Whereas Actually an Equal Number of Connections Are Made to Every Full-Sized Module.

Blum after the design by Kilmer. The input to the model is an environment, Σ, described by a binary number. A different sample of the bits in this number goes to each module through sensory systems S_1 to S_7. Responding to these inputs, each module yields a probability vector of four components, shown leaving the module at its bottom. (For module 7, these are labeled P_1 through P_4.) The same signals ascend (ASC) and descend (DSC) to other modules.

All of the signals with second subscript 1 go to threshold unit T_1, all of those with second subscript 2 to T_2, and so on. When the threshold of a T unit is exceeded, the robot enters the mode of behavior of its subscript. Only four modes of behavior are possible with this model, but with the addition

Table 1

Specimen Lists of Modes of Behavior
(Self Commands)

Vertebrate animal	Proposed Mars robot
1. sleep	1. look and feel
2. eat	2. advance
3. drink	3. retreat
4. fight	4. right itself if overturned
5. flee	5. maintain itself
6. hunt	6. chart its environment
7. search (or explore)	7. rest
8. urinate	perform incompatible
9. defecate	experiments, as follows:
10. groom	8. Experiment A
11. mate	9. Experiment B
12. give birth (or lay eggs)	10. Experiment C
13. mother the young (including suckling the young or hatching, retrieving, perineal licking, etc.)	
14. build or locate nest	
15. and special innate forms of behavior, such as migrate, hibernate, gnaw, hoard, depending on the species.	

of more modules and richer interconnections, more modes will be possible. The election of the mode and its strength are fed back into the computation by the box at lower right.

Modes that McCulloch identified in vertebrate animals are shown in the left column of Table 1. Possible modes of a Mars robot are shown in the right column. Our definition of a mode of behavior comes from Rioch as a pattern "in which the whole organism is integrated."[25]

Fig. 13. Arm and Hand Designed to Feel Shape of Terrain Where Cameras Are Looking.

Contact Subsystem

The minimum function of an arm and hand, we think, is to feel where the cameras are looking. Figure 13 shows an arm and hand designed to feel the shape of the terrain to where the cameras are looking. Mounted above the front axle of a small tractor, a binocular pair of TV cameras can look straight up or straight down as well as ahead and sidewards. The hand can reach to where the robot is about to go, to check on a perception, made through the visual subsystem, that the way is clear and the path smooth enough for the wheels.

A shoulder, pictured to the left of the cameras, provides three degrees of freedom for the arm: linear extension and rotations in elevation and azimuth. All motions, except that of the wrist, are polar-centric, that is, centered on a common point, so that transformation of coordinates can be as simple as possible. A spring-loaded pin, in the finger, indicates pressure by the amount that it is depressed.

Putting the Parts Together

As the model evolves it is to be expected that other parts will be incorporated. Examples are the hands that grasp as well as feel, employed at the Artificial Intelligence Laboratory at MIT,[26] the Department of Computer Science at Stanford[27] and the Department of Mechanical Engineering at MIT.[28]

Figure 13 shows how the outer loop of vision, previously diagramed as Fig. 3, may be joined by outer loops of contact and orientation. The axes of the two cameras (1) are parts of the outer loop of vision. The finger and arm (2) are part of the outer loop of the contact subsystem.

Orientation may be achieved through the readings of two pendulous accelerometers swinging in orthogonal directions (3) and readings of the resolvers on the gimbals that support the cameras. Pendulous accelerometers can be used because, in this design, the cameras may be used only after the robot has stopped. These readings will be organized by a vestibular first-stage computer.

The three loops will be integrated by a self-command computer which will resolve conflicts in the interpretation of the information entering it from the three loops.

It appears likely that all the computers required by the robot can be made small enough to be carried by the vehicle shown in Fig. 13. It also seems likely that operation of the robot will be attempted before this miniaturization has taken place. To operate with some computers on board and some remote, a radio link will be provided, using the antenna shown on the robot.

How will this robot differ from that already in operation at Stanford Research Institute (S.R.I.)? It will be oriented to perceive objects of any size or shape that it has been instructed to seek, whereas the S.R.I. robot can perceive only polyhedra. It will have binocular vision, a sense of touch capable of being manipulated, and a sense of orientation. If these senses disagree as to the robot's appropriate mode of behavior, the self-command computer will resolve the conflict.

The development of this McCulloch robot could come about through cooperation among the robot-developing laboratories.

What Good Is a Robot? An Agent? An Automaton?

We foresee a cooperative effort among laboratories leading first to a practical but low-level robot, then to an agent with some of the cognitive capacities of a human being. "The robot is a worker," McCulloch said, "obeying the order to get a job done, such as move across the surface of a moon or planet toward a designated destination, avoiding hazards and possibly seeking objects of particular shape, texture, or color.

"An agent we define as a higher level machine, able to think in elementary ways. It will act in the light of incoming information and in view of ends that we have pressed upon it. An agent will not quite be an automaton, because it will not go only by its own nod. It will listen to us. It still has its umbilical cord, so to speak.

"An automaton, as we use the word, is at present only a concept. It would be the manufactured equivalent of a higher animal, able to acquire habits," think, and act on its own.[12]

At the same time, insofar as we understand the functions of the nervous system, we will try to produce devices that simulate it. To quote Donald MacKay: "When a sufficiently rich sensory system is interlocked with a sufficiently rich motor system, the resultant possible combination of behavior patterns can readily exceed the capacity of the unaided imagination. Our purpose is to provide an aid to the imagination of the biologist seeking to formulate critical questions about the actual mechanisms of sensory-motor integration. In other words, we will provide him something to point to."[29]

Conclusion

Perhaps the models just described will support McCulloch's conclusion: "The main problems of the nervous system have been solved. Those that remain are parochial." Or perhaps these models will open the subject so that unsolved problems can be more squarely faced.

In any case, terms have been defined that apply to both animals and machines: robot, agent, automaton. A science has been defined that uses these terms to study self-command and control in animals and machines. This is cybernetics.

REFERENCES

1. L. D. Harmon. "Studies with Artificial Neurons, I: Properties and Functions of an Artificial Neuron," *Kybernetik*, (December 1961).
2. W. L. Kilmer. "A Model of the Brain's Hippocampal Computer," in this volume.
3. W. L. Kilmer, W. S. McCulloch, and J. Blum. "A Model of the Vertebrate Central Command System," *Int. J. Man-Machine Studies* 1, (1969), pp. 279–309.
4. K. Fukushima. "Visual Feature Extraction by a Multilayered Network of Analog Threshold Elements," *IEEE Transactions on System Science and Cybernetics* vol. SSC-5, no. 4, (October 1969), pp. 322–34.
5. K. Fukushima. "A Feature Extractor for Curvilinear Patterns: A Design Suggested by the Mammalian Visual System," *Kybernetik* vol. 7 (1970), pp. 153–70.
6. N. J. Nilsson et al. *Application of Intelligent Automata to Reconnaissance* (Stanford, California: Stanford Research Institute, 1968).
7. J. McCarthy et al. "A Computer with Hands, Eyes, and Ears," in *Proceedings of the 1968 Fall Joint Computer Conference* (Washington, D.C.: Thompson Book Co., 1968), 329–38. (hereafter cited as "Computer with Hands," *FJCC*).
8. A. Guzman. *Some Aspects of Pattern Recognition by Computer*, MAC-TR-37, Project MAC, Massachusetts Institute of Technology, Cambridge, Massachusetts, 1967.
9. J. Y. Lettvin. 'What a Frog's Eye Tells a Frog's Brain," in *Proceedings of the Institute of Radio Engineers* vol. 47, no. 11, (November 1959).
10. R. Moreno-Diaz. "An Analytical Model of the Group 2 Ganglion Cell in the Frog's Retina," Report E-1858, Charles Stark Draper Laboratory Division, Massachusetts Institute of Technology, Cambridge, Massachusetts, 1966.
11. R. Moreno-Diaz. "An Analytical Model of the Bug Detector Ganglion Cell in the Frog's Retina," in *Cybernetic Problems in Bionics*, ed. H. L. Oestreicher and D. R. Moore, (New York: Gordon and Breach, 1968).
12. L. L. Sutro. Notes of Conversations with W. S. McCulloch, 1958–1969.

13. N. Wiener, *Cybernetics*, (Cambridge, Massachusetts: MIT Press, 1961).
14. L. L. Sutro and W. L. Kilmer. "An Assembly of Computers to Command and Control a Robot," in *Proceedings of the 1969 Spring Joint Computer Conference*, (Montvale, New Jersey: AFIPS Press, 1969), p. 131, (hereafter cited as "Assembly of Computers," *SJCC*).
15. J. MacMurray. *The Self as Agent* (London: Faber and Faber Ltd., 1953).
16. J. da Fonseca. Personal communication to the author, 1967.
17. W. M. Brodey and N. Lindgren. "Human Enhancement beyond the Machine Age," *IEEEE Spectrum*, (February 1968), p. 89.
18. D. M. MacKay. "Ways of Looking at Perception," in *Models for the Perception of Speech and Visual Form*, ed. W. Wathen-Dunn, (Cambridge, Massachusetts: MIT Press, 1967).
19. J. B. Lerman. "Computer Processing of Stereo Images for the Automatic Extraction of Range," B.S. and M.S. thesis, Department of Electrical Engineering, Massachusetts Institute of Technology, Cambridge, Massachusetts, 1970.
20. B. Julesz. "Towards the Automation of Binocular Depth Perception," in *Proceedings of IFIPS Congress 1962*, (Amsterdam: North Holland Publishing Co., 1963).
21. L. L. Sutro and W. L. Kilmer. "Assembly of Computers," *SJCC*, pp. 122, 123.
22. J. Y. Lettvin. Personal communication to the author, 1966.
23. L. L. Sutro and W. L. Kilmer. "Assembly of Computers," *SJCC*, p. 124.
24. M. E. Scheibel and A. B. Scheibel. "Anatomical Basis of Attention Mechanisms in Vertebrate Brains," in *The Neurosciences—A Study Program*, ed. Q. C. Quarton et al., (New York: Rockefeller University Press, 1967), pp. 577–602.
25. D. McK. Rioch. "Psychopathological and Neuropathological Aspects of Consciousness," in *Brain Mechanisms and Consciousness*, ed. E. D. Adrian et al., (Oxford: Blackwell Scientific Publications, 1954).
26. M. L. Minsky and S. A. Papert. *Research on Intelligent Automata Status Report II*, Project MAC, Massachusetts Institute of Technology, Cambridge, Massachusetts, 1967.
27. J. McCarthy et al., "Computer with Hands," *FJCC*.
28. W. R. Ferrell and T. B. Sheridan. "Supervisory Control of Remote Manipulation," *IEEE Spectrum* vol. 4, no. 10, (October 1967), pp. 81–88.
29. D. M. MacKay. Personal communication to the author, 1969.
30. G. Sommerhoff, *Analytical Biology*, (London: Oxford University Press, 1950).
31. R. Herrmann. Personal communication to the author, 1970.

ADDITIONAL READINGS

Colonnier, M. L., 1966 "The Structural Design of the Neocortex" in *Brain and Conscious Experience*, John C. Eccles, ed., New York: Springer-Verlag, pp. 1–23.

Scheibel, M. E. and A. B. Scheibel, 1966 "Patterns of Organization in Specific and Nonspecific Thalamic Fields" in *The Thalamus*, D. Purpura and M. Yahr, eds., New York: Columbia University Press, pp. 13–46.

Scheibel, M. E. and A. B. Scheibel, 1967 "Anatomical Basis of Attention Mechanisms in Vertebrate Brains," in *The Neurosciences: A Study Program*, G. C. Quarton, T. Melnechuk, and F. O. Schmitt, eds., New York: The Rockefeller University Press, pp. 577–602.

Robots in the Home and Industry

M. W. THRING

*Queen Mary College, University of London
England*

Man's Use of Machines

The most justifiable reason that the human being invents machines is to have them act as his slaves, that is, to do the work which he wants done but which is too boring, elaborate, unpleasant, heavy, or dangerous for him to do himself. This is the work that, formerly, some aristocratic humans could arrange for others to do for them.

Now we have reached a stage in technology where we could free all humans throughout the whole world to do only the interesting, original, pleasant work (including designing and building and maintaining the machines) and to enjoy a short working life (perhaps 20,000–40,000 hours in place of the present 80,000). Machines could provide them with all the necessities, a reasonable number of luxuries, and enough leisure to do the creative things that are man's true self fulfilment.

In fact, however, we are not applying our ingenuity to this objective, but rather to the design of war machines and status symbols (both national and individual), with various unhappy results. Much of mankind has an inadequate standard of living. In parts of the world, we are rapidly destroying the environment with bad by-products of the thoughtless use of machines—noise, pollution, ugliness. We are exhausting our supplies of minerals, fresh air, and unspoilt country at a rate which will leave nothing for our great grandchildren.

However, in this paper I am going to adopt the optimistic hypothesis that before it is too late, humanity decides to make a better use of the magic powers given to it by the machines. I use the word magic because, in fact, all the wishes of the ancients, who went to magicians, can be satisfied now—flying carpets soaring round the earth, palaces, moving mountains, long life, and freedom from disease. All these technology can provide better than Aladdin's lamp.

We shall assume that a policy has been developed whereby everyone is properly and fully educated. Everyone then, is prepared to do interesting work to earn his living and to pursue hobbies or unpaid leisure activities. The leisure given man by the machines has become an opportunity for self-fulfillment. Also, the power of the machines to make five times as many goods per man hour as were producible in 1970 America has been harnessed to enable everyone to earn a good living in half as many working hours as at present and to receive a vast bonus in human services, especially professional, artistic, cultural, educational, and health services. I shall try to examine the role of the robots in such a society.

What Is a Robot and What Are Its Limitations?

Roughly, one can define a robot as a mechanical device to which a human being can give a series of sets of more or less detailed instructions to retain in its memory. Then, whenever it is ordered to do so, it can carry out these instructions to perform an appropriate, complex series of manipulative operations; it can be told to repeat them indefinitely or to do them every day at certain times. A complete robot must be sufficiently adaptable to do as wide a range of manipulative operations as a trained, albeit unimaginative human; for example, it must be able to operate the manual controls on other machines and use hand tools of various kinds. (These may well be modified to suit it, an electric drill, say, being fitted onto its arm with a bayonet fitting.) A complete robot must be able to move itself about in a certain limited environment. It must steer itself by dead reckoning to a position in that environment to which it has been instructed to go, carrying objects with it which it has picked up and can put down. A complete robot can be instructed to vary its movements according to its own sense impressions or observations of variations in the external situation, e.g., a variation in the position or orientation of the object it has to handle. (Fig. 1.) Thus, the two handling robots on the market at the present time, the Unimate and the Versatran, are incomplete in that they can neither move themselves about nor sense variations in the external situation.

Under this general definition the robot need not have the ability to learn craft skills or anything else. It does not have to carry out any complicated logical processes except, possibly, to interpret sense impressions to make the decision between two categories of objects, e.g., between a satisfied component and a faulty one. Some things, of course, the robot does require:

1. A hand and arm;
2. self-propulsion and self-steering;
3. power and control systems for 1 and 2;
4. a limited computer with memory for instructions and decision-making;
5. senses; these can be analog or digital observations of one or more of the following:
    a. touch, roughness, hardness and position, weight, thermal conductivity, temperature, proximity, and possibly shape and size, e.g., dimensional accuracy to a gauge;
    b. sight, shape, color, distance, size;
    c. smell, e.g., by gas phase chromatography;
    d. position of its limbs and weight by force on limbs;
    e. hearing—possibly a number of verbal commands or just one: Stop.

Of course, robots can be coupled to computers and so make

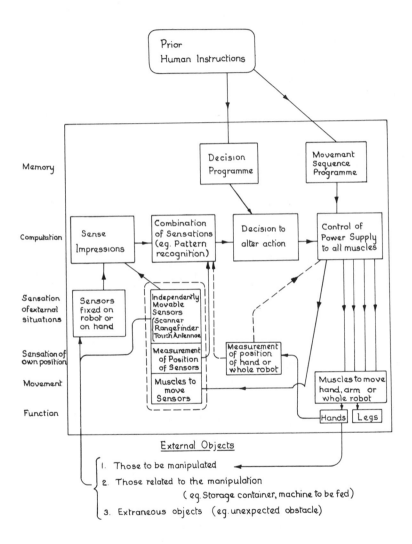

Fig. 1. Essential Mechanism of a Complete Robot; the Independently Movable Sensors Within the Dotted Region Are Not an Essential Part.

use of the latest developments in them. Thus, as computer design advances, they may be able to learn and carry out complex logical instructions, as the SRI robot is already doing. However, I am convinced that there are certain respects in which the human being will always be so superior to his arti-fact that he will need to have no hesitation in treating it as his slave.

The first respect corresponds to the second law of thermo-dynamics, that all systems become degenerate unless conscious-ness (Maxwell's demon) intervenes, and to the law of com-munication which states that a mechanical system can only make the message more garbled—it requires a human to make it clearer. This may be stated as follows:

> A robot can never do any task more sophisticated or organized than it has been instructed by a human to do. For example, it can sort things into categories that have been given to it, but it cannot discover a new category. It can carry out these instructions more patiently, accurately, and tirelessly than any human can do, but if it makes errors, they will be random and will neither constitute improvements nor be self-correcting. A corollary of this law is that robots left unattended by humans gradually will degenerate and become unable to continue their work because, however much the ability to repair each other's breakdowns is built into them, break-downs will occur which the human designers have not allowed for. Another corollary is that if robots are made capable of building copies of themselves, then by the third or fourth generation so many faults will have arisen that they will have become useless.

The second respect in which man-made machines must always remain qualitatively inferior to the men who made them flows from what may be called the "aesthetic law":

> The robot can never have true, human emotions or feelings. It can, of course, be programmed to produce all the external mani-festations of feelings, just as a tape recorder can sing as beautifully as the best artist recorded on it. A human being has three separate educable brains: intellectual (dealing with logical abstractions, con-cepts, mathematics, scientific theories), physical (the trained skill of the hands, eyes and body, e.g., in using tools or driving a car), and emotional (concerned with feelings, like happiness or loyalty; with human value judgments, such as that people matter quali-tatively more than machines; and with artistic appreciation). One

cannot prove any hypothesis about emotions, because they are essentially subjective and therefore not physically measurable; nevertheless, they matter more to a person's enjoyment, of life than anything that can be indicated on a dial. Still, I submit for consideration the hypothesis that we cannot build an emotional brain into a robot, and I believe that this view eventually will be proved, in the same way as the laws of thermodynamics are proved, by the failure of all attempts to build machines that can only work by contradicting these laws.

There are very important corollaries to this law, also. The emotional brain is essential for all really original, creative work, whether it be scientific hypothesis formation, painting a picture, composing a symphony, or inventing a new type of machine. It follows that a robot will be unpractical for all these activities. It also follows that the robot cannot make its own value judgments, and, therefore, that it must be provided with the value judgments that its human master decides are right. Thus, we have great responsibility, since we can make robots go berserk and kill humans or we can build into them the instruction never to harm a human even at the expense of their own self-destruction.

Design Principles for Robots

Quite apart from these laws of impotence of the robot designer, there are certain design principles which must be followed if artifacts are to be feasible, given limited human resources. These may be listed as follows:

1. There is no immediate possibility of producing an efficient robot which looks like a human being, because this shape and method of chemical operation via a bloodstream is impossibly restricting for a machine which is assembled from separate components and uses engineering materials, metals, and plastics. Thus, the robot must be designed purely functionally for the range of tasks that it has to undertake. For example, the complete robot will probably consist of a low trucklike base containing all the main machinery (computerbrain, power storage, motors for hydraulic operation, wheels, and steering device), with a single slender steel column rising to carry an arm and an eye (see Fig. 2). Specialized robots might have built-in workbenches and several arms, all of which can be doing different jobs at the same time, or a turntable on which successive components can be fixed onto a series of chassis.

Fig. 2. Storekeeping Robot (Model).

2. The control mechanism, with feedback of position and force which is available on nearly all the human muscles, is a very complex device to imitate mechanically, and therefore robots must have as few of them as possible. The complete robot will have to have seven such systems for positioning and orienting the hand and grasping with it. The hand has twenty separate muscle movements for grasping; the first robots will have a sophisticated design of hand with a single grasping movement (see Fig. 3), so it will not have the ability of the human hand to handle several objects at once.

3. Any device which has been found valuable in any industrial, domestic, or agricultural operation can be built into a specialized robot or can be given a simple locking device for use in the hand of a generalized robot. Moreover, operations which are very awkward or inconvenient for humans can readily be done by a machine with steel tubular skeleton, arms 2–3 m. (6½–10 feet) long, an eye, and a light on its hand and with a built-in tray for a collection of tools and devices.

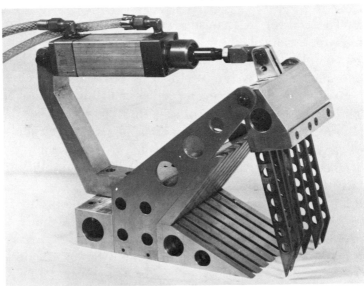

Fig. 3.   Hands for Robots (Models).

4. The designer must build in safety precautions against all foreseeable accidents, e.g., fail-safe devices and devices whereby a human can switch the robot off from a distance or take control of it verbally in an emergency.

Tasks for Robots

There are three tasks in industry which stand out as the most boring and unworthy of humans because of their repetitive nature, and, conversely, as ones for which robots can be developed in the next ten years. It is worth analyzing these in order to see how complex the brains of the first robots will have to be.

The first task is unloading incoming goods from a truck and putting them in an appropriate place in the store, informing the central factory computer or human controller of the stock levels, and then taking the appropriate materials from the store to the automatic machines in the factory as the robot receives instructions from the central controller. The whole factory would have a closed-loop radio system, so that all the robots in it could have two-way communication with the controller, and a standing wave navigation system, so that any robot could know its exact position in the factory, just as the central controller would know the robot's position. The robot would carry a map of the factory and a detailed plan of the x, y, z coordinates of all the racks in the store: these would be in its memory on two-dimensional, flat magnetic tape sheets, the z coordinates being recorded on the store-rack memory by the amplitude of magnetization. The factory map would have all permanent obstacles and permitted paths recorded on it, and the scanning head would move over the map according to the position of the robot in the factory: its orientation in space would be made known to it by a gyrocompass. It would obtain a slightly more accurate knowledge of its position by counting wheel revolutions, and the most detailed of all by an optical range finder at the top which would scan the direction of move-

ment for unexpected obstacles and take observations on known
fixed points. It would also have light touch bars on each side,
in front and behind, so that it could make an emergency stop
or change of course if it ran into an obstacle.

We will now consider what such a robot might look like, by
referring again to Fig. 2. It can run on ordinary wheels, but the
powered steering pair are on a bogey which can rotate full
circle, so that it has very great maneuverability. The mechanism is all in the base, which serves as a carrying surface onto
which it can place the goods. When it reaches its destination,
stabilizing feet come out on each side on the front, where the
column carrying the arm and hand are placed. The arm can
reach twelve feet all round, and the hand can pick up a weight
of 100 lbs. at this distance or 200 lbs. at six feet; a counter-
weight carrying a heavy but necessary mechanism, such as the
electrically driven hydraulic pump, automatically balances the
arm and hand as it moves out. The hand is a parallel jaw
mechanism which can open up to three feet. It can grasp a
package on the sides with a sensor control so that the grasp
is just enough to prevent slipping, or it can push one wedge-
shaped jaw under an object, while the other supports it on
top. The hand carries a special "eye" which can read magnetic
labels on packages.

The second industrial task is routine assembly of objects,
such as wrist watches, TV sets, and automobiles. Where many
million identical models are assembled consecutively, it pays to
build a special factory around the assembly line and have a
different specially designed machine to add each separate component. Where one or two experimental prototypes or special
models are to be made, it will be best to have human crafts-
men, but there will always be many products to be assembled
in the intermediate range of numbers, from three to 3 million,
where it will be humane to relieve humans of the repetitive
work, but will not be worth having a special factory. For this
it will be necessary to develop an adaptable specialized assembly robot which can be given a program to assemble any
one of a number of products with any number of components

whenever the product is required. We can imagine what such a specialized robot might look like (see Fig. 4). There would have to be a range of them for assembly of objects of different sizes, but each size would have an arm capable of picking up the chassis and holding it on a workbench, an arm rotatable about all three coordinates with a self-operated clamp whose positions are programmed for each job. The table is rotated so that the fixing position for the first component is in the correct place on top, and a third arm picks the first component out of the first storage bin, checks that it is not obviously faulty, and places it in position where a fourth hand holds it and fastens it by screwing, riveting, welding, soldering, or any other method. The second component is being picked up by the third arm and when the fourth is ready, it fastens the second component, and so on. Finally, a fifth picks up the finished assembly and gives it a test to verify that all components are correctly assembled before passing it on for packaging.

Fig. 4.   Assembly Robot (Model).

The main problems in developing this robot are:

1. Finding components randomly oriented and located in the correct bin, orienting them correctly in all three dimensional rotations, and signaling to the factory controller when any bin is empty;
2. accurate location of the components so near to the right position that the fastener can position it exactly;
3. checking components or final assembly and acting differently for accept and reject.

Where the run of identical assemblies is large, and the number of components is nearly constant from one model to the next, it will pay to use a different design of specialized robot. This design has a rotating turntable like a glass bottle blowing machine in which one operation (attachment of a component or checking assembly) is done in each station on the turntable simultaneously on a series of assemblies.

The third task is the least worthy of humans of all and is done by the greatest number of people. It is so boring that unless the workers have music to listen to or can talk about something else it will drive them mad. Millions of people sit in front of a machine, pick blanks out of one bin, feed them into the machine correctly oriented and positioned, operate the machine, take out the machined product, and pass it on. They may be operating punches or presses, filling gunpowder into fireworks, putting cartons round products or many other things, but always the job can be learned in a few minutes and is essentially repetitive every few seconds. It does involve the coordination of hand and eye to find the blank, orient it, and feed it accurately to the machine, but these are functions for which we can soon develop a robot. It will be faster and more accurate than a human, though not capable of any of the more exciting jobs a human can do.

We can imagine a rough model of one possible robot that can be programmed to feed and operate any machine that a seated or standing human can operate. It picks up the blanks from a belt, which brings them randomly oriented and positioned from a hopper, and then orients them about each of the

Fig. 5. Robot Machine Feeder/Operator (Model).

three axes in successive stations of the rotating table. A second arm transfers the fully oriented blank to the machine and signals the machine to operate, and a third takes the processed blank away to the next station on the turntable, where it is checked, e.g., by air gauging with a template; a fourth arm feeds it onto the accept belt or throws it into the reject bin. Here again, the main problem is to make a device which can be programmed to orient any object correctly in all three dimensions; if they are flat, rectangular sheets it is easy, but a completely asymmetrical shape like a TV chassis is much more difficult.

There is one group of tasks unworthy of humans which cries out for a generalized robot because relatively highly educated humans spend more hours on it than on any other. I refer, of course, to the group that makes up housework: cleaning, sweeping, scrubbing, dusting, clearing up floors, clearing and laying tables, washing up, making beds, and so on. One might ask, "why not have houses mechanically designed so that all these tasks would be eliminated?" Such homes, however, would not satisfy our human desires for variety, muddle, and fresh air. The only way to give humans freedom to have the individual homes they prefer without the need for excessive labor is to have a robot housemaid, which can be taught the various daily or weekly tasks and the correct positions for furniture, books, crockery, and so on, and then instructed to perform the tasks at fixed times. When one wishes to change the furniture around, one has to change the pertinent information in the robot's magnetic memory. Such a robot would be similar to the first factory robot in Fig. 2, but it is smaller and has four rimless wheels with twelve spokes on each, so that it can climb stairs. It does not have the stabilizing legs, because the arm support column is inclined so that most of the base is clear as a carrying tray, but the top (the "shoulder") is over the center of the base. It carries with it constantly a set of tools, operated from its own batteries, which it can pick up in the hand and use on ceilings, floors, the inside of ovens, bath tubs and so on. One of these is a special high-speed drive which can operate various concentric, annular brushes running in opposite directions and fed with various cleaning and scouring materials; an outer guard brush collects the materials and wipes them off. Another is a high torque, low-speed drive for turning handles, screws, etc., fitted with a large, three-jaw self-closing chuck with rubber pads on the jaws; a vice on the tray is used in conjunction with this for unscrewing bottle tops. A third is a vacuum-cleaner nozzle. Since the robot's arm can reach eight feet all around it, with this nozzle it can clean carpets, walls, ceilings, or furniture without moving itself. A simple table-clearing robot, which finds the objects in two dimensions and adapts its grasp to the size of the object also can be designed using the same principle (see Fig. 6).

There are many control problems that have to be solved in the development of this device, but its usefulness makes them well worth solving. It is necessary, for example, to develop the following:

1. Some pattern recognition, so that the robot can divide objects into a few tens of categories, each of which has

Fig. 6.   Table Cleaning Robot (Model).

to be treated differently; e.g., chairs, tables, books, cut-
lery, and crockery;

2. control of the hand, so the robot can pick up and deal
   with the objects it sees, a bedsheet to be folded;

3. The ability to vary a program according to variations in
   the instructions, e.g., in the number of places to lay at
   table;

4. the ability to see or feel dirt and apply extra cleaning to
   the dirty region until it is clean, e.g., in scouring cooking
   vessels;

5. sufficient delicacy of touch so as not to break glass or
   china while handling it.

Clearly none of these problems is nearly as difficult as getting
a rocket back from the moon; they can be solved if we decide
to solve them.

Robot Cybernetics

In the SRI robot work, it is necessary to have some computation on the robot itself, even though it is connected on a
time-sharing basis to a large fixed computer. In the case of the
Unimate and the Versatran, the memory is special to the robot
and built into it. I hope that the robot tasks which I have
described will show that small, specialized, hybrid or plain
analog computers specially designed for robots will be far
more efficient than conventional digital computers designed
for mathematical analysis. They will be more closely allied
to industrial control systems such as those on a boiler, with
feedback to give exact positional control of all the movements
and with the specially designed magnetic charts for recording
two- and three-dimensional maps with one-to-one positional
access. Even the pattern-recognition and reject sensors will
have a tailor-made hybrid computer with just enough elements
for the limited number of categories required.

The first robots to carry out the simple tasks outlined above
will not have any sophisticated learning ability—such as that
which the Cornell group is studying with the Perceptron—or
even any complex pattern recognition. They may be blind,
having only touch sensitivity, or they may have only a single
light-sensitive element, as in the table-clearing robot.

The main object of this paper is to suggest that the really
worthwhile applied research would be in the field of the
sensory and control systems of this first generation of true
robots.

III
Ecological Cybernetics

Cybernetics, Life, and Gene Action

C. F. ALBRECHT*

Oak Ridge National Laboratory
Oak Ridge, Tennessee

Introduction

A revolution has taken place in biology. What once was a descriptive science has now become one of the most active areas in modern research. All over the world, hundreds of teams consisting of biochemists, physicists, chemists, and in some cases even mathematicians are probing the living cell with sophisticated equipment such as the electron microscope, the ultracentrifuge, and the scintillation counter. A general aura of optimism prevails. A molecular biologist may even tell you that it is but a matter of time before we solve cancer, correct genetic mistakes, and even understand memory. Some, however, do not share this optimism. In his recent book, *Science and Survival*,[1] Barry Commoner expresses his doubts as follows:

*Postdoctoral Fellow on assignment from South African Council for Scientific and Industrial Research, Pretoria, South Africa. The author is engaged in the Molecular Anatomy (MAN) Program, which is supported by the National Cancer Institute, the National Institute of General Medical Sciences, the National Institute of Allergy and Infectious Diseases, and the U.S. Atomic Energy Commission. It is being carried out at the Oak Ridge National Laboratory, which is operated by the Union Carbide Corporation Nuclear Division for the U.S. Atomic Energy Commission.

"There is, I believe, a crisis in biology today. The root of the crisis is the conflict between the two approaches to the theory of life. One approach seeks for the unique capabilities of living things in separable chemical reactions; the other holds that the uniqueness is a property of the whole cell and arises out of the complex interaction of the separable events of cellular chemistry."

I will explore to what extent an understanding of the interactions occurring within and between cells and organisms may lead to a deeper insight into the nature of life. Because most of the processes occurring in living organisms are ultimately goal-directed in the sense that they maintain survival, and also because these processes in many cases are controlled by feedback signals, the subject matter to be discussed could be called the cybernetics of life.

Cybernetic Semantics

Before discussing living cells as cybernetic systems, it may be useful to clarify what is meant by a cybernetic system. To my mind, the essence of such a system is its inbuilt capacity for self-regulation, which is brought about by the interaction of a number of components, or subsystems. The number of components operating in a cybernetic system is usually dependent upon the complexity of the processes which are being regulated. To simplify the matter, four basic components can be mentioned. They are the program, process generator, transducer, and compare element. The program, which has also been called the goal,[2] is some kind of structure which contains inbuilt instructions for the execution of particular processes. Examples of such structures are computer tapes, genes, and nerve networks controlling the execution of instinctive behavior. For the program to be executed, information in the form of command signals must flow to the process generators, which do most of the work and consequently use up most of the energy available to the system. In a computer, the arithmetic calculation circuits are the main process generators.

The next step in the total process of self-regulation is to monitor the output of the process generators. This is done by sensing devices which can be called transducers. The output data which are sensed by the transducers and which are correlated to the process being controlled are then communicated as a feedback signal to a compare element. This crucial component contains a standard, which, when compared to the output data, determines whether the process output is sufficient or not. Most systems which are self-regulated are in a state of dynamic equilibrium. In other words, the feedback signals may change from positive to negative and vice versa. These fluctuations are sensed by the compare element, which then accordingly regulates the flow of command signals from the program. Thus, if the process generators are operating at suboptimal levels, the compare elements sense negative feedback and cause the flow of command signals to be amplified. Cybernetic theory has become quite complicated and now includes specific subdivisions, such as feedback oscillation theory, information theory, and bionics. In this presentation, however, emphasis will be placed mainly on the interaction of the four components discussed.

The First Cell and Gene Control

Five billion years ago, as far as we know, no cybernetic systems existed on earth. The atmosphere contained very little oxygen, for that element started to increase only with the advent of photosynthetic algae. According to evidence recently obtained,[3] sedimentary rocks in South Africa, which are at least three billion years old, contain fossils of organisms which look somewhat like present-day bacteria and blue-green algae. It is, of course, impossible to know what kind of control mechanisms were operating in these prehistoric cells, but their modern counterparts are, fortunately, well understood. Insight into bacterial gene control is mainly attributable to the revolutionary research of Jacob and Monod, published[4] in 1961. These French workers demonstrated for the first time that the bacterium Escherichia coli contains an elaborate system for the control of enzyme synthesis. Of considerable interest was the fact that the program of these organisms, which is contained in a linear deoxyribonucleic acid (DNA) molecule, contained instructions not only for the synthesis of particular enzymes (structural genes), but also for the control of the genes (regulatory genes). To understand how the bacterial self-regulating system works, consider a bacterium living in an environment which contains very little of the sugar lactose. The bacterial program contains a set of instructions for the synthesis of a special enzyme (beta-galactosidase) which can split lactose. In the absence of lactose, however, this enzyme is not made because the instruction for its synthesis is not being read out. Once lactose is added to the environment, an amazing sequence of interactions ensues. Some of the lactose gets into the bacterium, and when the concentration reaches a specific threshold value, these molecules bind to a protein (the repressor), which in turn is bound to part of the instruction sequence for the synthesis of the lactose-splitting enzyme. Once the "signal" molecule, the lactose, binds to the repressor which is bound to the DNA, the repressor drops off the DNA and the specific set of genes is ready to be activated. Activation is brought about by a special enzyme (RNA-polymerase) which makes a copy of the activated genes. This copy, which Jacob and Monod called "messenger RNA," is then translated by protein synthesizing factories, the ribosomes, into the specific beta-galactosidase enzyme which proceeds to split lactose molecules. Once the concentration of lactose molecules drops below threshold, they become detached from the repressor, which once again sticks onto the DNA at just the right place, and the genes in question are "switched off." The net effect of this remarkable process is that energy is only "invested" in the construction of an enzyme when its appropriate substrate is present. A number of other systems similar to this, involving molecules such as L-isoleucine and tryptophan, also have been described.

Bacterial Gene Control and Cybernetics

Analysis of the gene control system discussed shows that this interplay of molecules also can be described in general cybernetic terms. The main program, or goal, of the bacterium is growth and division. This main program is subdivided into many subprograms for the synthesis of hundreds of different proteins. Some of these proteins act as repressors, many of them are structural components, and most of them are enzymes. The total program is stored in a continuous thread of DNA which is about 0.3 mm in length and two millionth's of a millimeter in diameter. The entire program for the construction, maintenance, and regulation of a bacterium contains between 10^5 and 10^6 units (nucleotide-pairs) of genetic information. The translation of the genetic instructions into command signals occurs when messenger RNA is synthesized. The process generators in this system are the enzymes and enzyme-complexes, such as the ribosomes, which paradoxically also synthesize the enzymes. The output data of the process generators are the specific concentrations of particular metabolites. The sensing devices, or transducers, are the repressor molecules which sense and "measure" the metabolic feedback signals by binding with various metabolites only at specific threshold concentrations. Thus, in this system, the versatile repressor molecules act as transducers and compare elements by gauging the level of the metabolite and altering the flow of command signals accordingly.

Jean-Pierre Changeux[5] sums this up elegantly as follows:

"Regulatory enzymes appear to be built in such a way that they not only recognize the configuration of the specific subtrates as signals, but also gauge their response to whether or not the substrates and regulatory signals are present in certain threshold concentrations. (This is strongly reminiscent, of course, of electric relays and, one may add, of nerve cells which react only if the signal has a certain threshold strength.)"

The Advent of the Organelle

One of the characteristics of mammalian and other eucary-otic cells which make them more complex than bacterial cells is the compartmentalization of specific sets of enzymes and structural proteins into distinct subcellular structures called organelles. The most prominent organelle is the nucleus which contains the genetic program and is usually centrally located. The protoplasm surrounding the nucleus and enclosed by the outer plasma-membrane is called the cytoplasm and also contains organelles, such as the mitochondria, which act as the "powerhouses" of the cell by converting latent solar energy "trapped" in sugars into the "universal energy currency" of the cell, namely adenosine tri-phosphate (ATP). The effective surface area of the cytoplasm is also increased many times by a membrane system, the endoplasmic reticulum, on which the ribosomes are attached. In plant cells, the most distinct organelles are the chloroplasts, which trap photons. The development of organelles is a sophistication of the process generating component of the cybernetic system. Through the containing of most of the enzymes involved in one main process, i.e., ATP synthesis, within one "bag," the mitochondrion, new possibilities are opened up for the control of many enzymes simultaneously by altering the permeability of the enclosing membrane. It is thought that in some cases hormones may exert their control in this way. It is not yet entirely clear why the DNA-program, in the form of chromosomes, is contained in the nucleus. It has been suggested that the nuclear pores, which are not holes, may selectively influence the passage of messenger-RNA from nucleus to cytoplasm, thus exerting some form of control.

To gain a better insight into the structure and function of the nucleus, we have been isolating these organelles for the past year at the Molecular Anatomy Program, which is part of the Oak Ridge National Laboratories. The nuclei can be mass-isolated from about 1000 g of rat liver using a high-speed zonal-ultracentrifuge. The isolated nuclei were then subfractionated into nuclear membranes and certain small particles called informofers, the function of which is as yet unknown. These nuclear subfractions were further analyzed using the electron microscope and were separated into their protein components by disc electrophoresis. During these studies we also found some very long threads attached to the membrane, the composition and function of which are as yet unknown. Our lack of knowledge is both a challenge and a reminder of the complexity of the mammalian cell.

Cancer as a Cybernetic Disease

In recent years, more and more scientists have expressed the idea that the cancerous state is due to some kind of alteration in the cybernetics of the cell. Market refers to this unknown alteration as a "misprogramming of gene function."[6] Another worker in this highly active field, Moon referred to the problem as "a change in the basic regulatory mechanisms which determine the structure and function of cells."[7] Using our four-component model of a cybernetic system, we can ask whether the basic cancer-lesion represents a change in the program, process generators, transducers, or compare elements or in the communication-channels linking these components. Unfortunately, the cell is not like an electronic device, the circuits of which can be removed and checked out. Cells are microscopic, and, as far as we know, communication is brought about by the diffusion of molecules and is not "wired." This fact makes it very difficult to detect and analyze "communication pathways" in the cell because of the presence of hundreds of different molecules that would need to be separated. Furthermore, we are still very much in the dark about potential transducers and compare elements in the cell. In other words, we do not know how it is gauged within the cell whether all the process generators are performing optimally or not. The bacterial repressor system is a tantalizing suggestion but still needs to be demonstrated in mammalian cells. Some workers have assumed that repressors do act on mammalian genes and have proposed elaborate, albeit hypothetical, models of genetic regulation systems.[8,9,10] The search for mammalian repressors has been stimulated recently by the success of Ptashne and Gilbert[11] who have purified certain bacterial repressors. In our laboratory, we have attempted to determine how many different proteins there are in the nucleus and whether they are contained in the membranes, chromosomes, or particles. To facilitate this analysis, we have used a high-resolution gel-scanning device whose data-output can be analyzed by a digital computer. This is only a first step along a very long road.

The Importance of the Nervous System

Probably the biggest jump in the development of more sophisticated cybernetic systems in living organisms was the advent of nerves. As far as we know, prior to the development of nerves, the only communication channel in or between cells was the diffusion of molecules. With the development of large, multicellular organisms, one could expect that a number of fundamental problems would arise. First, little selective advantage could be gained by a mere proliferation of similar cells. With the advent of differentiation (the differential expression of different subprograms of the genome) a multicellular organism could be constructed out of a number of functionally distinct groups of cells. This can thus be regarded as a further step in the sophistication of process generators, i.e., proceeding from enzymes to organelles and then to functionally specialized cells which in higher organisms are organized to form organs. An organism containing functionally distinct organs would be severely handicapped unless these organs were controlled in a coordinated way. The advent of nerves was a remarkable solution to the problem of coordination and integration. This development also made it possible for control programs to be constructed in more versatile structures—the neural networks. Command signals could now also be conducted from the brain to the motor organs more rapidly and with greater precision. With the advent of neural networks, we also find more sophisticated transducers sensing not only internal but external stimuli. This development would be of very little use unless the signals being transmitted by the sense organs were interpreted by a compare element and then functionally integrated in the control of the generation of command signals by the main program. In other words summators or compare elements containing inbuilt standards would be required to measure the incoming signals and determine whether appropriate motor signals to cancel out positive or negative feedback were necessary.

We are now just beginning to understand how nerve networks integrate the functions of different organs. To simplify this extremely complicated problem, many studies are being conducted on simple organisms such as the marine snail Aplysia, crayfish, and leeches and various insects. Nervous systems in these organisms are ideal for investigation in that they contain perhaps 10,000 or 100,000 cells compared to the trillion or so in higher animals. Recently, Kandel[12] managed to map out the entire reflex wiring diagram for the contraction of the gill in Aplysia when the siphon of this organism is stimulated. The patterning of behavioral sequences is much more complex than reflex actions and far more difficult to study. Progress, however, is being made by Kandel and others who are now studying spontaneous fixed-action patterns. It is believed that these nerve-directed functions are controlled by as yet unidentified pattern-generating neurons. Studies such as these may yet lead to a day when we will have insight into the neural mechanics of such remarkable processes as the ability of birds to navigate by stars and of bats to catch insects in total darkness.

Man and His Machines

In terms of the theme of developing sophistication of cybernetic systems in biological organisms, the advent of man is probably the most dramatic "quantum" jump. Teilhard de

Chardin expresses this point forcefully in his book *Phenomenon of Man:*[13]

> . . . how utterly warped is every classification of the living world in which man only figures logically as a genus or a new family. . . . To give man his true place in nature it is not enough to find one more pigeonhole in the edifice of our systematization or even an additional order or branch. With hominization, in spite of the insignificance of the anatomical leap, we have the beginning of a new age. The earth "gets a new skin." Better still it finds its soul. . . . This sudden deluge of cerebralization, this biological invasion of a new animal type which gradually eliminates or subjects all forms of life that are not human, this irreversible tide of fields and factories, this immense and growing edifice of matter and ideas—all these signs that we look at, day in and day out—seem to proclaim that there has been a change on the earth and a change of planetary magnitude.

Probably one of the unique cybernetic abilities of man is his capacity for creating new programs and organizing their execution: man has the ability to shape his destiny. Unlike bacteria, which are programmed by their DNA, and other organisms, which are controlled by neural circuits (which in turn are also coded for by the genes), man can create his own programs which take the shape of ideologies, laws, mores, religions, systems of government, and life styles. In the case of man, not only has the nature of the program undergone a radical change—from prewired to creative—but the communication channels, process generators, sensing transducers, and compare elements also have changed drastically. The essence of the change has been the advent of man's technology, or the extension of his process generators into external machines. For millions of years, animals have been ultimately dependent on the energy released by their mitochondria for the execution of processes. First, man harnessed fire, water, and wind; then, electricity. Now, he controls power of the atom. We have also escaped from our inbuilt transducers for sensory input. The electromagnetic spectrum has been ripped open by our battery of machines sensing radio waves from distant galaxies and elementary particles from atoms. No longer are our communication channels entirely dependent upon the diffusion of molecules or the conduction of nerve impulses. The Gutenberg, Marconi, and Edison revolutions have made the rest of the planet our backyard.

How Far Will the Cybernetic Development Go?

A number of important cybernetic developments are upon us and will become more sophisticated in the future.

Of particular interest to me is the disenchantment of many young people with the sterile, nonintegrated presentation of facts in many university courses. I sense a yearning for a synthesis of this accumulated data into a meaningful framework. Fortunately, many educators sense this, too, and a number of universities have introduced courses, mainly in biology, which give the student a total view. For the past hundred years, the theory of evolution has been the main theme in the teaching of biology. It could be that the time has come to concentrate more on the control mechanisms operating in and between cells and organisms as a central theme. This shift in emphasis eventually may be necessary for the training of biologists who will be equipped with the necessary insight into the integration of biological processes. What is wanted is not a jack-of-all trades but a master of a new trade, and this will require a new synthesis of studies. Biology courses of the future may include studies of communications, servomechanisms, control theory, and computational techniques. Up to now, mainly electrical engineers have been involved in the growing science of bionics, the application of control data from biological systems to the construction of electromechanical devices. If biologists can be trained to communicate with electrical engineers, a two-way flow of information will result. Biologists may then understand their living systems better by also understanding the man-made analogs.

To save our environment, we will be compelled to formulate a specific program aimed at achieving this goal. For the execution of the program, specific process generators, including men

and machines, will be required. To monitor the concentrations
of pollutants and the concentrations of life-supporting molecules, batteries of sensing devices will be required. Probably
the most important sensing device will be a new breed of
ecologists well versed in the concept of cybernetics and with
deep insight into the interaction of biological systems.

Maybe then the development of a global, coordinated control network for the preservation of the environment will be
the final and logical extension of the grand pageant of sophistication of cybernetic mechanisms on this planet.

REFERENCES

1. B. Commoner. *Science and Survival*, (New York: Viking Press, 1966).
2. R. W. Avery. *A Functional Model of the Life Press*, published by the author.
3. E. S. Barghoorn and J. W. Schopf. *Science* 152, (1966), p. 758.
4. F. Jacob and J. J. Monod. *J. Mol. Biol.* 3 (1961), p. 318.
5. J. P. Changeux. "The Control of Biochemical Reactions," *Scientific Amercian* (212(4), (1965), p. 36.
6. C. L. Markert. *Cancer Res.* 28, 1908 (1968).
7. H. D. Moon. *Fed. Proc.* 29(3), (1970), p. 1243.
8. R. J. Britten and E. H. Davidson. *Science* 165, (1969), p. 349.
9. R. Tsanev and Bl. Sendov. *J. Theor. Biol.* 12, (1966), p. 327.
10. R. Tsanev and Bl. Sendov. *J. Theor. Biol.* 23, (1969), p. 124.
11. M. Ptashne and W. Gilbert. "Genetic Repressors," *Scientific American* 222(6), 36 (1970).
12. E. R. Kandel, "Nerve Cells and Behavior," *Scientific American* 223(1), (1970), p. 57.

The Knowledge-Transfer Problem and Its Contribution to The Environmental Crisis

SIDNEY R. GALLER

Smithsonian Institution
Washington, D.C.

Knowledge acquisition is the answer to the ecological crisis! As always, this is contemporary society's almost reflexive solution to any problem. Scientists have the answers, so let's do more scientific research, let's acquire more basic knowledge— more of that intellectual holy water that is the miraculous cure for society's ills. Unfortunately, the acquisition of basic knowledge by itself is no cure, only a promise. Without a means of transferring and transducing knowledge from the discoverer to the user, from the scientist and scholar to the technologist and the decision maker on the societal firing line of problem solving, we are left with magic incantations instead of therapeutic prescriptions. I am not a cyberneticist. However, it seems to me that the knowledge transfer problem—a problem of singular importance that has received but a modicum of attention—offers model makers, systems analysts, and those concerned with developing informational feedbacks some rather interesting opportunities to help in correcting environmental maladies.

If we can focus attention on knowledge transfer as an essen-

283

tial component in any communications system designed for
solving environmental problems, I believe we will have served
the cause of environmental restoration and enhancement rather
well. However, we cannot consider knowledge transfer in
limbo, separated from the other dimensions of the environmental geometry. I would like, therefore, to give you my perceptions of the general environmental problem. The knowledge
transfer issue is but one perspective on the global biosphere.
It must be considered in the context of the larger question of
how we propose to maintain and enhance the quality of life
on earth in a biosphere that is in danger of becoming so degraded that its life-support capacity will be irreversibly di-
minished. In searching for answers to that question, I have
come to believe that phrases like "environmental pollution"
and "the population explosion" are at best empirical descriptors of second-order effects rather than causes of the condition
expressed in that third catch phrase, "the environmental crisis."
At worst, these phrases are diversionary, focusing attention on
relatively superficial and easily discernible symptoms of environmental degradation. Society thinks it has obvious, relevant "palliatives" to prescribe, if not to follow. Turning attention away from the cause of the malady is an etiology not yet
fully understood. I have hypothesized that "the environmental
crisis" is a kind of self-created, societal flypaper produced by
a man-centered, self-serving civilization's search for "cheap"
security and plenitude. It's a kind of flypaper to which human-
kind is now in danger of becoming hopelessly, terminally stuck!
Basically, the cause of the environmental crisis is society's
unwillingness, at least to date, to recognize that the recurrent
theme and impetus for societal development over the last
10,000 years is an obsolete hangover dating from the primitive
hunter-forager phase of man's evolution. It is a kind of vestigial
impulse to take from nature without giving anything in return.

The notion that man can take free rides at nature's expense
is a time-honored but dangerous myth. The supposition that
nature will always be there to support man, come what may,
is just as faulty. Yet these are the fundamental syllogisms upon

which we have constructed a contemporary society whose success is based on maintaining the most inefficient way of exploiting both our renewable and nonrenewable resources. The renewability potential of our so-called renewable resources is, however, decreasing dramatically. Indeed, contemporary civilizations (with no political persuasion excepted) are almost irrevocably committed to the "freebie," to getting the largest short-term gain at the expense of the environment. All this at the least possible cost to the exploiter and without much thought given to long-term consequences for the viability of the environment. And all of this at a time when we can foresee the demands on the environment outstripping its life-support capability.

Nature can provide man with an ample living; indeed, it has done so. But it never intended to give him something for nothing, only a long-term mortgage on his terrestrial abode, the payment for which is now coming due. Society's social and economic infrastructure, its ethics, and its scale of moral values have been based on the illusion of the "freebie." Society considers the global environment as an open-ended system with an infinite regenerative capacity. In short, the Dostoevskian irony of this state of affairs is that man has created a society of law, order, and justice that is dedicated to protecting, preserving, and advancing an illusion that has become a prescription for civilization's self-destruction. The illusion persists in every portion of the globe, irrespective of its political coloration. To those who accuse the Western capitalistic imperialists of "perpetrating environmental crimes" against the whole of mankind, I can submit ample evidence to show that under communistic or other totalitarian systems, it is just as much a crime to interfere with the pollution of the atmosphere, the destruction of fisheries, or the rape of the land. The communists claim that in refraining from taking anti-pollution measures, they are allowing the lot of the proletariat to be bettered. Environmental carnage in the capitalistic world is considered an inalienable right of the private property holder, either individual or corporate. Thus, we must recognize that every nation has a stake in preserving the destructive status quo. Either we are members of nations which have already developed technologies that are depleting the environment for short-term gains, or we are members of underdeveloped nations aspiring to develop technologies for the same purpose.

In my opinion, the environmental crisis will be abated only when and if mankind recognizes that the earth is a closed, fragile life-support system of limited capacity, with a rapidly diminishing self-healing capability. The environmental crisis will be abated only when mankind recognizes that the global ecosystem is just that, global in character, with its component parts not only interrelated but interdependent. Locally caused environmental perturbations can proliferate and lead to regional and global environmental changes that are deleterious and irreversible. This can be so even though the changes may not be perceived for decades after the initial insult.

Finally, the environmental crisis will be abated only when we develop a more rational international *modus vivendi* based on the thesis that nature and her precious resources belong to the whole of mankind, irrespective of geopolitical social, cultural, or ethnic differences. It will only be abated with an international *modus vivendi* that is not derived from short-sighted, chauvinistic, and artificial economic incentives, such as increases in gross national product. The economic incentives must be based on a gross global product; i.e., profitability for the individual, the cooperating nations, and ultimately the global community. Such profits must be derived from free and competitive industry and commerce that incorporate a meticulous, indeed a parsimonious, husbandry of our limited global resources. The industry and commerce of tomorrow must have as their prime objective the equitable and efficient delivery of natural resources and manufactured goods in a manner that enhances the quality of life globally at a minimal cost to our common global environment.

Now that I have presented my general perspectives, allow me to come back to the knowledge transfer problem and its bearing on the environmental crisis. Today there are an estimated 52,000 scientific "repeat" publications, including periodicals, that frequently publish at least one article per issue on an aspect of the environment. However, most of these publications are discipline-directed, i.e., designed to communicate information within disciplines or to special interest groups. Very few of them are designed to convert information gained from the "producers" of fundamental knowledge and transfer it to those who need to apply the knowledge to solve environmental problems. The impedance mismatch between knowledge producers and problem solvers has been aggravated by the development of an "establishment" of professional information managers who have constructed elaborate, highly sophisticated and highly efficient systems for maintaining the informational *status quo;* i.e., for containing the information flow within disciplinary boundaries. However, these managers are almost totally ineffective in their efforts to transfer knowledge from producers to appliers!

The collation, synthesis, and transduction (not merely transfer) of basic knowledge to technological applications in environmental problem-solving is an extension beyond the capability of most existing professional information-exchange organizations. Further, most competent environmental scientists engaged in basic research are poor knowledge transducers. This is an understandable limitation, considering their academic backgrounds, experiences, motivations, and responsibilities, all designed to impart to their colleagues and students knowledge gained from independent investigations and to do so in the language and within the boundaries of their scientific specialties. However, whatever its genesis and history, we are confronted with a serious knowledge-transfer attenuation problem, one that is exacerbated by an innocent public that assumes a direct relationship between public investment in basic research and the flow of basic knowledge toward the solution of environmental problems.

We must develop a means for carefully and systematically reviewing and evaluating the existing publicly supported data and information exchanges, with the objective of improving the transfer of information gained from basic discovery and invention to those who are on the societal front lines of environmental problem-solving. In this connection, it is essential that we develop effective information translation and feedback systems designed to "nourish" self-improving models for playing predictive ecological games that incorporate retrospective analysis of existing biological and geophysical data.

Further, I believe we must establish a system of internships in applied ecology to expose young, academically oriented ecologists in training to actual environmental problem situations which will sharpen their perceptions of the complexities involved in the technological statement of environmental deterioration. Such exposure should also instill a sense of responsibility for the systematic transfer of their knowledge to engineers, technologists, and others concerned with practical problem-solving.

Next, I believe that we need to develop new knowledge transfer organizations based on the current realities of the environmental crisis. They must be capable of serving as knowledge transfer junctions for ecologists, sociologists, economists, and others who are producing potentially useful information and for decision-makers who need this information either to prevent environmental perturbations or to restore degraded environments. The new breed of knowledge exchangers must be able to convey useful environmental information and advice to industry, commerce, and entire communities. In the process, they should serve as bridging points and feedback loops to apprise those who are engaged in basic research of the types and qualities of information that engineers and technologists need to improve environmental protective technology.

Finally, and in the long run, the most effective solution to the environmental crisis (including the knowledge transfer problem) must be the development of carefully coordinated environmentally relevant curricula in the primary and secondary school levels. We must develop new educational strategies centered on the environmental protection theme. The next two or three generations must be educated to make sound environmental decisions if our society is to survive, at least in its present form. The whole educational infrastructure must be reordered to focus on improved communications leading to improved management of the total environment as the central theme. This theme must run through the teaching of reading, writing, and arithmetic. Intelligent management of the local, national, and global ecosystems must become the principal *raison d'etre* for education in history, anthropology, ethnology, sociology, economics, and the natural sciences. The recruits to the environmental protection banner are fond of saying that we all inhabit the same planet and thus are equally affected by the environmental changes. They are right, of course. But if everyone is to share the responsibility for maintaining and enhancing the global biosphere, we who are so fortunate as to be among the "haves" under a free and open society must be able to assure the "have nots" among the developing nations of the world that we are not making environmental decisions, for our own self-interest, that will foreclose their opportunities to achieve our status. This assurance can come only with an improvement in the knowledge transfer process that will enable the developing nations to benefit from our environmental mistakes. They should share in the insights and wisdom that we have gained from those mistakes, which, through God's grace, have not become irreversible catastrophies of the global environment—at least not so far!

Environmation

FREDERICK F. GORSCHBOTH

International Business Machines Corporation
Gaithersburg, Maryland

Twenty-five years have passed since Norman Cousins wrote his now famous essay, *Modern Man is Obsolete*. The thesis of this essay is that the pace of man's technological development is so far outdistancing that of his development of a governing philosophy that the survival of the race is in doubt. At the time of his writing, Norman Cousins was brooding about the atom bomb. When one considers the rate at which man is using up his resources, polluting his streams and poisoning the very air he breathes, it is apparent that the theme of this essay can, with validity, be applied in a wider, and perhaps more subtle, sense. Man may very well be polluting himself to death. Thus, man's technology may be bringing about his end—as speculated upon by T. S. Eliot. Man may indeed end not with a bang, but a whimper—or more precisely a cough.

It is fitting in a discipline concerned with the control of technology that consideration be given to the possibility of utilizing that technology to ensure, rather than threaten, man's survival. Two characteristics of modern technology may be most helpful in addressing this problem. The first characteristic is technology's capability of managing large amounts of data. The second is its capacity to define and address problems systematically. Some years ago we decided to consider the production of air pollution as a process like any other industrial process. If this concept is utilized, one would expect to find (and indeed is able to identify) the classical components of a process system: inputs, outputs, means of measurement, and means of control. Referring to Fig. 1, it is seen that the inputs to the system are the polluting sources and the controlling weather, and the output consists of an atmosphere of a certain air quality. Traditionally, the control programs of most political entities take the form illustrated in Fig. 1. Absent from such a system is any means for determining the air quality existent at the time or any means of measuring the effects of the variations in air pollution. Further, in such a system, it is seen that the only means available for control result from enforcement of codes that are enacted on the basis of a series of inspections or complaints. Absent from the enforcement system could be any technical basis for the codes' enactment, the cost for the implementation of the various control options required by the code, or the impact of the implementation of those codes upon the industries supporting the controlling community.

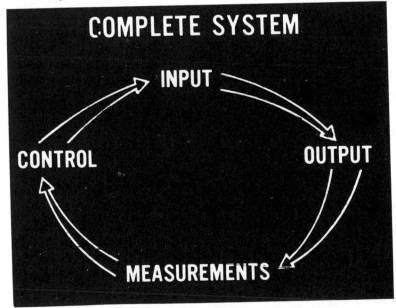

Fig. 1.   Components of Process Control.

As a result of the analysis of current programs, the process system concept was expanded to embrace the components illustrated in Fig. 2. The relationship among the components would now take the following form. The uncontrollable input to the system, the set of governing weather conditions, impacts the controllable input—the pollution sources; together they produce emissions that result in an atmosphere of a certain air quality. In the expanded system, the air quality can now be measured by an air monitoring system. But "air quality," as such, has a rather academic character. More important to the control problem are the effects upon the community of various levels of air quality. Thus, incorporated into the system is consideration of the effects of various air qualities upon property and the health of the population. It is clear that the most important consideration in the air quality program remains the effect of air pollution upon the health of the community. Therefore, a health-reporting system was added to the process. In addition to monitoring the effects of the various levels of air pollution, this system serves as the basis for establishing health standards; these standards ultimately will serve as the limits for the control program. The approach described represents the general sequence of action taken by the Federal control authorities in their relationship to the state and local controlling agencies. First, based on predicted health effects, the Federal criteria regarding allowable concentrations of air pollution in the atmosphere were established. These criteria are then to be interpreted by the state authorities in terms of required air quality standards. Finally, air quality standards are to be further defined in terms of the emission standards that will set control limits upon the system. In the control program, then, the air quality (as reported by the acrometric system), interpreted in terms of actual control limits, will serve as a basis for comparison with the established air quality standards. A comparison between the ambient air quality and the required air quality standards would serve, therefore, as an index to the type and extent of the control actions required.

The system can be taken one step farther. Instead of de-

294 FREDERICK F. GORSCHBOTH

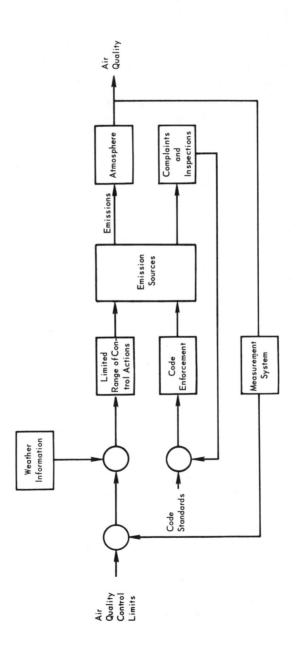

Fig. 2. The Urban System.

termining the effect of controlling weather conditions upon the pollutant emission and taking corrective action based upon those effects, with improved weather forecasts the anticipated effects of coming weather changes can be predicted, and control action taken in an anticipatory rather than a corrective mode. Thus, it is possible to consider a successful control program that, as a result of prompt and decisive control action, prevents the air quality criteria from being violated.

The system can be generalized to address other types of pollution, as well. In Fig. 3 it is seen that the components in the general area of the environmental control remain the same. For example, in a typical problem of water pollution, the controllable inputs again are the pollution sources. The uncontrollable input component of the pollution problem in this instance includes not only weather, but the complete climatology, the topography of the area, and the entire hydrological cycle—including such components as evaporation, transpiration, and run-off. The output again is environmental quality. Similarly, the underlying basis for adopted standards would be the effects of the variations of the environmental quality.

Whether addressing an air pollution, a water pollution, or any other polluting process, it is necessary to define and categorize in detail these areas and components of the process system. A typical air pollution problem may serve as an example. First, the inputs must be examined. The input components of the air pollution system have already been described generally, but it is necessary now to categorize them in detail. Three controlling weather components affect the air quality in any problem area: the local weather conditions, the mesometeorology of the area, and synoptic weather patterns dictating large-scale weather changes. The components of these three controlling weather systems are illustrated in Fig. 4.

Similarly, the controllable input component—the pollutants—must be identified and categorized. This categorization takes three forms. The first is a detailed breakdown of composition sources; the second is the relationship of these pollutants with their means of discharge. In other words, each pollutant com-

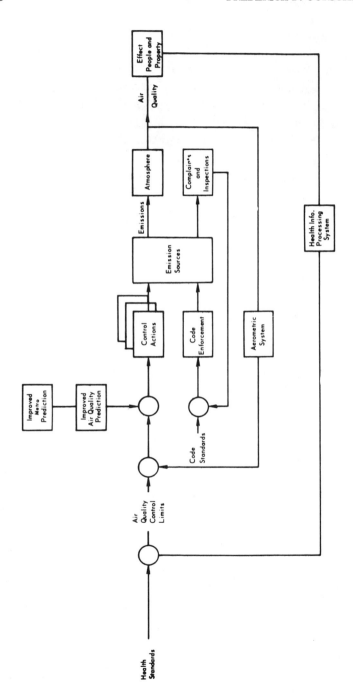

Fig. 3. The Fully Developed System.

ENVIRONMENT SYSTEM CONTROL

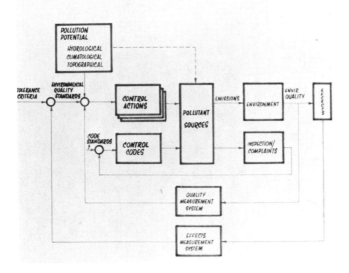

Fig. 4.   The System Generalized.

ponent must be identified with the smokestack or vent by which it is emitted to the atmosphere. Thirdly, the variations of the emissions as a function of time, reflecting the pattern of operation of the emitting activity, also must be determined. A systematic handling of these types of data is illustrated in Fig. 5. It will be noted that the data includes, for future control purposes, pollution emission devices that are located near and associated with the various emitting smoke stacks.

At this point in the control program, then, the output must be determined. A determination of the output may be made visually by personal observations or by photography; most frequently today, it is determined by the identification and quantitative assessment of the concentration of air pollutants by

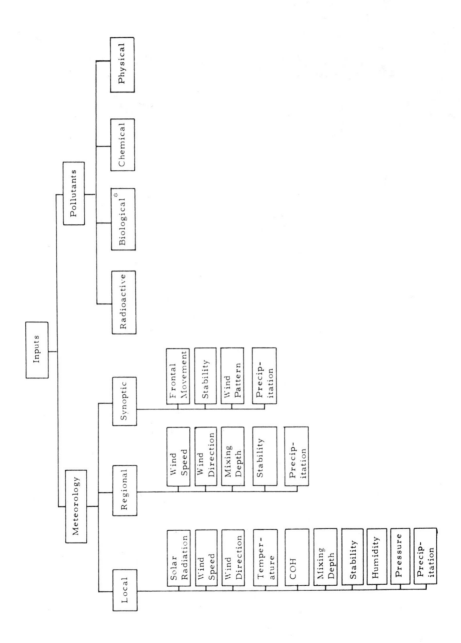

Fig. 5.   System Inputs.

remote monitoring systems. This determination of air quality, whether in chart form or represented by the compilation of digital data banks, the visual observation of air pollution, or the recording of ambient air pollution effects, to be of value must be related to the pollution sources which were the causes of the measured air quality.

The correlation between the inputs and outputs, as well as effects, describes the next step in a control process. This correlation can be determined in many ways. In controlled experiments, various aerosols analagous to pollutants were frequently released and their transport paths from the point of release throughout the controlled areas were observed measured, and analyzed. From such control experiments, the general diffusion patterns under the meteorological conditions existing at the time of the release could be determined. Since these experiments were applicable only for the conditions under which the substances were released, it became apparent that a more generalized approach to the determination of the diffusion patterns was required. This ordinarily is done by the use of mathematical descriptions based on earlier correlations which make it possible to model mathematically and predict the diffusion of the pollution from known sources, under various weather conditions, throughout a given area.

The earlier models of the predicted diffusion patterns were based on standard mathematical diffusion equations, generally statistical in nature, and were helpful—if not totally successful—in explaining pollution distribution. The models being developed today are more deterministic and less statistical in nature. They are based generally on the description of the dynamics of the hot gases described by the basic thermodynamic hydrodynamics and the general continuity equations employed to predict in a deterministic manner the pattern of pollution transport. Such models are able not only to give a better description of the effect of the effective stack height, but to describe to a greater extent than in the past the effect of the roughness of the surface over which the pollution diffuses.

The greatest utility of such models lies, not in accurate and

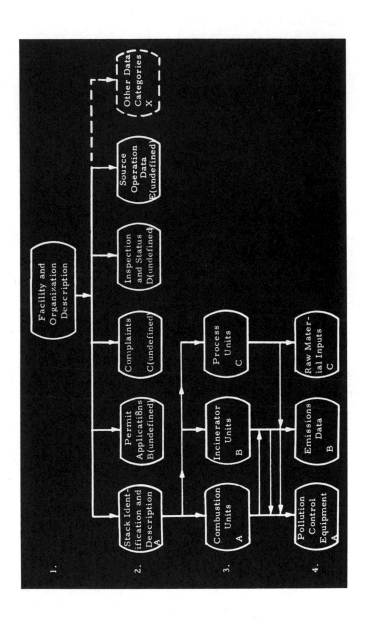

Fig. 6.   File Structure for Air Pollution Data Bank.

precise descriptions of the pollution transport pattern under all meteorological conditions, but rather in the possibility of predicting the seriousness of the pollution problem and determining the stringency of control measures required. This can be done most conveniently by looking at the predicitions of the worst-case conditions in a particular location under the worst historically anticipatable conditions.

We have termed this worst-case condition the "Maximum Credible Episode," and it provides the extremes of the problem. Thus, if a control program is proved effective in handling the maximum credible episode, it is reasonable to assume that all other, more probable, cases will likewise be effectively controlled. Modeling techniques as described above are most helpful in predicting the maximum credible episode. Thus, the limits on the emissions and the impact of various suggested control options can be determined.

The evaluation of the effectiveness of various control options requires careful and involved analysis. The results of this analysis are often very discouraging. In many cases, it seems that the means of control of the emission sources, under the expected and possible weather conditions, may prove insufficient. For example, it may be possible to consider a power plant whose production of pollution is so great, despite the installation of elaborate suppressing devices, that a small proportion (but a large quantity) of the sulfur dioxide generated is escaping to the atmosphere. It might be concluded from the worst-case analysis that despite the elaborateness of the suppression device, unacceptable levels of air pollution may be expected in the community. Harsh control alternatives may be required. From the point of view of the industry being controlled, the most effective, but obviously least acceptable, measure to be taken would be the complete shutdown of the activity. Variations of this approach, either in partial shutdown or temporary shutdown, may be considered. Another alternative possibility may be the modification of the process. This option is seldom exercised today because of the general lack of knowledge by the emitting operation of its own process.

Very few industries today know the process in which they are involved so well that they can predict the effects on emissions of possible changes in that process. What is required in most cases (and is most frequently unavailable) is the capability to simulate the process and to test process changes so that the effectiveness of a modification and the cost of it to the activity may be determined. In the above illustration of the power plant, the possibility of a fuel change on the levels of emission of sulfur dioxide might be considered by simulating the operation of the simple process. In many other industries, such a simple analysis of a modification requires much more elaborate simulation techniques.

In most analyses of processes, the process control approach is one aimed at maximizing profits. It may be in the future, however, that simulation of processes may be used as a means of assessing the various alternatives which have as their aim the control of the air pollution resulting from continued operation of the process based on a cost-benefit approach. By simulation analysis, for example, it may be concluded that a slight modification of the process, while slightly reducing profit initially, may result in an overall gain by making the problem of air pollution suppression less difficult. The simulation techniques described in the early part of this paper are of great interest to us today for this reason. The possibility of utilizing such techniques to simulate variations in the process and to determine the cost associated with various pollution control options, so that economic trade-offs among the various options may be made, is an interesting one for solving the environmental problems of this decade.

Systems Approach in Ecological System Simulation

TUNCER I. OREN

University of Arizona
Tucson, Arizona

Introduction

A combined digital simulation language, called the General System Theory implementer and referred to by the acronym GEST, has been developed to facilitate digital simulation of large-scale complex systems. A computer program to perform the simulation is to be generated by the GEST processor, whose input is provided by the user and has mainly two parts: (1) the mathematical description of the system under investigation, comprising the description of each component system and of the coupling of the systems; and (2) specifications about the simulation study. This paper explains some of the features which make GEST appropriate to digital simulation of ecological systems. The *world view* of GEST, which is based on the general system theory developed by Wymore[1] allows the teams of investigators to specify each component system separately. The input/output relationships of the component systems are specified by the *system coupling. Time-varying systems* can be modeled easily. *Nested couplings* can be used to define broader systems. Input generator systems provide the ability to have *nested simulation.* Provisions have been made to define commonly used systems and parametric systems, also.

Need for New Tool of Expression in the Ecological Community

Management of ecological systems requires the close co-operation of specialists having different backgrounds. In a pollution control study, for example, several teams may be formed to model component systems of the total system. In such a study, biochemists, microbiologists, chemists, sanitation engineers, mechanical engineers, process control engineers, and transportation engineers can model the systems dealing with the generation of several types of pollution. Similarly, physiologists, psychologists, geneticists, biologists, zoologists, and botanists can model systems dealing with the effects of several types of pollution on living organisms. Bacteriologists, engineers, urban planners, and educators, in their turn, can model systems dealing with alternative ways of decreasing pollution. Demographers, behavioral scientists, ecologists, oceanographers, economists, and legislators can model the systems dealing with the effects of alternative ways of decreasing pollution. A group of systems engineers can work with administrators and statesmen who will be responsible for the implementation of the pollution control system to formulate a figure of merit, or measure of effectiveness, of the pollution control system.

To be able to coordinate a project of this size, it is extremely important ". . . to have a powerful technique of expression worked out and accepted in the ecological community as in the physical sciences and then make each individual responsible for his manner of speaking."[2] GEST has been developed to be such a tool of expression.

The design goals of GEST are outlined after a review of the general system theoretic definition of "system."

System Definition

The intuitive black box representation of a system is elaborately defined in mathematical terms in general system theory.[1] For example, in the black box representation there are input, output, state, and state transformations.

In the general system theory formulation, input is represented by two concepts: a set not empty of input values and a set of admissible input functions. As far as state and state transformations are concerned, a set not empty of states, and a set of state transition functions are defined. Output is represented by two concepts: a set not empty of output values and an output function. The formal definition of a system in general system theory is as follows:

A system is a sixtuple $Z = (S,P,F,M,T, \sigma)$, where

S   is a set not empty of states,

P   is a set not empty of input values to the system,

F   is an admissible set of input functions defined on the real numbers R with values in P, i.e., $F \subset \mathcal{I}(R,P)$,

M   is a set of functions, each defined on S with values in S, i.e., $M \subset \mathcal{I}(S,S)$. In other words, M is the set of all modes of behavior available to the system;

T   is a subset of R containing 0. T is the time scale, or the period of time over which the system exists or over which the system is observed;

σ is a function defined on $F \times T$ with values in M such that σ is onto; i.e., $\sigma \epsilon \mathcal{I}$ $(F \times T, \text{onto}, M)$; σ is the state transition function and gives the time-dependent behavior of the system. $\sigma(f,t)(x)$ stands for the state of the system at time t, given the initial state x and the admissible input function f.

Furthermore, three basic conditions are satisfied:

1. *initial state condition:*

the identity mapping $\omega \epsilon M$ and $\forall$ $f \epsilon F \sigma(f,0) = \omega$;

2. *time invariant condition:*

if $f \epsilon F$, s,t, and $s+t \epsilon T$, then $\sigma(f \rightarrow s,t)\sigma(f,s) = \sigma(f,s+t)$;

3. *nonanticipatory condition:*

if f and $g \epsilon F$, $s \epsilon T$, and $f(t) = g(t)$ $\forall$ $t \epsilon R(s)$, then $\sigma(f,s) = \sigma(g,s)$.

In condition 1, it is required that at time $t = 0$ the state of the system is independent of the input function. In condition 2, it is required that the behavior of the system is independent of the choice of the time origin. Condition 3 states that if two input functions agree between 0 and s, then it makes no difference which input function is specified. Condition 3 does not exclude the possibility of modeling behaviorally anticipatory systems in terms of general system theory.

Design Objectives of GEST

The primary design objective of GEST is to provide a tool to be used in the mathematical modeling of *large-scale systems*. This goal has been achieved by having the ability to define a given system as a set of component systems having input/output relationships. A *component system* can have exogenous and/or endogenous inputs and outputs. An exogenous input of a component system is also an input of the total system. An endogenous input of a component system is an output of the same or another component system. The input/output relationships of component systems are specified by the *system coupling*.

The language should provide modeling facilities for systems which may possess some component systems having discrete time and some other component systems having continuous time. Since it is not a necessity that in a simulation study of a large system all the component systems have only discrete or only continuous time sets, one needs a combined discrete and continuous time digital simulation language. GEST is a *combined* system simulation language.

Broader systems should be easy to handle. By this requirement the following is understood: Suppose a mathematical model of a system Z1 within a given environment has been constructed. And suppose that after this phase of the study, one wants to model a system Z2 which will include the system Z1 and part of the environment of the system Z1. Then, it should be easy to model the system Z2 without being obliged to remodel the components of the system Z2 that were modeled in Z1. Broader systems are easily handled in GEST either by the provision of *nested couplings* or by the redefinition of the system coupling.

As an advanced conceptual tool, the language should provide the ability to handle *time-varying systems* where the component systems and their interrelationships can vary with time.

An example of the need for such a feature in a simulation language is as follows: In a simulation study of long-range international politics, not only may the structure of each country vary with time, going from monarchy to republic, for example, or vice versa, but also the relationships between several countries depend on their power relations, which are also functions of time.

Examples of the case where a component system may cease to exist can easily be generated in ecological systems, where a component system representing a given variety may cease to exist after the extinction of this variety.

Time-varying systems are handled in GEST by defining either couplings or component systems as functions of time. In the former case, the interrelationships of the component systems will change throughout the time. In the latter case, a given component system will be transformed into another one to perform another function.

The user should also be given the ability to specify *nested simulation* studies. In GEST, some of the parameters of some component system(s) can be chosen after at least one simulation run of another component system, called the *parameter generator system*.

Furthermore, GEST has been designed to allow an investigator to write the mathematical model of a component system independently of the details of the simulation study. The GEST source program is composed of two parts. The first part is the mathematical description of the system and consists of the coupling specification and the descriptions of the component systems. Monitoring of the whole simulation study or of a single simulation run, as well as monitoring the initialization of the model, the data collection, the integration, the input scheduling, the output, and the debugging, are declared mainly in the second part of the GEST source program. The GEST object program is generated by the GEST processor.

This approach requires from the modeler of each component system a minimum amount of information. Furthermore, the mathematical description of the component systems is not obscured by statements necessary to monitor the simulation study.

System Definition in GEST

Without going into further details, some statements in Backus-Naur form are cited to give an example of system description in GEST. In the sequel, the metasyntactic symbols " E ∃ " and " . . . " denote option and repetition, respectively.

< system description > ::=

{ E < coupling declaration > ∃ { < system declaration > }...}..

< coupling declaration > ::=
    < simple coupling declaration >|
    < general coupling declaration >
<simple coupling declaration > ::=
    COUPLING FOR < system name > (< system name list >)
    { < input name > (< system name >) E FROM ∃
        < output name > (< system name >)
    E < if statement > ∃ }...
< system declaration > ::=
    < simple system declaration >|
    < special system declaration >|
    < similar system declaration >|
    < parametric system declaration >|
    < full system declaration >|
< simple system declaration > ::=
    SYSTEM < system name > < is > < time scale >
        E < if statement > ∃
    E < integration monitoring > ∃
    E < local background type declaration > ∃
    < system input declaration >
    < system state declaration >
    < system state transition function declaration >

E < system output declaration >
< system output function declaration > ∃
< system input declaration > ::=
    INPUT E S ∃ E < is > ∃ E < system input port list > ∃
E CARTESIAN (< system input port list>) ∃
E < type declaration > ∃
E < equivalence declaration > ∃
E < random variable declaration > ∃
E < random variable control declaration > ∃
E < array declaration > ∃
E < set declaration > ∃
E < queue declaration > ∃
E < attribute declaration > ∃
E < data collection statement > ∃
E < function > ∃

REFERENCES

1. A. W. Wymore. *A Mathematical Theory of Systems Engineering: The Elements,* (New York: John Wiley & Sons, Inc., 1967).
2. R. M. Langer. "Comments," In *Ecological Technology—Space-Earth-Sea,* ed. E. B. Konecci, Transference of Technology Series no. 1, The University of Texas at Austin, 1967.

A Model For Pollution– Behavior Interactions

DAVID STONE
and
EDWARD MATALKA

*Worcester Foundation for Experimental Biology
and
Worcester State Hospital
Worcester, Massachusetts*

Introduction

Throughout most of man's history, he has been relatively submissive to his environment. His intellectual capacities, however, gradually lessened his dependence for survival on the fortunes of nature. His population increased. The slow reversal of the relationship of man to nature accelerated during the Industrial Revolution and is being completed at an alarming rate in our present scientific and technological era. While science and technology have undoubtedly been beneficial to mankind, a price has been, and will continue to be, paid.

Many have begun to believe that if this price is not controlled and drastically reduced, then instead of being the handmaidens of progress and civilization, science and technology will have become the sorcerer's apprentices.

Public concern with the now well-publicized problems of overpopulation, urban living and strife, and overproduction of unneeded goods; disposal of garbage, junk, and biological waste products; and industrial use of excessive amounts of limited natural resources and concomitant overproduction of pollutants and waste products will, it is hoped, lead to a real diminution in the disruption of our ecosystem.

The survival of the biological species including mankind is dependent on such action. But there is more. Man and animal will continue to be exposed to a variety of substances not encountered during their evolutionary development, and continuing efforts must be made to determine whether such materials are capable of causing genetic alterations reflected by permanent changes in physiological and/or behavioral characteristics. Subtle, easily missed changes caused by long-term exposure to low concentrations of pollutants, contaminants, and substances ingested voluntarily for other purposes can be particularly dangerous.

An example of the latter form of pollution, an innocent pollution of man's internal environment, lies in the story of the artificial sweeteners, sodium and calcium cyclamates. Until recently, these chemicals were *assumed* to be biologically inert and harmless to man and were used in numerous food products and ingested by millions of people throughout the world. Today, the FDA in the United States and the appropriate agencies in various other countries have banned the sale of cyclamates for human consumption because of recent evidence that it may be a carcinogen. Our studies, beginning with the demonstration that cyclamates can induce chromosome breakage in human cells, led us to investigate their possible effects on behavior and now to believe that our work on cyclamate provides a model for the interactions of pollutants and behavior.

A brief review of the cyclamate story is appropriate for reasons that will become obvious. Work in our laboratory demonstrated that far from being biologically inactive, cyclamate, in relatively high doses, had the capacity to induce chromosome breakage in human cells *in vitro*. That is, cyclamate was mutagenic. Soon afterward, others demonstrated that cyclohexylamine, a metabolite of cyclamate, was similarly active both *in vitro* and, more importantly, *in vivo* in rat spermatogonial cells. This was followed by the finding that both cyclamate and cyclohexylamine produced physical deformities in developing chick embryos. Despite the demonstrations that cyclamate was not biologically inert and that, though rapidly excreted, it could be converted to cyclohexylamine in the body; despite the demonstrations of mutagenicity of cyclamate and its chief metabolite; and despite numerous findings of activities in other biological areas, including our later work on effects on the behavior of offspring in the rat—despite all this—the unrestricted sale of cyclamate was allowed to proceed and it was allowed to be utilized in high amounts, even by pregnant women. It is fortunate that two groups of investigators finally demonstrated that high intakes of cyclamate appear to induce cancer of the bladder in rodents. These findings precipitated the crisis regarding these sweeteners, and some restrictions on usage were imposed by the office of HEW. Finally, and more recently, the FDA announced a total ban on cyclamate use.

The point is that these substances were allowed to be used unrestrictedly, in spite of all the adverse scientific evidence until a *clear* possibility of cancer induction was raised so that appropriate federal action could be taken. Evidence consistent with possibilities for irreversible biological damage, even in generations yet unborn—evidence too subtle, perhaps, to be easily discovered—was ignored and may have been compounded into the distant future.

It is in terms of such subtle, but important, effects that this discussion continues.

Soon after finding that cyclamate could induce chromosome damage *in vitro*, we decided to determine whether a *low* and continuing intake of cyclamate could produce functional changes in the living organism. Drugs with known behavioral effects, such as the psychomimetic LSD and the stimulant caffeine (in high doses), have been reported to produce chromosome breakage, similar to that seen with cyclamate and cyclohexylamine. Further, the literature is well documented with relationships between chromosomal abnormalities and mental function in human offspring (e.g., Down's syndrome, D_1 trisomy syndrome, trisomy 16–18, and Cri du chat syndrome). Therefore, as an overall measure of biological action, we determined to investigate possible behavioral effects of cyclamate intake.

Behavioral Effects Induced by Cyclamate Intake

We have now completed a series of behavioral studies on Charles River rats bred and raised on a 30 mg. per cent solution of cyclamate as their only source of fluid. The average intake of cyclamate is approximately 20 mg./kg. per day. Control animals in our studies were bred similarly and raised in the same animal colony room with tap water as their only source of fluid intake. We have not observed any significant difference in the amount of fluid consumed by control and cyclamate animals. While large amounts of cyclamate (1–10 per cent of the diet) have been reported to cause both a reduction in the average sizes of litters and the body weights of offspring in rats, the relatively small amounts used in this study produced no such effects. Appearance, growth, and mobility characteristics of the rats bred and raised on cyclamate resembled those of the controls.

Initially we began our studies on an empirical basis. A group of eleven cyclamate and eighteen control rats were trained, under food deprivation, on a spatial reversal in a Y maze. After a period of training in which the rats were trained to enter the left or right arm of the maze, they were further trained on two spatial reversals. Figure 1 shows the mean error scores for the cyclamates and controls. The cyclamates had lower mean error scores on original learning and both reversals. There was no overall significant difference between the cyclamates and controls. The cyclamate group did, however, make significantly fewer errors on the second reversal (Mann-Whitney U test, $U = 11.5$, $n = 11$, $n = 18$, $P = 0.002$). A second group of control and cyclamate rats were trained on a slightly different procedure. Figure 1 shows the mean error

Experiment 1:

	Original Learning	1st Reversal	2nd Reversal
Control rats (n = 18)	7.78	9.73	9.67
Cyclamate-treated rats (n = 11)	5.98	8.80	5.94

Mann-Whitney U test, second reversal:
$$U = 11.5, p < 0.002$$

Experiment 2:

	Original Learning	1st Reversal	2nd Reversal
Control rats (n = 8)	4.87	10.50	8.50
Cyclamate-treated rats (n = 8)	3.75	9.75	6.75

Mann-Whitney U test, second reversal:
$$U = 12.0, p = 0.019$$

*30 mg percent calcium cyclamate solution available ad lib.

Fig. 1.   Mean Error Score for Control and Cyclamate-Treated Rats in Y-Maze Reversal Learning.

scores; there was no overall significant difference, although again the cyclamate group did have significantly lower error scores on the second reversal (Mann-Whitney U tests, U = 12, n = 8, n = 8, P = 0.019). While the results were not decisive, they seemed important enough to warrant further investigation.

The apparent facilitation in maze performance suggested the possibility that cyclamate, even at the low dosage, might enhance drive levels under food deprivation. To examine this possibility, another group of animals was tested on wheel-running activity and straight runway performance under food deprivation conditions, since it might be expected that the cyclamate rats would show higher activity levels and lower running times on the respective tests.

Wheel-running activity was examined in a group of sixteen cyclamate-bred-and-reared rats and one of sixteen controls, each group consisting of eight males and eight females: Wahmann activity-wheels were used to measure running. After a twenty-four-hour habituation period, daily wheel revolutions were recorded for four days under ad libitum feeding, followed by four days under a twenty-three-hour food deprivation schedule. Total revolutions for each four-day period are presented in Fig. 2 in such manner as to reduce variations due to the estrus cycle of the female. In view of the fact that females are much more active than males, we analyzed the data by sex, comparing males to males and females to females. The results show that cyclamate males are significantly more active than control males under food deprivation conditions, and that cyclamate females are significantly more active than control females not only under food deprivation, but also during the ad libitum feeding period. Figure 3 shows the mean daily number of wheel revolutions of each group over the ad lib. and deprivation periods; the figure clearly demonstrates the higher activity of the cyclamate females and the large increase in activity shown by the cyclamate males.

Following testing on the wheels, all animals were maintained at 80 per cent of their initial weights and were trained on a six-foot-long straight runway. The times taken for the experi-

Control Male No.	4-Day Ad lib Period	4-Day Deprivation Period	Δ	Control Female No.	4-Day Ad lib Period	4-Day Deprivation Period	Δ
1	3,449	1,289	− 2160	1	2,724	9,496	+ 6772
2	2,541	2,793	+ 252	2	3,912	6,617	+ 2705
3	977	1,059	− 82	3	9,856	10,697	+ 841
4	1,453	1,548	+ 95	4	9,213	14,312	+ 5099
5	1,403	983	− 420	5	12,287	5,643	− 6644
6	1,319	1,327	+ 8	6	2,803	6,616	+ 3813
7	524	481	− 43	7	2,459	2,961	+ 502
8	1,402	1,208	− 194	8	5,524	5,663	+ 139

Cyclamate Male No.	4-Day Ad lib Period	4-Day Deprivation Period	Δ	Cyclamate Female No.	4-Day Ad lib Period	4-Day Deprivation Period	Δ
1	42	1,433	+ 1391	1	22,344	43,941	+ 21597
2	4,877	19,135	+ 14258	2	8,542	28,505	+ 19963
3	1,395	6,173	+ 4778	3	13,761	40,165	+ 26404
4	1,321	2,650	+ 1339	4	7,013	31,898	+ 24885
5	1,793	1,924	+ 131	5	8,392	21,431	+ 13039
6	505	1,134	+ 529	6	6,136	8,272	+ 2136
7	1,572	4,733	+ 3161	7	3,728	11,406	+ 7678
8	3,746	2,100	− 1646	8	9,967	19,204	+ 9237

Fig. 2. Total Revolutions Performed by Control and Cyclamate Rats in the *ad libitum* and Deprivation Periods.

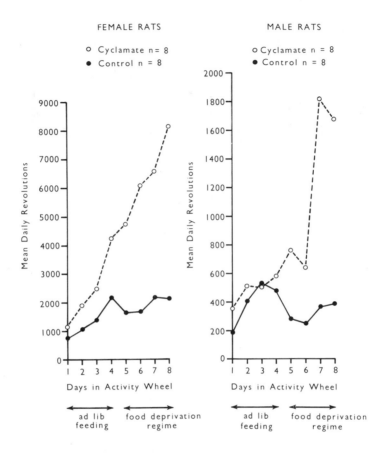

Fig. 3. Comparison of Activities (Activity-Wheel Revolutions) Between Control and Cyclamate Bred-and-Raised Rats under *ad libitum* and Food Deprivation Conditions.

mental and controls to run the runway were recorded, and all animals received five trials a day for five days. Since analysis of the data failed to reveal any suggestion of a significant difference between cyclamates and controls, this argues against the hypothesis that cyclamate enhanced drive levels.

In view of the higher wheel-running activity of the cyclamate rats, we decided to examine their activity in another situation, the open-field test. The open-field apparatus is simply a board 4 ft. by 4 ft. divided into 6-in. squares and with sides 1 ft. high. Each animal is placed in the center of the board, and two experimenters independently count the number of squares the animal enters within a three-minute session. In this experiment, the activity of cyclamate and control rats was recorded for five three-minute sessions. Both experimenters were blinded to the identity of the animals, and a correlation between the activity scores recorded by the experimenters was very close to 1.0. Further groups of twelve cyclamate-bred-and-raised rats and twelve controls (six males and six females in each group) were examined in this situation. Figure 4 presents the mean activity score for each session; it will be seen that both cyclamate females and males were higher than their respective control groups, with the cyclamate females again showing the highest level of activity. That is, the results are similar to those found with the use of activity wheels. Figure 5 shows the mean activity scores for each group for the five sessions. T tests revealed that both male and female cyclamate animals were significantly more active than controls. All animals were tested under ad libitum feeding conditions, so it appears clear that

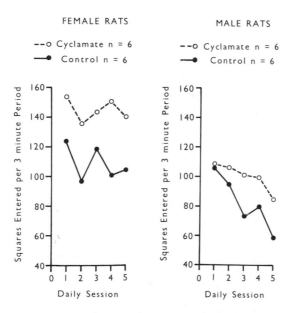

Fig. 4. Comparison of Activities (Open Field) Between Control and Cyclamate Bred-and-Raised Rats under *ad libitum* Conditions.

Female rats		Male rats	
Cyclamate	Control	Cyclamate	Control
686.0	549.0	488.0	414.0

t = 9.7; d.f. = 10   t = 1.87; d.f. = 10

p < 0.005   p < 0.05

Fig. 5.   Open Field Activity: Average Scores (Five-Day Sessions).

food deprivation is not a necessary condition for demonstrating a significant cyclamate effect on activity.

The "hyperactivity" of cyclamate rats in the open-field and activity wheels suggested that cyclamate animals might exhibit high response rates in operant (bar-pressing) situations and might even have difficulty in a task requiring response inhibition. We decided, therefore, to train a group of cyclamate rats on a DRL (Differential Reinforcement Low rate) schedule to test this possibility. The DRL schedule requires an animal to delay a response for a certain interval in order to obtain food reward, so that a hyperactive animal responding at a high rate on this schedule is unlikely to be efficient in obtaining food.

Eight cyclamate and eight control rats were available for this experiment, each group being composed of four males and four females. All animals were maintained at 80 per cent of their initial body weights and trained in LVE operant conditioning units. In this type of experiment, the animals must first be trained to bar press for food reward. Generally, the animal will begin exploring the conditioning box, occasionally striking a bar; the striking of the bar results in the automatic and immediate delivery of a pellet of food. The ratio of one bar press to one food pellet is called a Continuous Reinforcement Schedule (CRF). It is after the animal has learned to bar press for food reward that training begins on another (i.e., DRL) schedule.

Figure 6 shows the mean number of responses by the cyclamate and control groups over five forty-minute CRF sessions, in which, surprisingly, the cyclamate group were found to be retarded in the development of this rather simple response. By the end of the fifth session, only one cyclamate rat was responding within the range of the control animals. Four were virtually not responding at all, and it became necessary to "shape" (i.e., to artificially train) these animals to respond. Finally, when all cyclamate rats were responding at least three times per minute, training was begun on the DRL schedule. Figure 7 shows that the cyclamates, once trained to respond, had a significantly higher response rate on a DRL 10 second schedule than did the controls (t = 1.86 p .05 d.f. = 14). The response reinforcement ratio was also higher in the cyclamates, but this was not statistically significant.

We have no ready explanation for the apparent difficulty of the cyclamate group to acquire the simple bar-press response, but it suggests that cyclamate action may do more than produce hyperactivity. The results of the DRL schedule generally agree with the high response levels of cyclamate rats in the

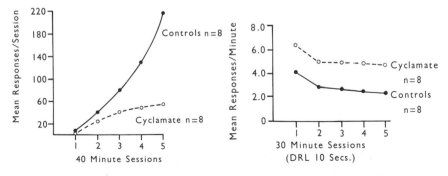

Fig. 6.   Mean Responses per Session under CRF Schedule.

Fig. 7.   Mean Responses per Minute under DRL 10-Second Schedule.

wheel and open-field situations, but also indicate that the cyclamate rats may, in fact, be impaired in response inhibition.

Permanency of Behavioral Effects Induced by Cyclamate Intake

All of the experiments so far discussed were performed with experimental rats bred and maintained on cyclamate throughout their lives. The fact that cyclamate has been shown to produce chromosomal damage (especially to germ cells) *in vivo* suggested that we investigate the possibility that cyclamate ingestion can produce permanent effects. Preliminary investigations were carried out using wheel-running activity as a convenient index, since in comparison to controls, rats bred and raised on cyclamate characteristically exhibit large increases in activity when food-deprived. The experimental and control animals of the first wheel-running experiment were employed in this one. After the initial wheel and runway tests, the animals were fed ad lib. until they attained stable body weights, and at this point one half of the males and females of the cylamate and control groups were switched to water or 30 mg. per cent cyclamate solution, respectively. The rats were randomly selected and the animals maintained on the new regime for four to six weeks before retesting. The remaining control and cyclamate animals were maintained on their original water or cyclamate solution. Wheel testing procedures and activity measures were made under the same conditions as previously described. Figure 8 shows the difference in activity in wheel revolutions for each animal when removed from ad lib. conditions of feeding to food deprivation. The results show that removing cyclamate from the cyclamate-bred-and-raised rats does not reduce their activities to control levels. One cyclamate male which did appear to show a decrease in activity when switched to water was the particular animal which exhibited a decrease during the first wheel-running experiment (see Fig. 2). Conversely, it appears that young adult control animals switched to cyclamate solution are no different than control

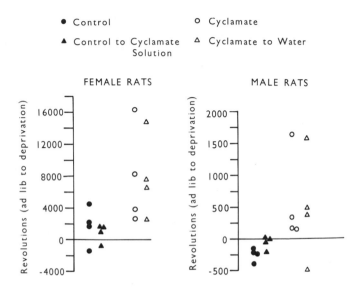

Fig. 8.   Increments in Activity-Wheel Revolutions (Four-day Totals) Due to Food Deprivation in Rats Kept on or Switched from Original Water or Cyclamate Regimes.

animals retained on water. Apparently, the cyclamate effect is not easily reversed, nor is it easily induced in young adults, and this suggests the possibility that the cyclamate exerts its effect during embryonic or neonatal stages to produce "permanent" behavioral changes. In a similar manner, it might be pointed out that neonatal steroid treatment or early dietary manipulations also can produce permanent behavioral changes in rats.

Naturally, it is of interest to determine whether cyclamate intake can produce permanent changes in behavioral patterns other than wheel-running. Presently, we are conducting a series of experiments using not only wheel-running behavior but also operant conditioning tasks as indices of cyclamate action; in these additional behavioral tasks, we can present some preliminary evidence consistent with the induction of permanent alterations by cyclamate. As previously mentioned, all cyclamate animals used in the above studies were bred and maintained on a 30 mg. per cent cyclamate solution, from parents receiving cyclamate for approximately eight weeks prior to mating. Further experimental groups have now been added. One group (designated SW) are the offspring of cyclamate • rats maintained on cyclamate until two weeks before breeding. At that time, tap water was substituted for cyclamate, and the pregnant female maintained on water throughout gestation and suckling, so that the SW offspring never received or ingested cyclamate. The second group (designated CSW) are the offspring of control (i.e., water-reared-and-maintained) parents, in which the pregnant female was given a 30 mg. per cent cyclamate solution only during gestation. In this group, the cyclamate was then removed immediately after the birth of the pups, and water substituted during the weaning period. Thereafter, the CSW offspring were maintained solely on tap water.

We have now examined the behavior of our experimental and control groups in several situations, although data collection is still in progress. Figure 9 shows the results of a further study of wheel-running activity, with some procedural changes. Instead of four days we measured activity for four weeks and also allowed for a five-day habituation period before tabulating the scores. Figure 9 shows the total activity scores for a twenty-day period for cyclamate, control, SW, and CSW males.

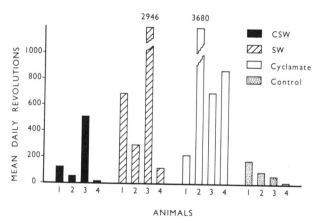

Fig. 9. Mean Daily Activity of Individual Rats (Twenty Days) under *ad libitum* Feeding.

Although there are only four males to each group, it is clear that not only are the cyclamate males more active than the controls, as expected, but also the SW males are overall much more active than the controls. (While one CSW male is quite active, it seems unclear as to whether the CSW group is, in fact, different from the controls.) When our experimental and control animals were subjected to a twenty-three-hour food deprivation schedule for four days, the results on activity were as shown in Fig. 10. Both SW and cyclamate animals exhibit the large increases in activity which characterized cyclamate action in our first activity-wheel study. Food restriction did not lead to large increases in activity in either the control or CSW (except for one animal) groups. Thus, these data show that for wheel-running activity, the SW rats behave like cyclamate-bred-and-raised animals, while the CSW rats behave like the controls. The latter result indicates that, *as far as the wheel-running index* of cyclamate action is concerned, in utero effects have not been demonstrated. On the other hand, the results with the SW animals indicate that cyclamate-bred-and-raised

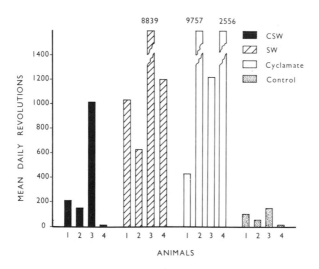

Fig. 10. Mean Daily Activity Score (Four-day, Twenty-Three-Hour Deprivation Schedule).

parents, even when removed from cyclamate ingestion, produce offspring with this characteristic behavior of cyclamate
action.

Studies of cyclamate effects also have been made employing
another type of behavior, that is, the avoidance of mild electric
shock, and currently we are examining the operant (Sidman)
avoidance performance of cyclamate, control, SW, and CSW
rats. The animals are trained in LVE operant conditioning
units, wherein shocks are delivered to their feet from a constant
current shock generator fitted with a scrambler. Shocks are

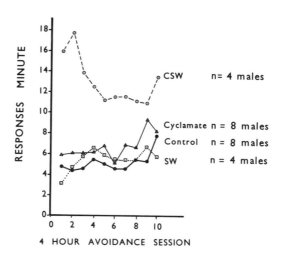

Fig. 11.   Mean Responses per Minutes (Four-Hour Avoidance Session).

applied for a duration of 0.5 seconds at a level of 1.4 m.a., with a shock-shock interval of 5.5 seconds and a response—shocks interval of 16.5 seconds. In other words, the animal receives a shock until it bar presses so as to delay the shock for 16.5 seconds. Each succeeding press delays the shock for a further 16.5 seconds. Figure 11 shows the mean response rate and mean shock rate for each group over five four-hour avoidance sessions. The CSW group shows a strikingly high response rate compared to all the other groups and, therefore, as was to be expected, they also show the lowest shock rate. It is interesting to note that the rats in the CSW group exhibited a simultaneous drop in response rate (as indicated in Fig. 11), suggesting that their performance became more efficient over the sessions. Relative to the CSW group, the differences in response rates between the cyclamate and control groups seem rather slight, but, nonetheless, the cyclamate group consistently responds at a higher level than the controls. The shock levels of the cyclamate group are lower than those seen for the controls and appear to decrease more rapidly. The SW group, so far, does not appear to differ significantly from the controls, although their initial response rate was lower than that of any of the other groups.

It would be premature to draw any firm conclusions until more data has been collected. However, even on the basis of the small groups studied, it appears that the ingestion of cyclamate *during gestation* markedly affects the avoidance behavior of the offspring. It will be remembered that with the activity wheel we saw a somewhat different picture: the CSW rats were not clearly different from controls, whereas the SW offspring were clearly more active than controls. The results of the avoidance and activity measures taken together suggest that cyclamate ingestion does produce permanent changes in behavior, whereas cyclamate ingestion during pregnancy only appears to be affecting behavioral systems which are different from those altered by prolonged cyclamate ingestion prior to mating.

Summation of Results

In summation, our data shows that rats bred from parents
whose diet contains cyclamate and then retained on cyclamate
throughout suckling and young adult life (i.e., bred and raised
on cyclamate) are behaviorally different, in a variety of tests,
from normal, control rats bred and raised in the complete absence of cyclamate. Furthermore, such alterations appear to be
permanent in that the removal of cyclamate for long periods
does not cause these characteristics to disappear. Because
cyclamate does not produce observable effects when given for
the first time to young, adult, control animals, the results suggest that the cyclamate effect may be induced in the newborn
(e.g., during suckling), in the gestation period (i.e., in embryonic development), or in the development of the egg or sperm
(i.e., during meiosis).

The preliminary results obtained on activity wheels with the
SW rats (i.e., rats never receiving cyclamate, but whose parents were bred and raised on the material) suggest the possibility, which we are now actively investigating, that cyclamate
can act during meiosis. The data obtained to date in Sidman
avoidance tests with the CSW rats (offspring bred from normal
parents, and whose exposure to cyclamate was during gestation
only) indicates that cyclamate can also induce certain behavioral changes during embryonic development. The types of
behavioral systems altered appear to depend upon whether the
cyclamate acts during meiosis or embryonic development. As
yet, no tests have been carried out to determine whether cyclamate can cause behavioral alterations in infant life (e.g., during suckling).

Conclusions

Concern has been voiced by many geneticists, notably the
late H. J. Muller, regarding the apparent "genetic load" of
deleterious genes carried in the human population. Muller assumed that if medical technology continues to reduce deaths

due to deleterious genes, a point could eventually be reached where the entire resources and energies of a society would be expended on coping with genetic defects. While Muller clearly regarded this situation as hypothetical, he was basing his calculations on what was then known about mutation rates. If, however, radiation and various other pollutants are accelerating mutation rates, we may find that in a relatively few generations mankind will be faced with inordinately large numbers of genetically defective individuals, imposing immeasurable grief as well as impossible financial burdens. If pollutants can affect the organism during the development of the germ cells or of fetal or infantile life, we will likely find out much sooner.

It should again be stated that we have come to regard our research on cyclamate as a model for further studies on pollution-behavior interactions. While pollution and overpopulation can be regarded as behavioral problems to begin with, it is likely that the behavioral patterns initially responsible for pollution were primarily culturally determined. Our work, however, points to the real possibility that pollution can feed back biologically and influence behavior. Indeed, it is unreasonable to expect that pollutants capable of inducing biochemical lesions to produce gross physical deformities (including those acting as teratogenic and mutagenic agents) are not also capable of inducing those biochemical lesions in the central nervous system, which circumstance would only be reflected by behavioral alterations. It is, of course, impossible to say at the moment which particular pollutants can (and do) affect physiology and behavior, and at what levels they might be active. It seems likely, however, that low levels of heavy metals (including methyl mercury), pesticides, and defoliants do have the capacity to disturb behavioral mechanisms. Courtship, feeding, reproduction, and aggression are all examples of behaviors of the wild species in adapting to their environment. Disruption or alteration in the spectrum of these patterns might produce deleterious effects with respect to survival of species. Man is no less dependent on intact behavioral mechanisms for his survival; the inability to inhibit finger pressure on a trigger or on the legendary red button could have tragic and irreparable consequences.

Much of what has been said is speculative, some of our data is preliminary, and it is conceivable that cyclamates and all other chemical pollutants to which man is exposed are totally harmless. On the other hand, if our results are verified, and cyclamate can, indeed, serve as a model for pollution—behavior interactions which might be applicable to the human species, then future generations will have one more reason to curse the thoughtlessness and greed of their forebears. The stakes are terribly high.

Index